# Social Security and Pensions in Transition

# Social Security and Pensions in Transition

## *Understanding the American Retirement System*

**BRUNO STEIN**

THE FREE PRESS
*A Division of Macmillan Publishing Co., Inc.*
NEW YORK

Collier Macmillan Publishers
LONDON

The Free Press
A Division of Macmillan Publishing Co., Inc.
866 Third Avenue, New York, N. Y. 10022

Collier Macmillan Canada, Ltd.

Library of Congress Catalog Card Number: 79-7632

Printed in the United States of America

printing number

1 2 3 4 5 6 7 8 9 10

**Library of Congress Cataloging in Publication Data**

Stein, Bruno
Social security and pensions in transition.

Bibliography: p.
Includes index.
1. Social security—United States. 2. Old age pensions—United States. I. Title.
HD7125.S73 368.4'00973 79-7632
ISBN 0-02-930850-X

*To Judith:*

Wenn ich bei meiner Liebsten bin,
Dann geht das Herz mir auf;
Dann bin ich reich in meinem Sinn
Und biet' die Welt zu Kauf.

# Contents

# List of Figures and Tables

## LIST OF FIGURES

## LIST OF TABLES

**APPENDIX: ADDITIONAL TABLES TO CHAPTER 4**

# Preface

SOCIAL SECURITY HAS long been taken for granted as a normal aspect of modern industrial society. After the stormy debates surrounding its passage in 1935, relatively little attention was paid to it by scholars and policy analysts. From time to time, discussion would flare up regarding the need for extending and improving benefits, but only a handful of scholars paid continuing attention to the topic.

This period of calm was shattered in the 1970s. The precipitating factor was the fear that the system was headed for bankruptcy. Although the conventional concept of bankruptcy hardly applies to a program that taxes one group of the population in order to pay benefits to another group, it became increasingly clear that something bad was happening.

As a result—or coincident with it—economists and actuaries began to take a closer look. When they did, they discovered not only a horrendous technical flaw that was legislated in 1972, but also a variety of other issues. These included questions of equity, the relationship of Social Security to other income maintenance programs, and the possibly deleterious effects of the system on the economy.

The tenor of the debate began to change. One need only compare the relatively calm analysis by Pechman, Aaron, and Taussig, published in 1968, with the more urgent tone that can be detected in the work of Alicia H. Munnell, published almost a decade later. I mention these two analyses because both came from the Brookings Institution and did not diverge significantly in ideology.

By the time I began this book in 1977, writing on Social Security had become a major industry. Material appeared so rapidly that unpublished papers cited other unpublished papers. Although Congress altered the law in 1977 to reduce—or postpone—the impending crisis, the momentum of the literature is unabated. The topic continues to be a lively one.

Ideology necessarily plays a role in the examination of a social policy. The recent spate of economic literature on Social Security is noteworthy because much of it contains a high quality of analysis, regardless of the ideological leanings of the authors. There is considerable agreement on what the main issues are and disagreement on what to do about them. Underlying the discussion is a sense of pain. Social Security is an expensive program and will become even more expensive as time goes by. This has already been noticed by the public and its representatives.

Policymakers tend to demand a simple answer, but no simple answer can be supplied. The entire topic is extremely complex. That is not surprising, inasmuch as Social Security directly affects virtually all of our population, as taxpayers, beneficiaries, and potential beneficiaries. Its operation affects the entire economy at both microeconomic and macroeconomic levels. It even spills over into international trade and capital flows. More to the point, it concerns the welfare of individuals and families, young and old.

One purpose of this book is to clarify these complex issues and to present a reasonable set of alternative policies. This necessarily involves specifying the possible goals of Social Security in order to identify means for accomplishing such goals. For reasons of brevity I have omitted such peripheral policies as means-tested veterans' programs. In addition I have avoided policy proposals that, in my judgment, are not politically feasible. For example, I do not believe that Social Security can be abolished, nor do I believe that it can be used to replace all preretirement income at preretirement levels. Neither proposal strikes me as politically achievable, even if it could be shown to be workable.

The plan of the book is as follows. I begin with a brief introduction describing the bare elements of Social Security for those readers who are not acquainted with it. The three chapters that follow lay the groundwork for the analysis. Chapter 1 provides an overview of the principal issues and problems. Chapter 2 adds historical perspective on the development of both the social insurance and public assistance traditions that merged in the Social Security Act. It then presents a combined view of both Social Security and other public income maintenance programs as part of a unitary structure. Chapter 3 adds to the structure by examining occupational pensions.

Chapter 4 analyzes the retirement system as it functions in this time of change. The needs of the retirement population are examined, both in theoretical terms and in terms of income replaced by Social Security and pensions. Changing needs caused by changes in family behavior are looked at, along with changing needs resulting from a social distaste for the sex discrimination inherent in Social Security. Interactions between Social Security and other retirement programs are analyzed to detect dysfunctional behavior. Finally, the chapter deals with problems of equity, for the political acceptability of the system depends on whether it is perceived as fair.

Chapter 5 deals with issues that were not envisioned by the founders of Social Security but must be faced today. Specifically, it examines the impact of the system on labor markets and on capital formation. This involves the economy's ability to support both its working and retired populations; the issues owe their present prominence to the pioneering works of Martin Feldstein, Alicia H. Munnell, and their critics.

In Chapter 6 the financing of Social Security is scrutinized, both for the present and for future needs. The nature of the Trust Fund is explained. The chapter concludes with a review of the proposals to alter financing in order to stimulate economic growth. The final chapter summarizes the issues covered in the book, compares goals and means, and presents alternative options for dealing with the changing role of Social Security.

Throughout the book, an effort is made to present the material in a nontechnical fashion so that it can be accessible to interested lay persons as well as to economists and other specialists. At times this is difficult, and I ask the reader's forebearance in stretches where the analysis gets a little hairy. All tables and diagrams are explained in the text. Only specialists may need to examine them closely.

A small technical note is in order. All after-tax computations of benefit were made on the basis of the federal income tax law that was in effect in 1978. Changes that are in effect for 1979 have no significant impact on these computations. In addition, calculations involving changes in average annual earnings were made before the Social

Security Administration decided on the precise definition of this variable. Accordingly, attempts to replicate these calculations may yield results slightly different from mine.

I am indebted to the Ford Foundation for its support of this project. The section on private pensions benefited from a supplementary grant given by Industrial Relations Counselors, Inc., and I am grateful for this help. An abbreviated and somewhat different version of Chapter 3 was separately published by IRC. Diane Diamond, my research assistant, unearthed mountains of data and other materials, and our daily discussions were a valuable ongoing seminar for me. Various officials of the Social Security Administration patiently gave their time to explain some of the mysteries of the system that they administer and to provide unpublished data. Their help was crucial because, partway through the book, the law was significantly changed. The work also reflects the insights that I gained from many years of collaboration with Peter S. Albin.

The administrative details of the topic are so complex that some errors pertaining to details may unavoidably have crept into this work. I have tried as best I could to guard against errors, and I am grateful for the help I received on this from several anonymous referees. Needless to say, the responsibility for any remaining errors is mine.

BRUNO STEIN
New York, April 1979

# Introduction

## THE ELEMENTS OF SOCIAL SECURITY

The principal focus of this work is on Social Security as a vehicle for obtaining retirement income. Social Security has a number of other functions: providing income to survivors of workers and to disabled workers and their dependents, and medical care to the aged and disabled. Although these secondary benefits will be referred to in passing, our chief concern here is how the Social Security system functions with respect to our growing population of older persons, those who have completed the greater portion of their working lives.

The system operates within a larger framework of retirement provisions. It is sometimes described as a three-tiered system, a three-legged stool, or a three-layer cake. The underlying tier is Supplemental Security Income, a sort of safety net for those whose assets and income are insufficient for retirement. Social Security (more precisely, Old Age Insurance), is the second tier but constitutes the primary retirement system for most of the population. In the jargon of the literature, it is often called the cornerstone. On this cornerstone, people are expected to accumulate savings during their working lives to enable them to retire. Savings may be individual, such as by building up equity in a home, or collectively through a pension plan. Some saving, including home ownership and pensions, is encouraged by favorable income tax provisions.

In essence, Social Security levies a payroll tax on workers and their employers and uses the proceeds to pay benefits to the retired population. During periods when tax collections are greater than benefits, the surplus is credited to a Trust Fund and invested in federal government securities. The Trust Fund is merely a contingency fund, unlike the sort of fund used in private and some public pension plans. Again, to use the jargon of the trade, the system is on a pay-as-you-go basis. Each generation of workers pays for the benefits of its elders in the expectation that it, in turn, will be supported by its successors.

About 90 percent of workers are covered by the system. The normal retirement age is sixty-five. Reduced benefits are available at age sixty-two (at a lower age for certain dependent survivors), and increased benefits are payable to workers who postpone retirement past age sixty-five. Thus, the amount of the benefit depends partly on age of retirement. It also depends on average lifetime earnings of the claimant, subject to certain adjustments, and on the number of the claimant's dependents. The structure of benefits, before taking account of dependents, is shaped to favor lower wage earners. All benefits, once received, are adjusted to changes in the Consumer Price Index. Benefits are reduced 50 percent by earnings past a limit imposed by the law.

In order to qualify for retirement benefits, a person must have worked in jobs covered by the system for a minimum number of years, thereby attaining the minimum quarters (quarter years) of coverage. A quarter of coverage is credited for every $250 earned in any year, up to a maximum of four quarters per year (before 1978, it took $50 to earn a quarter of coverage). In general, a worker needs a quarter of coverage in at least one-fourth of the years between 1950 (or attainment of age twenty-one, if later) and the year before age sixty-two. Ultimately, forty quarters of coverage will be needed. This will occur in 1991. The system is financed by a tax on wages up to a limit called the wage base. In 1978 employers and employees each paid 6.05 percent of wages up to $17,700 (the rate for self-employed workers was 8.1 percent). This tax includes provision of survivors, disability, and health insurance for the aged. Neither the tax rate nor the wage base is fixed. The tax rate is scheduled to rise to 7.65 percent in 1990. The wage base moves to $29,700 by 1981, after which it will be changed by changes in the nation's average annual earnings.

The description above covers the rudimentary aspects of the system and will be elaborated upon in the pages that follow. In practice, the details are so complex that a five-hundred-page book is needed to explain them. The interested reader is referred to the *Social Security Handbook,* published from time to time by the Social Security Administration.

# Social Security and Pensions in Transition

# CHAPTER ONE

# An Overview of the Problem Issues

## THE CRISIS OF THE 1970s

IT WAS WITH considerable shock that the nation awoke in 1975 to an apparently sudden threat to Social Security. The system was said to be going broke. The authorities for the statement were the three Cabinet members who constitute the Board of Trustees of the system,[1] and the Treasury Secretary added to the air of panic with an article in the *Wall Street Journal*.[2] It was the 1974 *Annual Report of the Trustees* that first broke the bad news,[3] but that is not a publication with wide circulation. However, as word spread, it engendered an understandable amount of fear among some of the elderly population,[4] although most Americans probably did not believe that Social Security would simply stop one day.

Whatever the feeling among the elderly, both experts and policymakers knew that a genuine problem existed. The system was paying out more in benefits than it received in revenues. Inasmuch as the system was expected to be self-sustaining, this could not go on forever, or even for very long. Under a reasonable set of assumptions about the future, the Old-Age and Survivors Insurance Trust Fund was due to be wiped out in 1984, and more pessimistic assumptions put the date at 1981 or 1980. The Disability Insurance Trust Fund was headed for extinction in 1979.[5] As the Trust Fund pays out the difference between revenues and benefits, no one knew what the implication of "bankruptcy" might be.

Some of the founders of the Social Security system would not have been surprised by this turn of events. Although their original bill, passed in 1935, was much more restricted and less liberal than the law now in force, some at least foresaw the need for external financing by 1980,[6] although they could not have foreseen the particulars of this crisis.

Relatively high rates of unemployment have led to a relative diminution of revenues to the system. In absolute terms, revenues are fed by rising employment combined with the higher revenue yields from the rising wage base against which the tax is applied. Nevertheless, revenues would have been higher if unemployment were lower, say 5 percent. Thus, in fiscal year 1975 the Trust Fund would have risen by $6.7 billion instead of $2.1 billion. In the following year (July 1 to June 30), the fund declined. Had unemployment been at 5 percent, the size of the fund would have *increased* by $4.3 billion instead of declining by $3.0 billion.[7]

Unemployment is worth noting, because high rates may become chronic in the future unless we succeed in finding better macroeconomic policies. In the long run, high rates of unemployment help to diminish the system's financial problem, since they will lead to lower benefits at the far end of a worker's life cycle. Benefits are based, in part, on average monthly earnings (the five lowest years can be dropped). Hence, prolonged stretches of unemployment yield lower retirement, survivors, and disability benefits. In the short run, however, high unemployment may increase the system's outlays, if it leads to earlier retirement and greater use of the option of retiring at sixty-two at a reduced benefit.

## Indexing

From time to time, Congress had raised benefits in response to rising prices and had raised the tax rate and the wage base (the maximum wage on which Social Security taxes are levied). Raising the wage base meant raising future benefit levels. These actions were not evenly distributed over time, causing retired persons to suffer from inflation in the intervening lags.

In 1972 Congress decided to index the system so as to make it unnecessary for it to engage in periodic legislation. Beginning in 1975, benefits were tied to the Consumer Price Index whenever it rose more than 3 percent per year. By itself, this simply maintains the real value of the benefits to those who currently draw them. But Congress went a step farther. It also adjusted the benefit computation formula for price changes. In addition, the maximum taxable wage was to go up with changes in average annual earnings. The higher wage base would increase the system's revenues and thus help to pay for the higher money benefits that inflation now brought to retirees. As will be seen in the next chapter, Social Security is financed largely on a pay-as-you-go basis. Today's taxes pay today's benefits.

A short-run result of the 1972 amendments was to drive up benefits as the rate of inflation in 1975 and 1976 rose dramatically, faster than average wages. But a longer-run consequence now became apparent. The coupling of price-indexed retirement benefits to a price-indexed formula for future benefit calculations served to overcompensate future retirees for inflation, if a rising ratio of benefits to previous earnings (the replacement rate) is taken as a measure of overcompensation.

This would happen because inflation raises wages as well as prices. When inflation activated the benefit computation formula, future benefits would rise. As time went by, more and more workers would arrive at the point of retirement with benefit rights that already reflected inflation. From that point on, their benefits would be further protected from inflation. They would get several bites at the cherry.

What was worse, the behavior of the interaction on replacement rates was erratic, depending on whether wage or price changes were dominant. If real wages and prices had moved together at the same rate, average replacement rates would have been stable. This had, more or less, been the experience in the past, which is why the problem was not perceived in 1972. But when price rises exceeded real wages, average replacement rates went up, leading to the paradoxical situation that a working population with declining standards of living was financing retirement at rising real benefits for a retired population.[8]

### Demographics

To complicate matters further, the age distribution of the population is changing. The baby boom that followed World War II was succeeded by a sharp drop in fertility rates. The war babies are reproducing far more slowly than their parents. At the moment the fertility rate is 1.8, and we are moving toward zero population growth (it takes an average of 2.1 babies per family just to maintain a population of a given size, aside from immigration). Even if the fertility rate ultimately moved back to 2.1, the ratio of the aged population (sixty-five and over) to the productive population (twenty to sixty-four) would rise from 18.9 percent in 1975 to 30.6 percent in 2050.[9]

This represents a 62 percent increase in the ratio between the aged population and those in their prime working years. It implies either an extremely heavy rate of taxation levied on the prime-age population to support its aged, that is, a relative reduction in their living standards, or a relative reduction in benefits to ease the burden on the working age population. Decoupling solved part of this but it did not solve all of the problem generated by the demographic change.

Part of the solution, as will be shown in later chapters, also lies in the drop in fertility rates. Let us take another look at the dependency ratios calculated in the *1977 Annual Report* just cited. The dependent population of a country does not consist entirely of its aged and disabled. It includes children, who, on net balance, consume more resources than they produce. The total dependency ratio is computed by taking the over-sixty-fives plus those below age twenty and dividing the total by the prime-age population (twenty to sixty-four years of age). Again assuming a fertility rate of 2.1, the total dependency ratio falls from 82.9 percent in 1975 to 66.2 percent in 2010, thereafter rising a bit and declining again to 79 percent in 2050. At no point is it estimated to reach the 1975 level. A lower fertility rate would reduce the total dependency ratio. Even a return to a fertility rate of 2.3 would produce declining total dependency ratios from present levels in all years, except the period 2030 to 2040 when it would rise slightly above the 1975 level.[10].

If we think in terms of real goods consumed by real humans, then the total resources that need to be devoted to the dependent portion of our population are not due to change very much. Indeed, they decline. To put it more simply, we shall need to spend less on children, both as private individuals and through the public sector, via schooling and similar services. Clearly, some of these savings can be used to help support the aged. Whether or not society chooses to do so will depend both on the private preferences of consumers and on the political preferences of voters. Whether or not the society is able to make such a transfer will depend on the prices of child services relative to other goods and services.

This line of reasoning will be pursued in the chapter on financing social security. Insofar as the long-run demographic problem is concerned, it is sufficient in this overview to note that our prime-age successors in future decades will not be asked to support an ever growing ratio of dependents. Hence, the demographic change does not necessarily present a catastrophe or an immutable crisis. What it does present is the very serious problem of reallocating resources from the diminishing number of children to the growing number of the aged. Politically, it will not be a simple problem. But it may be one that is capable of solution.[11]

## SOCIAL SECURITY AND THE ECONOMY

### Social "Saving" Versus Private Saving

The original Social Security Act, as legislated in 1935, established a system of compulsory private saving, very much in line with the European (especially German) systems from which it drew its inspiration. The "savings" consisted of the revenues from a tax levied equally upon employers and employees in jobs covered by the act. Leaving aside for later the question of who really pays the employer's share, the savings were to be invested in U.S. government obligations.

The 1939 Amendments essentially changed this by shifting to a system by which current Social Security taxes (called "contributions") paid current benefits. Still, the excess of contributions over disbursements led to the building up of Trust Funds for the Old Age and Survivors Insurance (OASI), Disability Insurance (DI) and Health Insurance for the Aged (HI). The OASI Trust Fund, which concerns us here, grew until 1975 and served as a contingency reserve. Its projected decline thereafter precipitated the crisis that led to a major change in the law in 1977.

Whether or not compulsory saving is proper is an ideological and political question. For the time being, it seems to have been accepted by the greater part of the American public. However, certain economic questions have been raised in recent years regarding the consequences of such social savings and whether one can even think of them as savings in the ordinary economic sense of the word. It is worth reminding ourselves that an individual can save for the future by accumulating claims against future resources (for example, by depositing money in a bank for later withdrawal), but a nation cannot do this.[12] This is because people consume goods and services that are currently produced and not stored up.

A flow of private savings, both corporate and individual, is needed to build up future stocks of capital. The word capital is used here in its sense of goods that are used to produce other goods (e.g., machinery). Public savings, in the form of the OASI Trust Fund, do not directly produce a similar effect, although they may indirectly lead to an increase in the stock of private capital.[13] During the years that the OASI Trust Fund was built up, the excess of revenues over disbursements simply entered the federal government's flow of general revenues. The bonds purchased by the Trust Fund were claims against future general taxpayers.

Since they were used as general revenues, most of the monies financed the ordinary operations of government. These were principally national defense,[14] health, labor, welfare, and education. Although some of these expenditures might also be thought of as capital to the extent that they enhance the nation's productive capacity—for example, some outlays on health, training, and education—it is safe to say that most of the expenditures were for the current services rendered by government.

In contrast, the bulk of private savings flows through the money markets to be used for the financing of private investment (the purchase of capital goods). In a capitalist economy, private capital yields a return to its owners and thus to savers, since their savings have generated a claim against the capital. The nation's ability to produce goods and services, given its resources, depends on the quantity and quality of its stock of capital and the extent to which it is used.[15] It follows that any policy that may diminish its ability to produce goods and services will diminish its ability to redistribute income to the aged.

Hence the question: Does the Social Security system act so as to reduce the flow of "real" savings to the economy? If so, does this reduce the economy's ability to engage in capital formation? It can be seen that the problem presented here transcends the operation of the system itself and affects Americans of all ages. For if we produce less in the future, we will be forced to consume less and thus enjoy an absolute or (at least) relative decline in real income. Such a decline would certainly put pressure on the benefits that our retirement system can pay.[16].

One reason why Social Security reduces savings is simply that it reduces the worker's ability to lay money aside by the extent of the tax on his or her earnings. If the employer's share is, in reality, shifted back to the worker, in the sense that wages would be higher by the amount of the employer's tax, then the worker's ability to save is reduced by the full amount of the joint tax.[17]

If the employer's share is not shifted,[18] it will reduce *his* ability to save and invest his profits. If the tax is passed forward to consumers, in the form of higher prices, their ability to consume and save is thereby diminished. Less consumption, in turn, reduces the demand for capital goods.

A second reason why Social Security may reduce private savings is that workers regard the tax (their share, if not both shares) as savings. They are certainly encouraged in this belief, because the tax is called a contribution on their pay slips (the employee's share is deducted under the heading Federal Insurance Contributions Act) and because it carries a promise of benefits. Accordingly, workers may respond by reducing their savings. If, alternatively, workers view their benefit rights as annuities, they may regard such annuities as wealth that reduces their need to save by an equivalent amount. Such wealth is not real wealth in the sense that there is no underlying stock of capital to produce goods and services. Instead, it is a claim on the taxes of the generation behind them.

Martin Feldstein estimates that in 1975 Social Security taxes reduced private savings by 40 percent, which implies an enormous reduction in the nation's potential stock of capital and, therefore, in its Gross National Product (GNP). Taking a more conservative estimate of 35 percent, he shows that the increase in capital would have led to an increased GNP in 1975 of $285 billion, or more than $3,500 per family.[19] If Feldstein is correct, this is no trivial sum but a significant impairment of the nation's ability to generate income now and in the future.

Although the consensus on this subject is growing among economists, the opinion is far from unanimous. As Professor Lampman reminds us, the presence of savings is no guarantee that they will be invested.[20] This is a Keynesian view, and if we take it a step farther, an upward shift in private savings can reduce consumption, income, and therefore savings.[21]

The issue will be explored in greater depth in a subsequent chapter. At this introductory point, it is sufficient to note that a serious issue about the impact of Social Security on savings and capital formation exists. Any thoroughgoing reform of Social Security will have to consider the issue, determine the extent of the problem, and examine the possible policy alternatives to solve it.

### Impact on Labor Markets

As we have just seen, the operation of the Social Security system may have ramifications on capital markets if the tax reduces the total amount of savings in the economy. The system also impacts on the nation's labor markets, principally through its provisions for retirement, including the retirement test that reduces or eliminates benefits between the ages of sixty-two and seventy-two.

The Civilian Labor Force (CLF) consists of all persons above age sixteen who are working or looking for work and are living outside of military installations or institutions like hospitals or prisons. The Labor Force Participation Rate (LFPR) is the proportion of persons in the population who are in the labor force. These concepts will be helpful as we try to analyze what is happening.

There is widespread agreement among experts that the advent of Social Security helped to solidify sixty-five as a "normal" retirement age. Like all markets, the labor market has a demand side and a supply side. On the demand side, employers were probably encouraged to make sixty-five a mandatory retirement age. Employers have a preference for younger workers in any case. Therefore, older workers may be forced out of a job on the one hand, and find it difficult to get another, even if they prefer work to retirement. When they stop looking, they are classified as out of the labor force (OLF).

On the supply side, the existence of benefits (as well as private pensions, savings, and so forth) helps to induce workers to leave the labor market. This, as we shall see, was one of the purposes of Social Security. In economic terms, the presence of income maintenance reduces the cost of leisure relative to work[22] for individuals or family members. As with capital, a nation's ability to produce goods and services depends, in part, on the quantity and quality of its labor force and the extent to which it is utilized (employed). Thus, a reduction in the labor force can lead to a reduction in the nation's output. The effect can be especially deleterious where persons who leave the labor force have skills that are in demand.

Clearly, this is not an unmitigated evil. Many, perhaps most, of our older population want to be out of the labor force. They have worked most of their lives, often in jobs that were unpleasant or psychologically unrewarding, and want to enjoy their remaining years. Since we value the welfare of people above the welfare of machines (if there be such a concept), much of the voluntary withdrawal of the elderly from the labor force is a social good, not a social evil. The loss of output from such voluntary withdrawals is then part of the price the society pays to enable its aged to enjoy retirement.

Unfortunately, it is not easy to distinguish statistically between those who are glad to be finished with their working lives and those who would prefer to work, either because they like it or because their retirement incomes force a reduction of their standard of living upon them. Whatever the case may be, the statistics on labor force participation rates for the elderly have shown persistent decline in most categories. Not all of this can be attributed to Social Security. Our elderly are more affluent today, and more of them enjoy benefits of pensions from their jobs. However, Social Security undoubtedly makes a big difference.

Statistics on the Labor Force Participation rates for the over-sixty-fives tell an interesting story, as pictured in Figure 1–1. For married men (spouse present) the rate has dropped from 54.5 percent in 1947 to 20.9 percent in 1977, a decline of 61 percent. However, married women over sixty-five (spouse present) increased their participation from 4.1 percent to 7.0 percent. This is a 71 percent increase (on a small base, of course). For persons widowed, divorced, or separated, the LFPR for males dropped from 32.8 percent in 1947 to 12.4 percent in 1977. For the same class of females, the rate remained relatively stable, although it showed a rising trend until 1973.[23]

Labor Force Participation Rates fluctuate from month to month and tend to decline with unemployment as people stop looking for work. However, the secular trend is clear. The participation rate for

**FIGURE 1-1** Labor Force Participation Rates, 1947 and 1977 — People Aged 65 and Over

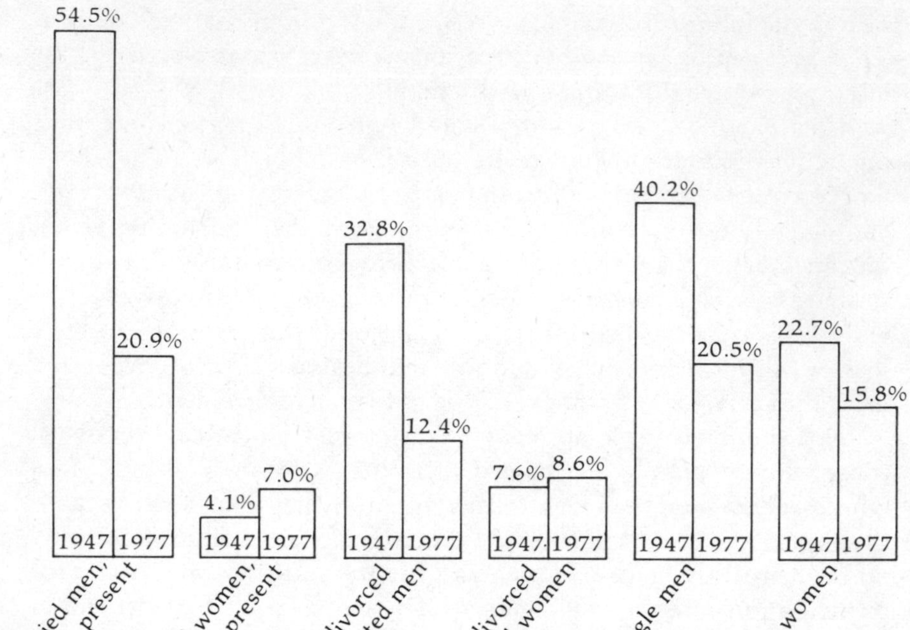


Source: *Employment and Training Report of the President* (Washington: U.S. Government Printing Office, 1978) pp. 235-36.

the elderly is falling, with the exception of married women. The rate is also declining in the adjacent age groups (fifty-five to sixty-four and forty-five to fifty-four). Obviously, the latter cannot be attributed to Social Security, although the fifty-five to sixty-four bracket may be influenced by the early retirement provisions available at age sixty-two.

The Social Security Administration projects further declines in participation rates, but it predicts that the trend will slow down. In the fifty-five to fifty-nine group of males, whose participation rate was 89.5 percent in 1970 and 83.6 percent in 1976, the expectation is that the rate will reach 82.1 percent in 2000.[24]

Various factors are at work in these withdrawals from the labor force, and it is evident that Social Security only plays a part—a part whose magnitude is hard to estimate. The retirement test undoubtedly influences the decision as to whether to withdraw completely or partially, especially for low-income elderly persons who rely principally on Social Security.[25] The issues to which all this points are: (1) Inducing people to stay longer in the labor force can increase the nation's output and, in the long run, help to finance the system; (2) the participation rate of the elderly can be increased by a liberalization of the retirement test; but (3) this would involve a significant increase in the cost of the system, at least in the short term. We shall return to this issue in Chapter 5.

## SOCIAL SECURITY AND OTHER MAINTENANCE SYSTEMS

Few people are aware of the complexity of our income maintenance systems. The *Handbook of Public Income Transfer Programs* lists a total of thirty-eight public programs, including cash transfers, health care, housing, and food, both for the general population and for such special groups as American Indians and Cuban refugees.[26] As Chapter 2 will show, various programs were developed over time and tended to be treated separately rather than as part of a comprehensive system. One by-product of this development was that some programs interact with others, yielding results that were not intended by the policymakers. This introductory chapter will touch upon a few of these interactions, both within the structure of public programs and with the structure of employment-related pensions, both private and public, that have emerged over the years.

**Public Programs.** One of the controversial overlaps between systems is the Social Security's minimum benefit and the public assistance system's Supplementary Security Income (SSI). Social Security benefits are progressive, that is, they yield relatively greater benefits to low wage earners than to high wage earners. The lowest benefit bracket has been set especially high to encompass and aid not only very low wage earners but also persons whose attachment to the labor market has been sporadic. As of June 1978, it took twenty-seven quarters of coverage (6¾ years) for a person aged sixty-two to attain fully insured status to qualify for retirement or disability benefits. (This figure will rise, in stages, to forty quarters, or ten years, by

1991). At age sixty-five, in July 1978, someone with average annual earnings of $921 ($77 per month) was eligible for a Primary Insurance Benefit of $121.80 per month. With a spouse aged sixty-five, the benefit was $182.70 per month ($167.50 if she claimed benefits at sixty-two).

SSI is available on a means-tested basis and provides a federal minimum of $189.40 for an aged individual and $284.10 for an aged couple.[27] The means test counts Social Security benefits as unearned income and excludes all but the first $20 per month from SSI benefits. Since many SSI beneficiaries are likely to be eligible for low or minimum Social Security benefits, the cost of supporting them is partly borne by the Social Security tax instead of the general federal (and state) taxes that support SSI. This is because the SSI benefit and not the Social Security benefit is reduced. Whether an increase in Social Security benefits helps such persons depends on the state in which they live. States that supplement SSI on a mandatory basis (those whose Old Age Assistance benefits were higher than the minimum SSI benefit in 1974) need not pass the Social Security increases along. Furthermore, an increase in Social Security benefits can jeopardize Medicaid benefits in those instances where double coverage of Medicare and Medicaid is possible, if it throws people over the state's income test for Medicaid.

Social Security contains two provisions whose purpose is to help indigent persons. One is the minimum benefit, available to anyone who qualifies by having the necessary years of coverage, regardless of how low his or her earnings record may be. The second is the special minimum benefit for low wage earners who have spent more than ten and up to thirty years in covered employment. These minimums are more in the nature of a welfare payment than replacement of previous income. The function of SSI is to provide for elderly and disabled indigents. It clearly serves a welfare function. Although we may assume that our society wishes to provide for the poor among our aged and disabled, it is not at all clear what the source of the financing should be. If we are worried about the fiscal integrity of the Trust Fund, then the minimum benefit places a burden upon it that, arguably, is better borne by the broader-based general federal and state tax systems.

This argument is reinforced by the fact that the miminum benefit is available to quite a few people who are not poor. It is widely utilized by persons who benefit from public sector retirement systems not covered by Social Security, especially federal employees, who "moonlight" (i.e., hold second jobs) or retire early and work long enough in covered employment to achieve eligibility. In short, the minimum benefit is an inefficient way to reach the target population.

Thus we have two issues here. One is: To what extent shall we separate the welfare and income replacement functions, or at least their financing, in Social Security? The second issue concerns the interactions between the social insurance and public assistance systems that have undesirable effects.

**Employment-related Pensions.** An issue that may develop over time pertains to the integration of Social Security with pension plans. In the private sector, plans that specified a defined benefit inclusive of Social Security (called integrated plans) were popular in the early 1950s. Since private pension plans covering most eligible workers are noncontributory (that is, the employer is the sole contributor), increased Social Security benefits accrued as windfalls to employers. The tendency to liberalize benefits led to the decline of integrated plans, and Social Security was viewed as a supplement rather than as a complement. However, the realization that changes in Social Security taxes and benefits can be expected regularly is now leading to the reappearance of integrated plans or other plans that treat Social Security as a complement rather than as a supplement.[28] This trend is likely to be reinforced as the 1974 Pension Reform Act increases the cost of pensions through its requirement that pensions be vested.

Unfortunately, data are not readily available on the extent to which integrated plans are returning, nor is it clear what the consequences of this reappearance might be. In the short run, as Social Security benefits rise with rising money wages, integrated plans shift at least part of the cost of defined benefit plans from employers to the Social Security system, to which both employers and workers contribute. To the extent that earlier pension plan liberalizations were anticipations of inflation, integrated plans shift the cost of the inflation adjustment to the Social Security System. They also stabilize the proportion of earnings that are replaced by the combined pension upon retirement.

Virtually all state and local government workers are covered by pension plans. In 1951 states and localities were given the option of joining the Social Security system by election of the workers in question. By 1973, 73.8 percent of state and local government employees were covered.[29] Initially, many of the systems became integrated plans (at least in part), by providing differential benefits below and above the Social Security wage base. However, they have tended not to follow the upward movement of the wage base, so that integration is now vestigial and Social Security benefits supplement rather than complement the pensions.

This raises questions regarding public pensions. Because they are generally higher than private pensions, the combination can lead to extremely high replacement rates. From the point of view of this book, however, the questions that are likely to arise in the future are (1) whether coverage should be total and (2) whether public systems should be permitted to withdraw.

The 26.2 percent of public employees who have chosen to stay out of Social Security have probably done so because their options were better in staying out, at least at the time the decision was made. Presumably, Social Security taxes were a poor investment for them, especially if they could persuade their pension systems to make equivalent contributions into funds with higher yields. Withdrawal (which is the option of state or local government) can benefit workers with ten years of coverage who are near retirement. Even if retirement is ten or twenty years away, such workers may still benefit, as the benefit formula is progressive, so that benefit loss is not proportional to the decline in covered earnings to zero. The five lowest years of earnings are dropped from the benefit calculation in any event. Thus, if public employers withdraw, the Social Security system will continue for a long time to carry the burden of paying benefits, without receiving the taxes to finance those benefits.

## THE GOALS OF THE SYSTEM: DIVERGENT VIEWS

The preceding overview has dealt with questions that are currently asked. Answers, as always in social policy, depend not only on technical considerations and actuarial calculations, but also on the more fundamental issue of what the system is intended to accomplish. Given the goals, the appropriate means must be chosen, for it is possible that the means will not achieve the goals, defeat them in whole or part, or possibly offset the goals of other programs or the means chosen to accomplish them. Goals are, after all, good social intentions, and the road to hell is paved with many such intentions.

### The Goals of the Founders

The underlying goal of the original Social Security Act was to provide some economic security for families whose income was cut off by the advent of old age, short-period unemployment, or loss of a male breadwinner. Indeed, the original proposals submitted by the administration were called the Economic Security Act (the change of name was made by the House Ways and Means Committee). Emphasis was on social insurance, not public assistance. The traditional means for social insurance is a tax levied upon workers (and/or employers) specifically earmarked for the purpose, at a rate that can be expected to provide the specified benefits.

Public assistance, unlike social insurance, tends to be financed from general revenues on a year-to-year basis. Of the original act's two public assistance provisions, one (Old Age Assistance) was intended to be transitional, providing help to the indigent aged until the social insurance system for the aged (Old Age Insurance) matured so that, over the years, coverage would become widespread as older workers died off and younger workers became fully insured. The second public assistance provision (Aid to Dependent Children) was for poor children without a father in the household.

For the Committee on Economic Security, the group that drafted the Administration's proposal, unemployment compensation had the highest priority. For Congress and the general public, the provision for the aged was more important.[30] This might be because WPA and similar programs already provided relief for the unemployed, and there was still hope that New Deal economic policies would reduce unemployment. The aged, however, were not directly affected by such programs, and economic recovery would be of little direct use to them. Furthermore, they were politically vocal and becoming politically organized under the aegis of the Townsend Movement.

During the discussions of the proposed Old Age provisions of the law, many divergent views emerged. Harry Hopkins, a man with a social work background who was close to President Roosevelt, wanted to lump relief and social insurance together, with payment as a matter of right and not as a matter of need. In effect, he sought a demogrant for the aged (as well as for the unemployed). That was strong stuff for 1935, and Roosevelt had a great aversion to the dole.[31] Treasury Secretary Henry Morgenthau was concerned with the need to make any program self-sufficient. There were conflicts between those who wanted high payments immediately and those who preferred to begin with minimal benefits until revenues accruing in a reserve fund were great enough to finance higher benefits as the system matured.

Some of the founders of the law, like Murray W. Latimer, stressed the need to remove older people from the labor market in order to keep them from depressing wages and blocking the opportunities of younger and middle-aged persons. He also noted what many modern writers overlook, the need to relieve adult children of the economic strain of supporting their parents.[32] Labor Secretary Frances Perkins saw the system as "making almost [*sic*] compulsory a habit of a slight saving . . . which I think most of us find very difficult unless there is some rather systematic way by which we can compel ourselves to do so."[33]

The Report of the Committee on Economic Security listed many goals. These included (1) preventing dependency in old age; (2) retarding the growth of public assistance; (3) encouraging thrift because public assistance discourages savings with its means test whereas social insurance has no means test; (4) preventing a decline in wage standards (by removing older workers) and providing opportunities for younger workers; (5) promoting economic stability by maintaining the flow of consumption expenditures by the aged; and (6) providing for the basic needs of the aged (i.e., not necessarily for full needs). Among the basic principles it listed: (1) a long-term goal of 50 percent replacement of average earnings and a short-term goal of 15 percent; (2) a relatively high minimum benefit, inasmuch as initial benefits would be seriously inadequate; (3) benefits graduated relative to contributions to favor low-income workers and those who entered the system late. With respect to this last point, it saw old age benefits as a social mechanism that adjusted, in some measure, to the relative needs of various classes of beneficiaries.[34]

Undoubtedly, many of the founders were incrementalists in the sense that they settled for what they could get from Congress in 1935 and expected to build a broader and more comprehensive system over time. Roosevelt himself favored a "cradle to the grave system;" indeed, he claimed to have coined the phrase and was miffed when Lord Beveridge used it in 1942.[35] The work of an Advisory Council that developed the changes enacted in 1939 marked the initial victory of the incrementalists. From the fairly narrow Act of 1935, the system has become comprehensive, encompassing not only more people but more contingencies.[36].

The means to achieve these goals, and those that emerged with the development of the system (see Chapter 2) were to levy a payroll tax equally divided between employers and employees covered by the act (the self-employed were later included at a special tax rate). Although many European models supplement payroll taxes with subsidies from general revenues, Roosevelt, Morgenthau, and the more conservative faction wanted a "self-supporting" system. Opinion on this was by no means unanimous. Although Wilbur Cohen lists this as a "basic principle,"[37] J. Douglas Brown saw the need for eventual government subsidies, as did others. The self-support principle has been breached several times with the federal payments to the OASI Trust Fund for certain veterans and special age seventy-two benefits for persons who lacked coverage. The issue is not settled and promises to remain lively as policymakers search for ways to resolve the problem of high payroll taxes.

Once the decision was made to divide the tax, the fifty-fifty formula seemed fair—it was not, and is not, grounded in technical considerations or in any inherent logic. In 1977 the Carter Administration proposed to alter the fifty-fifty principle by increasing the tax paid by employers on behalf of workers earning more than the wage base. The proposal was not passed.

The choice of sixty-five as the basic retirement age was also somewhat arbitrary. When is a person too old for the labor market? In looking for models, the original policymakers saw state public assistance programs for the aged with age requirements ranging from sixty-five to seventy for men (one state had sixty for women). Foreign models showed similar variations, although Germany and Britain, being among the best-developed systems at the time, used sixty-five. The Railroad Retirement Act, passed by Congress in 1934, used sixty-five. Perhaps the overriding considerations were the high cost of retirement benefits below sixty-five, and the desire to get older workers out of the labor market, which precluded an age like seventy.[39] Sixty-five has a sort of esthetic neatness about it (after all, why not 64 or 65½?), and was chosen.

Sixty-five remains the basic retirement age in the law, although retirement as early as sixty-two is permitted with actuarily reduced benefits.[40] It is important to keep in mind the retirement test, which sharply reduces the beneficiary's ability to work without loss of some or all benefits (at this time, the test no longer applies past the age of seventy-two and will be reduced to age seventy in 1982). The retirement test was a means to accomplish two goals: (1) reduce costs, and (2) remove older workers from the labor market by establishing a work disincentive. The test has been liberalized since the original act, and the 1972 and 1977 amendments indexed the amount that can be earned, before loss of benefits, to average wages.

Needless to say, the retirement test remains a continuing political irritant. If people are led to believe that Social Security is a form of saving, then it is difficult to explain why they must stop work or limit their work activity in order to receive their benefits. The test does not cover income from physical or financial capital, and thus favors the well-to-do and discriminates against those who accumulated human capital in the form of education, training, and experience. Thus, it raises issues of equity, the economic issue of whether it is desirable to deplete the nation's stock of human capital, and finally, whether the incentive to retire creates personal and social problems among active and capable people whose mental and physical health may deteriorate as a result of inactivity. Like many other "basic principles," this issue is by no means settled.

An important means to achieve the goals of Social Security is compulsion. All who are covered must pay the tax, although they are free to reject the benefits if they like. Compulsory social insurance has the advantage of pooling all risks and thus overcoming market failure. Because private companies that sell insurance and annuities are free to reject poor risks, not all persons would have access to insurance and annuities. But there was a deeper argument in the decision to make social insurance compulsory. In a society that will make some provision for its indigents anyway, social insurance compels people to "save" so as to minimize the number who would otherwise become public charges. The founders of the Social Security system, following the lead established in countries like Germany and Britain, believed not only that the uncertainties of the labor market made it difficult for people to save systematically, but also that many would simply not do so.

In the first of these beliefs, they were influenced by the Depression of the 1930s. This created havoc not only in the labor market but also in the capital market. The collapse of banks, insurance companies, and private pension plans led them to believe that only government could provide the necessary security. The second belief—that many people would choose not to provide for their old age—was an equally powerful reason for the decision in favor of compulsion. As noted above, an explicit goal of the act was the reduction of dependency on public assistance. Compulsion would achieve such an objective by overriding personal choices.

Thus the founders of the system can be accused of paternalism. This is an ideological charge, although both economic theory and observed behavior support the proposition that people prefer goods now to goods later. It is doubtful whether the charge of paternalism would have disturbed either the New Dealers or the corporate and union officials who were on the Advisory Committee of the original Committee on Economic Security. The last were, of course, carefully chosen, but not all were especially liberal in their political outlooks.

As Milton Friedman has noted, the compulsion takes three forms. One is participation in a redistributive system both among beneficiaries and between generations. The second is the compulsion to "purchase" the "annuities" (if that is what the benefits may be called) from a nationalized insurance company. The third form is the compulsion to use current income to provide for old age. To Friedman, the third is the key issue. As a libertarian (or liberal, as he prefers to be called), he believes that individuals have a right to make their own mistakes.[41]

However onerous compulsion may be to individuals who prefer to make their own choices, the Friedman position has not attracted much of the electorate. Social Security is widely accepted in principle, and few argue about its compulsory nature as such. However, this acceptance may depend on the ability of the system to perform well. When and if it does not, the points made by Friedman may assume greater political importance.[42] This may occur in the next century, when the ratio of the aged to the younger population rises sharply and the younger population, through its higher taxes, comes to realize that the Social Security tax is not a "purchase of an annuity" but primarily a transfer of income from the younger to the older generation.

### Transfers in Cash and in Kind

With the exception of some federal aid to states for public health, the Social Security system provided income strictly in cash until the advent of Medicare. Public assistance had always had a tradition of providing some income in kind, that is, in the form of the commodity or service itself. This has been the case from the soup kitchens of yore to public hospitals for the poor, public housing, and today's food stamp program (not to mention Medicaid). As will be noted later, some of the founders of Social Security wanted to include national health insurance in the original bill, but opposition from the medical industry persuaded them to drop it.

The emphasis on cash was not coincidental. In a society that stresses individualism and the market mechanism, cash gives the individual the widest range of choice in how he or she wants to allocate personal income. Given the income constraint, cash allows the individual to buy more of one commodity and less of another, as a matter of personal choice. Income in kind does not provide this freedom.

The rise in medical costs that followed World War II presented problems both to the population and to the aged. In the nature of things, the aged are heavy users of medical care. The better the care (including self-care and medical care during their prime years), the longer they live and the more care they will need. One approach to the problem would have been to increase benefits to cover the average amount of care that an aged person needs and let him or her purchase it on the open market. Presumably this could have been financed by increased Social Security taxes like the payroll tax for Medicare.

Unfortunately, no one is average. Some people need more care, and some need less. Since an individual cannot foresee the amount of care he or she will need, the service lends itself to a pooling of risks, by which all members of a group pay an "average" amount to cover total needs, but some draw more upon the pool while others draw less. That is, of course, the principle underlying health insurance, although the word insurance is something of a misnomer—health insurance is largely prepaid medical care for the "insured" group.

The rise in population, combined with the increasing popularity of health insurance sharply increased the demand for health care without a corresponding increase in supply. As health-care prices went up, the aged (and the disabled and the poor) were particularly affected. The rise was compounded by the peculiar relationship among consumers, providers, and third-party payers. When the consumer pays himself, he makes choices about the amount of medical care he desires, subject to the constraints of family income and the possibility that the need is so great that savings, if available, must be used. Chances are taken and judgments are made that illnesses that appear to be minor will not require treatment. Most illnesses cure themselves anyway, but you never can tell for sure.

When the patient is insured, the temptation is great to make full use of the insurance. The premium has been paid, either by the individual or in his behalf by his employer (about 60 percent of the population carries some health insurance). Once he goes to his physician, the decision about how much care shall be rendered is in the physician's hands. Deductibles and coinsurance reduce the incentive by the individual to seek care, as well as by the physician to order extensive care, but they do not eliminate it. Third-party payers are in a poor position to second-guess the doctor's judgment. The leading one, Blue Cross/Blue Shield, was organized by doctors and hospitals and thus particularly dislikes second-guessing its patrons. The response is to raise premiums.

Where income transfers are concerned, a service that lends itself to risk-pooling is better suited to a transfer in kind rather than a cash transfer. When Medicare was under consideration, few voices were heard to say that, as a transfer in kind, it would rob its beneficiaries of individual freedom.[43] It made sense to cover the elderly with a federally financed form of health insurance (this was later extended to persons receiving Disability Insurance). At the same time, Medicaid was enacted to give the poor more equal access to the market for health care.

The impact of Medicare and Medicaid was to increase further the demand for care, both by individuals and by those who provide the care, again faster than the increase in supply. Wildavsky's Law of Medical Money states that costs will always rise to the level of available funds.[44]

It is not surprising that the Trust Funds covering Medicare are not in healthy shape under present circumstances. The Hospital Insurance Fund will be depleted by 1988. The Supplementary Medical Insurance Fund is financed on an incurred basis from premiums and general revenues. It does not make long-term projections. Despite a run of deficits, assets now exceed outstanding liabilities. However, costs are rising, which will require higher premiums and greater contributions from general revenues.[45]

Passage of a national health insurance bill will exacerbate the cost problems described above. Focus is already shifting to methods of cost control, including more efficient utilization of a more integrated health-care system and the removal of incentives by patients and providers to overuse the system. If the quantity of health care is equated with the level of national health, then an implicit policy decision is being made to transfer resources from other uses to health care. This is because, in the long run, the cost of health care can be stabilized only by increasing its supply or productivity. Whether or not more health care leads to better health on the whole is an issue beyond the scope of this work.

Whatever the case may be, present trends show that individual purchase of health care is on the wane. Medicare beneficiaries do not feel the stigma or restriction of freedom commonly associated with transfers in kind. A national health insurance system might subsume both Medicare and Medicaid but will undoubtedly contain an income transfer component to give the elderly, disabled, and poor relatively equal access to health care along with the working population.

## THE SOCIAL BENEFITS OF THE SYSTEM

It is difficult to talk about social benefits without introducing either private value judgments or the social value judgments that emerge through the political process. Those who value individual liberty above all may see no social benefit at all in the system. Such people see the system as depriving working individuals of the ability to make their own consumption and investment choices, to the extent of the tax. Since the system may be redistributive within a given generation, it robs Peter to pay Paul. Why, it is asked, should Peter be responsible for Paul? Furthermore, the system is redistributive between generations. It can be described as a social compact between generations by which the younger generation is compelled to abide even though it was not a signatory to the compact. The pure laissez-fairist can argue that all individuals are responsible for their mistakes, misjudgments, and misfortunes, and should bear the consequences thereof.

More socially minded libertarians, like Milton Friedman, are willing to make some provision for income transfers to those in need and recognize the obligations created by the System for the present generation of retirees and workers, although they may wish to abolish it for the future and replace all existing income transfers with a negative income tax.[46] This is not my point of view, nor is it widely held among the population.

The benefits to society are both tangible and intangible. Since labor is the principal source of income for most people, cessation of labor at the advent of old age makes the aged peculiarly vulnerable to poverty. In the absence of transfer payments, the aged would constitute the largest single group below the official poverty line. With luck, those of us who are not yet old will reach our "golden years," and the prospect of a high probability of poverty is not a pleasant one to contemplate. It will be too late then to correct the errors, misjudgments, and misfortunes of earlier years, too late to learn from experience.

Nor is the spectacle of poverty a pretty one for the rest of the population. There may be dispute over the extent to which the community should support the able-bodied poor who—arguably—could take steps to correct their situation by finding work. But age is a condition that is altered only by death. The fountain of youth has eluded us, as it did Ponce de Leon; the aged elicit sympathy from us. Social Security provides the aged with at least partial support. The belief that the benefits were earned, as well as the absence of the means test, do this without impairing their dignity.

Intangibles like dignity and the feeling of some security for those now old and those who will be old are beyond the scope of economic measurement. The alternatives to a social insurance system are liquidation, poverty, greater reliance on public assistance, and greater reliance on support from the family. The last was simpler in an agricultural society; to this day, children are the social security of parents in less-developed countries. Industrial society, with its urbanization (high cost of space) and labor mobility has helped to put an end to the extended family. It has also reduced the ability of the aged to contribute to some production. On the idealized farm, the old folks took care of the kids, helped with the cooking and the lighter chores, or tended the kitchen garden. Those days are gone forever, as the saying goes. Today, we even worry about the break-up of the nuclear family.

Thus social and economic forces beyond the control of individuals make the state a substitute for the economic support once provided by the family. The existence of income maintenance programs may speed up this process, although I doubt whether this is the original causative factor.[47]

Given the alternatives, social insurance has proved to be a "good thing," on net balance. The question is not whether to abolish it but how to deal with aspects that are beginning to make it dysfunctional. All social policies must change over time as needs and circumstances change. Social Security is no exception.

## THE NEW LAW AND THE OUTLOOK FOR CHANGE

Change there will be, and it will come in several stages. The immediate problem of erosion of the Trust Funds has apparently been solved, although short-term pressures may arise again in the early 1980's. Many people are unhappy with the solution. It means higher Social Security taxes and relatively lower future benefits. The "principle of self-sufficiency" has been preserved, albeit by diverting part of the Hospital Insurance tax into the Old Age, Survivors, and Disability Trust Funds. Decoupling has been accomplished, and the system no longer overcompensates for inflation. However, long run problems remain.

The increased participation of women in the labor force and the rising divorce rate may lead to changes that attach benefit rights to individuals rather than families. At some point, two-earner families will realize that their taxes are "buying" relatively less protection than that obtained by similarly situated one-earner families. Higher divorce rates may further increase the female labor force participation rate but will leave some nonworking wives stranded outside the system after divorce. To a certain extent, this may be offset by frequent remarriage, but as in musical chair games, some will fall off, as long as women live longer than men.

Some of the other issues touched upon in this overview will have to be dealt with. These include the system's impact on capital markets (if Feldstein is right) and labor markets. On the latter issue, there will probably be further political pressure to ease or abolish the retirement test. Whatever the pros and cons of this may be, retired workers consider it unfair. At some point, the existing crazy quilt of social insurance, public and private pensions, and public assistance may bear re-examination to bring it into a more coherent whole. Finally, the cost problems associated with Medicare (and Medicaid) are bound to lead to revisions in the present Hospital Insurance program.

On the farther horizon is the demographic change that occurred after World War II, which will mature in the twenty-first century (happily after I am gone). It may be wise to begin to plan for it now, but I do not know of any politician who, in 1980, is worried about re-election in 2028.

All change is painful, for there will be some who gain and some who lose. The intentional gains and losses will be worked out through the political process. The unintentional ones will manifest themselves later and may lead to further change in efforts to correct them.

At all times, it must be remembered that the entire structure of income maintenance, including Social Security, operates within the context of the economy's ability to produce goods and services. No amount of tinkering with the Social Security Act will alter this, for distribution depends on production. A growing economy can distribute more; a declining economy *will* distribute less. Hence, the success of changes and reforms in Social Security and in the other income maintenance systems will depend on the future course of the economy.

In this chapter an attempt was made to survey the issues that now becloud Social Security and appear to threaten its future. The present system was not created in one fell swoop but grew in bits and pieces, along with the rest of our income maintenance structure. For an understanding of why our problems have come about, it may be instructive to trace the development of public income maintenance and of the employment-related pensions system that has grown to supplement and complement it. In the chapter that follows, public income maintenance will be examined for its traditions and historical development. Its two parts, social insurance and public assistance, will be viewed as components of one (perhaps somewhat incoherent) structure of income transfers. The analysis will help to explain how we got to this point and how the problems developed. Pensions will be examined in Chapter 3, after which it will be possible to view the total structure and examine it in greater depth.

## CHAPTER TWO

# Public Income Maintenance Systems in America

THERE ARE ESSENTIALLY two traditions from which public income maintenance systems are derived. The first and older is a charitable function assumed by local and state governments—and later the federal government—as private charity and family support eroded over time. This can be called public assistance and has two characteristics. One is a means test: The applicant must show some evidence of need and lack of alternative sources of income. The second is that support is offered without necessary regard for the applicant's previous record of work or tax contributions to the community's fisc. Until the twentieth century, all public income maintenance systems in this country were, in one form or another, in the nature of public assistance. In a larger sense, this included veterans' benefits, inasmuch as these were generally offered on a means test basis, although it might be argued that they constituted a kind of deferred payment for service to the nation.

The second tradition is social insurance. The earliest form of social insurance was Workmen's Compensation (now often called Workers' Compensation) and made its appearance at the beginning of the twentieth century in various industrial states. Unlike the social insurance programs that were to follow, Workers' Compensation was insurance in the usual actuarial sense of the word. The worker injured on the job was entitled to medical benefits, compensation for damages, if need be, and possibly a pension for himself (or his dependents if the injury was fatal). Because the risks for groups of workers were predictable, they were insurable. Employers complied with their state laws by purchasing insurance in the open market. To this day, the bulk of Workers' Compensation is funded through private insurance companies. Where publicly owned insurance companies are found, as in New York, they compete with private firms and also pick up the poor risks at correspondingly high premiums. One of their chief functions is to substitute for the assigned risk pools commonly found in automobile insurance.

Although the word "insurance" came to be used for other public benefit programs, especially those that developed from the Social Security Act of 1935 and its amendments, the concept of insurance became attenuated as it applied to them. If insurance is used to pertain to a spreading of risk that is predictable for any group and is funded accordingly, then the programs that we shall call social insurance hardly fit into this category. Nonetheless, the word insurance remains important for its symbolic connotation. Benefits are a matter of right, as distinct from the charitable notions of public assistance. The right is "earned" by the characteristics commonly associated with social insurance: (1) Contributions (taxes) are paid by or on behalf of the covered worker, based in part on his earnings, and (2) benefits are paid to the worker and his dependents based on his earnings record, that is, his previous tax contributions. Invariably, there is a fund, resembling an insurance carrier; a corollary is that (3) no showing of need is involved, as all that needs to be proved is that the insurable contingency occurred, that is, that the claimant is indeed disabled, aged, or unemployed.

The symbolic value of the term insurance, even as modified by the word social, cannot be overstated. The claimant, having paid his contributions, is not a supplicant for charity. His dignity is unimpaired, at least in principle, by the receipt of the benefit. In practice, the process of applying, standing in line, and dealing with a civil servant may contain the seeds of some humiliation, but perhaps no more so than an argument between a consumer and a large enterprise. Be that as it may, the symbolic value of the word insurance is politically potent, its potency reinforced by the fact that virtually all members of our working population have contact with social insurance, whereas only a minority deal with public assistance.

In the paragraphs that follow, I shall trace the emergence of both the public assistance and the social insurance traditions in the United States. It will be seen that the two overlapped as they developed and that the distinction, though analytically and politically convenient, is not a clear one. Social insurance, as embodied in Social Security programs, has taken on some of the aspects of public assistance. The latter, in turn, has assumed some aspects of social insurance, at least in localities where welfare has become more and more (perhaps properly so) a matter of right.

## DEVELOPMENT OF THE PUBLIC ASSISTANCE AND SOCIAL INSURANCE TRADITIONS

### Public Assistance

The history of public assistance is worth reviewing here, not only as a prelude to its interactions with other forms of income maintenance, but also to demonstrate the conflicting goals and purposes that are carried forward to the present day. Private charity is an obligation that was established by many religions since time immemorial. It is clearly found in the teachings of the Old Testament, the New Testament, and the Koran, to name but three writings that have had a powerful impact on religious belief in much of the world. In medieval Europe, the charitable obligation was carried on both within the family and through the intermediation of local Church bodies.[1] But changing agricultural technology, with corresponding changes in serfdom and land tenure, and the growth of cities began to generate a population of paupers—now with work and now without it—that transcended the willingness or ability of the Church to serve as a welfare department. The increasing separation of Church and state—at least, the emergence of non-Roman Catholic religions in the West—probably added to the need to bring government into the picture.

The last point should not be stressed too much, although it is important in the derivation of the American tradition from the English Poor Laws. It is worth noting that even in Catholic Bruges, the local burghers asked Juan Luis Vives to develop a plan for relieving the large number of unemployed workers laid off because of the recession in the wool trade.[2]

Although pauperism and public assistance made their appearance in various parts of preindustrial Europe, it is to England that we turn for the evolution of a comprehensive system of poor relief. Parliament began to legislate on the subject even before the passage of the celebrated Act of 43rd Elizabeth I Chap. 2, the first Poor Law. The early laws under Henry VIII and his immediate successors contained, in essence, the mix of charity and deterrence that we still encounter today. The well-to-do were to contribute to parish charity, and persistently idle rogues were to be branded and whipped.[3] Deterrence was important. Tudor policymakers, like their modern counterparts, entertained the fear that, with relief provided at subsistence level, some part of the population would be tempted to forgo work (often at or near subsistence) and prefer the leisure of a subsidized pauper. Although the formal economic theory of this phenomenon was not to be developed for some centuries, it was intuitively believed, possibly on the basis of casual empirical observation.

In any event, the English[4] Poor Law set into place a formalized system of public assistance, some of whose elements were brought to North America by English settlers. Its essence was a decentralized system of poor relief mandated upon local government jurisdictions (parishes). Each locality was compelled to levy taxes for support of its poor and to establish some administrative mechanism to determine the tax levy (commonly property taxes) and to disburse aid. Although Tudor England, like other rising nation-states, had a centralized government, it was far from reaching the high level of centralization in government encountered today. The mechanism of using the national state to deal with local problems made particular sense here: Westminster was merely compelling localities to do something that they had, in some quasi-voluntary fashion, been doing all along. Certainly, the appointment of a Crown official to administer such a law would have been an unthinkable act in seventeenth-century English political and constitutional theory.

The decentralized nature of the system gave localities considerable scope for variation in tax rates, benefit levels, and the manner in which benefits were given out. For example, parishes would choose to make payments in cash or kind, or to construct almshouses. It was taken for granted that work was compulsory, except possibly for those too aged or disabled, and children and their mothers were certainly included among candidates for work. Furthermore, law and custom placed great reliance upon intrafamily income transfers, making relatives legally responsible for the support of indigents within the family.

To put the last point more succinctly, the primary obligation for the support of poor persons lay within the family. The community's obligation was secondary and constituted a last resort. There may still be those who yearn for the simpler days and decry both the decay of the family as a mutual support group and the locality as the reliever of last resort. However sentimental one may wish to be on this subject, the decay, if that is the proper term, was caused by economic forces that were external to the family and to the community. Both were caught in economic changes over which they had no control and had no choice but to respond in some fashion. As always, the response lagged behind the economic reality by a long time. I shall return to this point later.

The tradition that the local community was responsible for its own poor was reinforced in the seventeenth century by the Act of Settlement.[5] Each person had a "settlement" in his place of origin or in some place to which the local authorities formally admitted him on proof that he had adequate means of support. The law was intended to protect localities from having to support actual or potential indigents who came from other parts of the country. It was not unknown for miserly localities to push their poor elsewhere,[6] although much of the population movement was undoubtedly the result of a rise in the mobility of labor that followed the beginnings of industrialization. In effect, the law permitted the locality to deport persons who did not have a legal residence there. The economic folly of this practice was noted by a number of observers, not the least being Adam Smith,[7] who showed that preventing workers from seeking employment outside their communities made the country poorer by diminishing the supply of labor available to it.

As noted previously, the English colonists who came to our shores brought with them a public assistance tradition based upon the Poor Law of the mother country. As might be expected, they adapted it to an economy in which land was more easily available, especially after the Revolution, when trans-Appalachian settlement became possible. At the minimum, some of this land was available for subsistence farming, and in relatively small lots, unlike the land tenure system in Great Britain which was more in the nature of latifundia (with a relatively small group owning large tracts). This helps to account for the American emphasis on self-reliance, an ethic that persisted throughout the nineteenth-century influx of a landless group of industrial workers.

**Private Charity.** It is time to shift this historical survey from England to the United States. Before doing so, it should be noted that private charity had existed in England and in the rest of Europe. So too, Americans contributed to charitable causes long before the income tax made it cheaper and more advantageous to do so. Private institutions to aid the poor began to assume importance in the early part of the nineteenth century, especially in cities, which received an accumulation of a poor, landless population. At first such organizations preferred "indoor" relief, that is, the use of homes for the indigent aged and disabled—really private poorhouses. The private sector feared public outdoor relief in that it lent itself to the buying of votes, not an entirely irrational fear. The political machines that grew in nineteenth-century cities after manhood suffrage became universal based their power, in part, on the ability of local political leaders to provide services to their constituents. The advent of industrialization made unworkable a system of aid developed for small agricultural communities.

The response of both sectors was to offer aid on an outdoor basis, often in kind and within the established tradition of distinguishing between the able-bodied (who were expected to offer work), and those who could not be expected to participate in the labor market. Private organizations developed coordinating systems to avoid duplication and to place the granting of aid on a more businesslike basis. They tended toward social reform, such as tenement laws. Their utilitarian philosophy did not conflict with a generally social Darwinist view of society, which regarded most paupers as more or less responsible for their own condition, to be reformed if at all possible.

The income maintenance role of private charity was ended by the massive entry of state and federal programs in the 1930s. Because the federal programs in that decade were largely aimed at the unemployed, such institutions as private (often religious) orphanages and old age homes survived. Orphanages have well-nigh disappeared and charitable old-age homes, like their profit-making counterparts, make use of government funds that are disbursed directly or indirectly (through Medicaid) to them.

**Summarizing the Charitable Tradition.** As the foregoing historical survey indicates, the public assistance tradition developed as a charitable function, an aspect reinforced during the heyday of private charity. This applies as much to support for the aged as for the able-bodied. The applicant was a supplicant, to be judged on his worthiness and the existence of responsible relatives or other means of support. Acceptance of charity, either public or private, stigmatized the recipient and his or her family. (Devotees of old movies will remember *The Bank Dick*, in which W. C. Fields's mother-in-law threatened to "go on the county" and thus bring shame on the family.) As for benefit levels, they were adjusted to need on a case-by-case level by a social worker or a similar functionary who made judgments not just on overall needs but on the components of the family budget.[8] Later refinements were to standardize aid budgets, partly for administrative convenience, but the general principle survives to this day.

### The Social Insurance Tradition

The English Poor Law had made its impact in Western Europe as well as in the United States.[9] The impact of the preindustrializing and industrializing stages of capitalist development subjected poor laws to extreme strains. Europe, furthermore, had a lively and growing socialist movement that grew with the development of an industrial working class. If the specter of communism was something of a figment of Marx's and Engels's imaginations in their 1848 *Communist Manifesto*, it became a nightmare to the upper classes by the second half of the nineteenth century. The need to provide more security to the working population became apparent to a wide variety of respectable opinion-makers, ranging from Pope Leo XIII to Otto von Bismarck. The Pope was neither pro-capitalist nor violently antisocialist. Bismarck, on the other hand, had an almost neurotic fear of socialism, even the revisionist Social Democracy that emerged in Germany.

The latter part of the nineteenth century saw a considerable search for reform on the part of a variety of people with varying and conflicting motives. This search for at least a partial replacement for the Poor Laws led them first to the concept of insurance, a familiar device for persons of even middling wealth. From there it was an easy step, at least in Europe, to the concept of social insurance as a compulsory device through which workers and their dependents could achieve at least a modicum of security.

Commercial insurance was not available to working people. Premiums and cost of administration would have been too high for the bulk of the population. However, skilled tradesmen in a number of occupations here and there formed Friendly Societies. These were, in many cases, indistinguishable from trade unions, but some behaved as mutual benefit societies to aid in cases of illness or death. The British were particularly advanced in this concept, and British Friendly Societies were encouraged by legislation to provide for registration and orderly administration.[10] As the Germans moved to establish themselves as the pioneers of social insurance, they took note of their own miners' societies,[11] and several German states in the pre-Imperial period encouraged the formation of benefit societies for sickness and accident cases.[12] Germany also took an interest in the operation of British Friendly Societies.[13] It was natural for German reformers, when they took the next step, to organize their social insurance system along occupational lines (a number of other European countries were to follow this example, although Britain itself was to move to a simpler national system.)

Germany stands as the first nation with a fairly comprehensive system of social insurance. Any attempt to trace the origins of the social insurance tradition must take at least a brief glance at the origins and motives for this remarkable law. Bismarck was undoubtedly the driving force behind the reform: Two of the three laws that constitute the package of legislation were enacted under his administration, and he wanted all three. In view of the fact that he was not a man noted for compassion toward the less fortunate, it is worth examining his motives.

His legislation to repress the Social Democrats was successful, but he was a man of great political sense who knew that social unrest cannot solely be dealt with that way. Being a Prussian, he may also have been influenced by the paternalist traditions of that region. In any event, his stated motives can be summarized as follows:

1. Workers were to see the state as something that serves their needs and interests, and not only those of the propertied classes.

2. To gain the loyalty of the workers, they should be given something they could not secure themselves. In his proposals, benefits would exceed the value of workers' contributions, because employers also contributed and the government was to add to the benefits.

3. The system was a "more dignified form of poor relief and a development of the idea on which relief is based."

4. It would create a class of rentiers who, like French rentiers, would develop a conservative attitude and a stake in the status quo.[14]

5. Localities that gave public assistance to their poor would have their local tax burden lightened by a national system that maintained aged and infirm persons.[15]

As can be seen, a principal purpose of the scheme was to wean workers away from a rival political ideology: socialism. Bismarck did not entirely succeed, for the end of the anti-Social Democratic laws saw a rise in the power of that party even before the advent of World War I. However, because Social Democrats are the moderate wing of the socialist movement, it can be argued that Bismarck's purpose was not entirely frustrated. Certainly similar political reasons for social insurance systems obtained in the other industrial nations that followed suit. Even in the United States, a latecomer to such programs, the Social Security Act's development and passage were triggered by the politically potent Townsend movement and by Senator Huey Long's "share the wealth" movement.[16] Thus: *Principle 1*: Social insurance serves an important political need, not merely to gain votes for the sponsoring political party but also to achieve a level of social stability.

*Principle 2*: In industrial countries, where other mechanisms of mutual aid have broken down, social insurance serves this purpose better than public assistance.

*Principle 3*: Locally financed public assistance programs create disproportionate tax burdens in the face of national labor markets, leading to demands for fiscal relief from the heavily burdened areas.

A social insurance system overcomes part of this problem by spreading the risk across a larger pool of the taxpaying population.

Looking back at the early German system, it can be seen that it was not especially redistributive among social classes but served to redistribute income within the working population (and, as will later become apparent, between generations). In the Bismarckian system, contributions were regressive and benefits were progressive, thus balancing out the income redistribution. True, the government added to benefits out of general revenues (thus adding a welfare element), but the overall structure of German taxes was not progressive. Thus: *Principle 4*: Social insurance systems are not necessarily intended to redistribute income from the rich to the poor. However, even nonredistributive systems can enable workers, as a group, to pool risks and thus overcome the failure of commercial insurance to provide security. Compulsory participation is a key element in this principle.

The first German social insurance laws required contributions from both employers and employees, although not necessarily in equal proportions. (Industrial accident insurance, however, was entirely financed by employers because it replaced, as in the United States, the employer's common law and statutory liabilities).[17] Sickness insurance contributions were, generally speaking, paid on a ratio of ⅔ by workers and ⅓ by employers. Old Age and Invalidity insurance contributions were equally divided. Efforts were made to establish contribution rates on an actuarial basis, subject to change with changes in experience.[18] Both contributions (except accident insurance) and cash benefits were wage-related, although not in precise proportions. Benefits calculations were exceedingly complex.

From this we get:

*Principle 5*: The beneficiary's claim is seen as a matter of right and not subject to a means test. It is, in effect (or gives the appearance of), a combination of insurance and savings, albeit compulsory.

It may be that Bismarck did not concern himself with the question of whether the employer's share of the contribution would be shifted back to his employees through a relative diminution of wage rates. German economics at the time was antitheoretical, and the theory of shifting and incidence of taxation was not, in any event, well developed. Socialist critics saw the employer's contribution as part of the worker's rightful wage, a position grounded as much in ideology as in the fundamentals of Marxian economic theory.[19] Modern economists almost uniformly assume that all of the social security tax is borne by the employees, but this cannot be deduced as a principle from early social insurance programs.

*Principle 6*: Regardless of who bears the employer's share, the linking of benefits to contributions introduces an element of fiscal soundness. This serves as a political limit to popular demands for higher benefits and diminishes the resistance of wealth-holding groups to the introduction of the system.

Although the evidence is somewhat mixed, it appears that the advent of social insurance in Germany reduced the amount that lower wage workers deposited in savings banks (the only investment vehicle open to them). Obviously, such workers' ability to save was diminished by the new tax (contribution) and, quite probably, their need to save was diminished by the prospect of benefits that were greater than those purchasable out of their meager savings. Principle 5 above indicates that workers were intended to see the social insurance tax as savings. If so, they made a rational adjustment in their personal investment portfolios.[20]

If we count the funds contributed for the total package of the German social insurance system, not all of it was invested in government securities. The early years show a surplus of inflows over outflows. From this we get:

*Principle 7*: Contributory social insurance systems may have a negative impact on private savings. The resulting impact on capital formation may depend, in part, on whether the system runs surpluses and how such surpluses are invested.

Finally, the early German experience revealed a decrease in the ratio of the relieved poor to the whole population (Bismarck's fifth stated purpose, above) but a general *increase* in the cost of public assistance. Unemployment had been excluded as a social insurance contingency, new responsibilities were mandated upon the relief authorities, there was a natural increase in population, and poor relief benefits rose not only in response to rising prices but also in response to the social insurance system's benefit levels.[21] Thus, from the very beginnings of social insurance we encounter the puzzling phenomenon that public assistance, with all its objectionable features, retains an important and often growing role in income maintenance, notwithstanding the development of social insurance. Hence:

*Principle 8*: Public assistance is only partly displaced by social insurance. It retains a complementary role, and its growth may result from the growth of problems not covered by social insurance.

It is not my intent to spend too much time on the early German system. Although the Germans influenced the social insurance systems that evolved in the developed world, the nations that followed on the heels of Germany would probably have developed similar systems from which much the same principles would have emerged. Rather, it has been my intent to draw from the early German experience the traditions of social insurance as they developed historically. The details varied from country to country. Over time, the systems matured. They became more complex and more comprehensive.[22] The basic concepts concern us as we turn now to the formation of the Social Security Act in the United States, which drew upon both the English public assistance tradition and the European social insurance tradition.

## THE MERGER OF THE TWO TRADITIONS

Inasmuch our focus is on old age issues, much of the discussion surrounding the Social Security Act will have to be omitted for the sake of conciseness. The discussions were wide-ranging and were stimulated by the work of a remarkable committee formed by Executive Order 6757, dated June 29, 1934.[23] The staff of this committee, headed by Prof. Edward E. Witte of the University of Wisconsin, conducted a series of comprehensive research reports as underpinning for the committee's legislative recommendations and as grist for the mills of Congress.

One of the studies, quite naturally, dealt with foreign experience, since so many countries preceded the United States in the enactment of public systems to support the aged. These were divided into two types: (1) noncontributory general old age assistance laws, or public assistance and (2) compulsory general old age insurance laws,[24] or social insurance for the aged. There was, of course, some overlap. However, as of 1933 the committee found thirteen means-tested public assistance systems and twenty social insurance systems. Of these, two (in France and Britain) also had a public assistance tier. Some combined old age insurance with invalidity insurance and/or survivor's insurance. With the exception of Germany's, all but one were enacted in the first two decades of the twentieth century. They were not, with the exception of Poland's, responses to the Great Depression.[25]

The twenty countries with social insurance laws encompassed nearly all the industrial nations of Europe. The committee noted two principal reasons for the shift in emphasis from "gratuitous old age assistance" to "contributory insurance." These were (1) the widespread objection to the means test and a desire to make benefits a matter of right, and (2) objection to the financial strain upon the public exchequer stemming from the increasing percentage of aged persons in need of help.[26]

Both of these reasons are related to the motives discussed with reference to the German experiment. A growing population of indigents (aged and otherwise) is likely to become politically restless when faced with the indignities of the means test, and this will be especially true in urban industrial countries where community and family support systems have disintegrated. The second reason is as politically significant as the first. If the aged (and others) are to be publicly supported—at least in part—then the tying of limited benefits to an earmarked tax serves as a way of controlling the fiscal growth of the system in some orderly fashion. This is a matter of considerable concern to middle- and upper-income taxpayers. The committee found it significant that virtually all systems it studied covered only employed workers, required contributions from both employers and workers, and provided supplements from the general exchequer, either in the partial payment of premiums or in contributions to the annuities.[27]

It was the committee's conclusion that a fully funded system (which it favored) should be financed by joint contributions. However, its actuarial estimates indicated that even a funded system would require subsidies after the first twenty-five years. At that point the projected revenues from its proposed contributions would fall short of the projected aggregate cost of the benefits it proposed, and government subsidy would become necessary.[28]

The 1939 Amendments shifted the system from more or less full funding to pay as you go. However, some provision for public assistance would have been needed in any event, at least as a transitional measure until the system matured. Accordingly, the committee also proposed a system of old age assistance on the public assistance principle to be built on pre-existing state systems, but with the federal government as a partner.[29] But even in respect of its insurance proposal, the committee wanted a welfare component in the benefit structure rather than a wage-related benefit system computed on a one-to-one basis,[30] so that benefits should favor persons of lower income. Such a benefit structure was enacted and has been considerably reinforced with the relatively high minimum benefits (that is, relative to contributions) that now prevail.

Thus, the charitable and the insurance traditions overlapped from the very beginning—indeed, in the proposal stage. The intent of the law was to provide some redistribution of income in the benefit structure within the covered segment of the population.[31] Both traditions, as embodied in the Social Security Act, developed further and changed in the decades that followed the passage of the law. Accordingly, an examination of the present structure of public income maintenance for the aged requires us to look at how the components of our public assistance system changed over time, and we must do the same for the changes in the Social Security system. This will then enable us to pull the two threads together and to view the two systems as components of *one* structure—components that are troublesome because they conflict, overlap, and sometimes interact so as to defeat one another's purpose.

Having completed this analysis, it will then be possible to discuss in Chapter 3 employer related pensions, which, together with social insurance and public assistance, form most of the income maintenance for the aged.

## DEVELOPMENT OF THE STRUCTURE OF PUBLIC INCOME MAINTENANCE

The committee's recommendations (which included health insurance) went to Congress, where they were subject to considerable debate. The law that emerged from the deliberations is the Social Security Act (Ch. 531, 49 Stat. 620, August 14, 1935), one of the few remaining monuments to the New Deal. Some of its proponents saw it as a foundation on which a larger and more comprehensive structure might be built. They were right, as opponents of the act feared. As the years passed, the act has been amended many times to add new provisions, to liberalize existing ones, and, incidentally, to depart from the original principle that the insurance portion be funded on a full reserve basis.

In the ensuing paragraphs, I shall summarize the original act[32] and then trace the growth of its two principal components: the public assistance part and the social insurance part. Although the focus will remain on the provision for the aged, it will be necessary to make reference to other provisions, inasmuch as we are dealing with a complex system whose parts affect each other as well as the behavior of families who are trying to provide for their old age.

**Summary of the Act**

Title I of the act is the public assistance provision to the aged that became known as Old Age Assistance and is now encompassed in Supplemental Security Income. Essentially, Congress retained the Poor Law traditions, which by the beginnings of the twentieth century had led states as well as localities to establish old age pensions for their aged indigents. In many cases, these worked cooperatively with private charities. However, the Depression served to decrease both public and private funds for this purpose, while drastically increasing the size of the indigent population. The latter phenomenon came about in a variety of ways: unemployment of older workers, unemployment of younger workers who had previously been able to help parents and relatives, the collapse of many private pension systems then in existence, and the wiping out of savings not only by the drop in security prices but also by the collapse of banks and other financial institutions. The need was not only relief for the aged poor but fiscal relief for the states and localities whose laws provided for such aid.

Title I enabled states to set up statewide programs of Old Age Assistance for persons over sixty-five (until 1940, states could use seventy as the minimum) at the option of the state, and provided partial federal participation in the financing of such programs. The conditions on the state were designed to ensure that the state's plan would have uniform conditions and benefits, regardless of whether it was administered by the state itself or its subdivisions. This, in effect, mandated a state agency either to administer or to coordinate the plan. In addition, the scope of the residence requirement that any state might want to impose was broad in order to allow it to minimize its outlays. The restriction was quite generous to the states. It established a maximum residence requirement of five of the nine years preceding the application. The act thus carried forward a variant of the old Poor Law tradition that the community (but now the state) was responsible only for its own poor. States were free to establish more liberal residence requirements, and some, in fact, imposed only one year.

The original benefit structure of the Old Age Insurance system would have provided very low benefits (see below) and excluded many workers. Accordingly, Old Age Assistance had important transitional functions—helping low benefit insured workers until the system matured and aiding those excluded from insurance.

Title II, called Federal Old Age Benefits, established the Old Age Insurance system. It is interesting to note that its first provision, Section 201, established the Old Age Reserve Account on an actuarial basis and an interest rate of 3 percent per year compounded annually. Portions of the fund not needed for immediate benefit payments were to be invested in obligations issued or guaranteed by the federal government. The possibility of investment in the private capital market was thus excluded from the very beginning. It would have led, over time, to ownership by the government of a large block of private securities. In the words of Senator Arthur Vandenberg, "that would be socialism."[33] The fear of a capital shortage obviously did not haunt anyone in 1935, when so much capital was idle. If anything, there was the fear that, over time, the fund would generate large increases in the national debt and, as will be shown, this fear was allayed in 1939 when the system moved from full funding to a pay-as-you-go basis, although the Reserve Account (now called the Trust Fund) was maintained.

Section 202 provided for the schedule of benefits to begin in 1942. Benefits were based on total wage earnings after 1936. The schedule was progressive, i.e., it favored the lower-income workers, and had a maximum of $85 per month. Since the system's full funding made it resemble an annuity, Section 203 provided for lump-sum payments to the estates of deceased workers, amounting to 3½ percent of covered wages earned after 1936. The next section provided a lump sum benefit for workers who did not qualify (see Section 210 below) at age sixty-five. This was apparently intended to be transitional, to phase out as more and more workers became qualified.

Section 210 defined qualified workers by excluding from coverage a considerable portion of the labor force, including agricultural workers, all government employees, casual workers, seamen, domestics, and employees of religious or nonprofit (charitable, educational, etc.) institutions. Railroad workers were also excluded but had coverage under a separate program, established by the Railroad Retirement Act. By implication, the self-employed were also excluded. Evelyn Burns noted that the exclusions pressed heavily upon women and blacks, who were concentrated in the excluded occupations, and noted that there was some truth to the charge that this part of the act was a plan to provide security for white male wage earners.[34]

Financing of Old Age Insurance came from Title VIII, so that it would be obvious to a hostile Supreme Court that benefits and contributions were entirely separate. Nowhere is the term "contributions" found here or anywhere else in the original act. Instead, we find an income tax on employees covered by the act and an excise tax (really a payroll tax) on employers, both presumably constitutional under the taxing powers of the federal government. The maximum of wages on which these taxes were levied was $3000 (the original wage base), and the rate was 1 percent on employees and 1 percent on employers. This was to rise, by stages, to 3 percent each in 1949. Note that whereas the benefits were (and are) progressive, the tax was regressive past the wage base, as in the original German system.

The other social insurance provision of the act was Unemployment Compensation. As in Old Age Insurance, Congress was careful to satisfy the constitutional issues by dividing the law between widely separated titles. Title III provided grants to states for administration and placed conditions on state plans, including the use by them of a federal Unemployment Trust Fund for the accumulation of funds and payment of benefits. However, no benefit schedule was provided, and states were relatively free to establish their own systems. Title IX, which dealt with funding, was a tax law on employers of eight or more workers (again, with a list of exclusions similar to those in Old Age Insurance). The tax began at 1 percent in 1936, rising to 3 percent by 1938.

The kicker, which really mandated unemployment insurance on the states, was the provision that 90 percent of the tax could be credited to a certified state plan. The remaining 10 percent provided for the grants to states for administrative expenses. Thus, any state that might not want such a law would find its employers paying a tax without the state's receiving any benefits from it. The predictable result was that all states passed such laws. The fund was invested in federal obligations, but separate accounts were, and still are, kept for each state.

Two more public assistance provisions were contained in the act. One was Aid to the Blind (Title X), with provisions similar to Old Age Assistance (OAA). The other was Aid to Dependent Children (ADC). These were on a cost-sharing basis, like Old Age Assistance. The cost-sharing formula indirectly helped to determine benefit levels by limiting federal participation, although states could be as generous as they liked with their own funds. For the aged and the blind, federal participation was limited to 50 percent of a $30 monthly benefit, plus 5 percent of a $30 benefit usable for administration or benefits. Thus, the maximum federal grant per person was $16.50 per month.

The ADC formula was somewhat more restrictive. The maximum grant was 33 percent of an $18 benefit for the first child, ($6), 33 percent of $12 for each additional child ($4). No payments were made available for persons caring for dependent children. However, the maximum residence requirement for ADC was limited to one year.

The rest of the original act need not concern us in detail here. Briefly, it created an administrative agency, originally known as the Social Security Board, to carry out the functions of the act. Although health insurance was not provided for, the act provided funds to states for maternal and child health services, vocational rehabilitation, and public health work.

**Development of Public Assistance**

The basic public assistance system for the aged and blind remained relatively unchanged for several decades after 1935, except for the addition of a program of Aid to the Totally and Permanently Disabled (APTD) passed in 1950 on terms similar to OAA and AB. As time passed, benefit levels rose, spurred by changes in the federal cost sharing-formulae. ADC became Aid to Families with Dependent Children (AFDC) that year with the inclusion of payments for persons caring for such children. In most cases these were mothers. The purpose of the program was to aid fatherless children; intact families were not eligible for benefits. Since our concern in this work is primarily with the aged, the development of the AFDC program into the great "welfare crisis" will not be followed here.[35] Needless to say, that segment of the adult poverty population whose primary dependence has been on AFDC for much of their lives is likely to graduate to the public assistance components of the income maintenance system for the aged.

The first really radical change in public assistance for the aged (and disabled) was Medicaid (Medical Assistance), which came with the 1965 amendments that also created Medicare (Health Insurance for the Aged). The federal government had participated in cost sharing for medical payments in behalf of welfare recipients since 1950, and in 1960 it added Medical Assistance to the Aged for those of the aged who, although not on OAA, met a means test of medical indigence. Medicaid (Title XIX of the amended Social Security Act) was initially intended to consolidate the cost-sharing programs for the categorical and medically indigent.[36] Like other public assistance programs, it is administered at state (and local) levels, a continuing tribute to the Poor Law tradition.[37]

The initial hope of the policymakers was to provide medical care for all needy persons, but within two years rising costs led to the federal government's establishing an income limit beyond which it would not share costs (133 ⅓ percent of the highest amount payable to a comparable AFDC family). Because virtually all the aged are eligible for Medicare, the federal government attempted to reduce the overlap between the programs by withholding cost sharing for services that could have been rendered under the Supplementary Medical

Insurance (SMI) part of Medicare. The Medicare system will be described below.

The Medicaid program has proved to be an important structure of income maintenance for the aged, although its importance varies from state to state. All states must cover the categorical poor but may limit recipients of public assistance for the aged and disabled (currently called SSI) to those who would have been eligible under standards in effect in 1972. Sixteen states have such limitations, subject to the restriction that they must allow all aged, blind, and disabled to qualify by spending on medical care that portion of their income which is in excess of the medical assistance standard (that is, if the standard for an aged family is $2,200, and a family receives $2,600, it becomes eligible when it has spent $400 on medical care.[38]

The importance of Medicaid can be seen from the fact that 17 percent of the aged received Medicaid payments in 1975 and accounted for 37 percent of payments. If we add the blind and disabled, we get 28 percent of the three population segments accounting for 61 percent of Medicaid expenses.[39] Clearly the Medicare program, which covers virtually all the aged,[40] has not been sufficient, especially as it does not cover extended stays in nursing homes. One of the results of Medicaid has been the growth of such homes for the aged who can no longer take care of themselves. Given the high costs of health care in the United States, it does not take long for ill, aged persons in their declining years to spend so much of their remaining assets on medical care not covered by Medicare or private insurance that they meet the means test for Medicaid.

Accordingly, Medicaid has become a large and growing source of maintenance for the older population in the very last years of their lives. This includes persons who, throughout most of their active lives, were relatively well off. The extent of the phenomenon varies from state to state, depending on the state's eligibility restrictions. No state may treat adult children as legally responsible for the well-being of their parents, but all states treat spouses as responsible for each other. This creates an interesting incentive for divorce among couples where one spouse needs nursing home care and the other would rapidly impoverish himself or herself in an attempt to finance long-term care at rates that can easily run from $7,000 to $10,000 a year. In short, Medicaid is acquiring a middle-class clientele and must be considered a significant part of the structure of income maintenance for the aged that has developed over the years.[41]

The basic reform of cash public assistance for the aged, blind, and disabled occurred with the passage of H.R. 1 in 1972. Beginning in 1974, this combined all the former federal adult welfare categories into one system called Supplemental Security Income (SSI).[42] The legislative objective was to establish a national program providing a uniform minimum cash income to the aged, blind, and disabled.[43] Funds for the minimum come from general federal revenues, thus providing a measure of fiscal relief for states (and some localities). Administration of the minimum is by the Social Security Administration. Like its predecessor programs, SSI is means-tested for both income and assets. The original minimum benefit levels to persons with no other income were $146 per month for an individual and $219 per month to an eligible couple. Benefits have been indexed to the Consumer Price Index since 1975. There is no work requirement, but a work incentive exists by which $85 per month of earned income plus 50 percent of the remainder are excluded from "countable income" (i.e., income to be deducted from SSI benefits).[44]

In a 1973 amendment, Congress required all states to supplement the federal minimums to the extent that persons receiving state administered assistance at higher levels would not suffer a reduction in benefits. These are called mandatory supplements. In addition, states were encouraged to provide optional supplements above the federal minimums. The mandatory supplements are transitional, as the beneficiaries will die off over time. States may opt to have supplements administered by the Social Security Administration; an incentive for them to do this was provided by (1) federal assumption of administrative costs and (2) a "hold harmless" provision that protects states from the costs of increasing caseloads at benefit levels that obtained in each state in January 1972.

As a result of the supplementation, eligibility requirements and benefit levels continue to vary considerably from state to state, and states that administer their own supplements retain considerable freedom to apply their own standards and administrative practices. This has detracted from the original goal of uniformity, although it has, of course, prevented the sharp reduction in benefits that would have occurred if only the federal minimum were payable as the benefit. The consequence has been that the new system is, in some states, as complex and irrational as the older one.

Nevertheless, SSI represents a marked improvement, especially in the poorer states, toward the objective of reducing the incidence of poverty among the aged. At its inception in 1974, the system's combined minimum and supplemental benefits ranged from 90 percent to 170 percent of the poverty line for couples.

The interactions between SSI and other parts of the income maintenance structure for the aged will be discussed later. At this juncture we may note two interactions of some importance. One is with Social Security. Like other unearned income, all but the first $20 per month of Social Security benefits are deductible from SSI. This has a particular impact on persons receiving both Social Security and SSI benefits,[45] because an increase in Social Security benefits is deductible from the federal portion of SSI (note that this drains the Social Security Trust Fund while relieving the pressure on general tax revenues). The second interaction is with private pension plan benefits, insofar as these are "countable income." Again, the impact is on retired low wage workers who managed to accrue pension benefits low enough to satisfy the SSI means test, but whose income is the same as if they never received a pension. This now affects only a small number of people but will assume greater importance in the future as the Employee Retirement Income Security Act increases the number of retired workers who are likely to get some pensions.

No discussion of the structure of public assistance is complete without reference to food stamps. Like Medicaid, food stamps are a transfer-in-kind that has grown rapidly over the last few years. They are treated here because SSI recipients (except in a few states), along with other indigents of all ages (including the working poor), are eligible.

Originally a Depression measure, food stamps were relegislated in 1964 on an optional basis to states and localities. In 1973 Congress made the program nationwide and extended it to SSI recipients whose state supplements did not "cash out" the bonus value of the stamps. The purpose of the law was twofold: (1) to alleviate hunger and malnutrition in low-income households, and (2) to increase the market for domestically produced foods (i.e., to benefit farmers). It is the latter purpose that has provided political support for the program in constituencies that are not usually sympathetic to welfare measures.

As a public assistance program, food stamps are subject to a means test covering both assets and income. The latter uses a concept of "net income" that excludes from gross income such items as taxes, high medical expenses, and high shelter costs. However, there is an upper limit to deductions from gross income. The amount of the allotment is a function of family size and net income,[46] with a benefit–loss ratio of about 30 percent for each additional dollar of income.

The federal government pays 100 percent of the stamp value. Administrative costs are equally shared between states and the federal government. A 1973 survey of food stamp participants showed that 15 percent were retired and over sixty-five.[47] The absolute numbers of aged who use food stamps to supplement their income can be expected to increase if the program remains in existence, especially if food prices go up, inasmuch as the bonus value of stamps is indexed to food prices. Usage will also rise because recipients after January 1, 1979, no longer need to buy the food stamps with cash.

The main items in the public assistance system for the aged and disabled are (1) SSI, which developed from the Old Age Assistance and Aid to the Blind provisions of the original Social Security Act, plus the Aid to the Permanently and Totally Disabled program that was added to the Act in 1950; (2) Medicaid, which comes from the Amendments that also established Medicare as a social insurance program; (3) food stamps; and to a certain extent (4) Aid to Families with Dependent Children, which serves as an assistance program for survivors, although much of its clientele comprises households whose male heads or fathers have deserted or divorced rather than died. Considerations of time and space preclude mention of a variety of smaller programs, such a public housing, that serve some of the aged. However, some mention may be made of (5) Pensions for Veterans with Non-Service Connected Disabilities, since any indigent veteran over sixty-five is considered disabled for the purposes of this law. Both the means test and the benefits are more liberal than for SSI. In 1973 there were 650,842 veterans over sixty-five who received such pensions.[48] The number should rise as the large World War II cohort matures between 1980 and 1990, to be followed by the

Korean War and Vietnam era groups. A provision for survivors of veterans (widows and children) also exists.

We turn now to the development of the social insurance system. Unlike public assistance, this covers the larger part of the population. It is politically more sensitive than public assistance, because the nonpoor substantially outvote the poor and because changes involve alterations of what the general population conceive to be their rights. Its purpose is more to prevent poverty than to alleviate it. Economically, its importance is great, if for no other reason than that it involves a lot more money and resources.

## Development of Social Insurance

As we saw earlier, the basic social insurance provision of the original Social Security Act was (in addition to unemployment compensation) a pension payable to retired workers at age sixty-five, based on total wages earned by covered workers between 1937 and their attainment of retirement age. Benefits were calculated at ½ percent of the first $3,000, 1/12 percent of the next $42,000, and 1/24 percent of the next $84,000, to be payable "as nearly practicable" in equal monthly installments. No more than $3,000 would be countable in any one year. The maximum monthly payment was limited, in any event, to $85. Although there was no direct provision for survivors of workers, the estates of such workers would receive 3½ percent of total wages (less any benefits already paid). The system was financed by a payroll tax levied jointly upon employers and workers and invested in U.S. Government obligations. The first payments were scheduled to begin in 1942.

Clearly, it would have taken quite some time for the system to mature so as to provide any but minimal benefits, hence the use of Old Age Assistance as a transitional supplement. Take the monthly benefits for a retired worker with average monthly earnings of $100 for ten years before retirement. The benefit for such a person would have been $22.50 per month or $270 per year. In effect, the benefit would come to 22½ percent of his average earnings. As younger workers passed through the system, their replacement rates would rise. Thus, our $100 per month worker who stayed in the system for forty years (fully employed) could look forward to $51.25 in benefits, or 51¼ percent of his average wages. It is useful to remember that most wage earners were not subject to any income tax except for the Social Security tax at that time, and that wages of $100 per month were not uncommon in the 1930s. Judging from the rate of wage replacement contemplated by the act, benefits were progressive, that is, the replacement rate diminished with rising average wages. Workers who paid taxes but did not qualify (for example, because they earned less than $2,000) would receive their payments as a lump sum or death benefit.

Accordingly, the system could be described as compulsory saving with an insurance feature for those who lived long enough,[49] with some income redistribution from higher- to lower-paid workers. Full funding meant that the system would build up reserves over time to support the gradually rising benefits. By 1980 this would raise the national debt to $47 billion, a figure unthinkable at a time when the debt was $27 billion and conservatives wanted to reduce it further.

While conservatives worried about the rising national debt to be generated by the system, the early Keynesians worried about the fiscal drag of the growing reserve as something that would retard recovery. The imposition of a tax beginning in 1937, with benefits not payable until 1942, was in clear violation of the new fiscal doctrines being imported from England. Furthermore, popular pressures built up to speed up payment and liberalize the system by raising benefits and providing coverage for widows with children and to the dependents and aged survivors of retired workers.

Under pressure from both conservatives and liberals, Congress modified its handiwork in 1939. The amendment of that year drastically altered the act. On the financing side, the new law moved away from full funding toward a pay-as-you-go basis, thus quelling the conservative fear of a huge national debt (some may think it ironic that conservatives deserted full funding). Although a trust fund would still build up, it was to be more in the nature of a contingency reserve whose growth was limited to about a year's benefit obligations.

The tax increases were deferred (until 1950) and benefits were increased and extended. The increases were accomplished by basing them on average monthly earnings (AME) instead of lifetime earnings, and eligibility criteria were changed (the present method of quarters of coverage was adopted) so as to make the first payments possible in 1940. Provision was made for aged dependents of retired workers and for survivors. This changed the system from an individual savings-cum-insurance system to a family protection system that placed greater emphasis on social adequacy than on individual equity.[50]

It may be argued that the 1939 amendments, and not the 1935 act, were the true bases for today's Social Security system. The former was an individual retirement system with a philosophy of full funding. Actually, genuine full funding was not possible at the tax rates initially contemplated, and subsidies would have been necessary by 1965.[51] But even if full funding was a somewhat illusory principle, both Congress and the President agreed that the social insurance system should be "self-sustaining," a principle that has generally survived until this day.

The shift toward pay as you go was a major philosophical departure, because it clearly established the system as one of intergenerational income transfers: Today's productive workers and their employers finance today's retirement benefits. One can view this as a sort of social contract between generations, whereby each generation undertakes the support of its aged in the expectation that the generation that follows will do likewise. Thus, it socialized what was an old family tradition. However desirable this might be, it hardly qualifies for a conservative notion of "soundness," for future generations may not wish to observe the contract. Unlike private contracts, social contracts are breakable by new legislation.

The inclusion of an aged wife marked a philosophical shift away from the more individualistic approach of the 1935 act. The pensioner was expected, originally, to take care of his aged wife by whatever means he might have accumulated (or with the help of his children), or fall back on Old Age Assistance, to the extent that it was available in his state. If he died before exhausting his benefits, the remainder would be paid to his estate and go to whomever he designated in his will.[52] In other words, the benefit rights accrued solely to the worker who had earned them.

Granting benefits to a dependent wife over sixty-five increased the total benefits available to an aged couple, but it did so on the basis of need or social adequacy. Again, however desirable this may have been, it further attenuated the link between contributions and benefits and strengthened the principle of social adequacy, a principle that owes more to assistance than to insurance concepts. It also introduced an inequity that seemed minor at a time when fewer than 20 percent of married women were in the labor force, many in occupations not covered by the act. This inequity between two-earner families and one-earner families (to be discussed in detail elsewhere) has become an important issue with the dramatic growth in the female labor force and extension of coverage to virtually all working women. It means not only that the taxes paid by a two-earner couple of about equal wages buy less than twice the benefits of a one-earner couple, but also that the tax paid by a low-wage member of the family "buy" no retirement benefits at all, in cases where the same or higher total benefit would be available through the dependents' coverage.

The inclusion of Survivors' Insurance (SI) for widows with dependent children can be seen either as an extension of the social adequacy principle or simply as an additional benefit based on insurance concepts. Leaving aside the progressive structure of benefits, SI can be viewed as a form of insurance. After all, it has some of the elements of life insurance, including the bet that the insured will die before his policy is paid up. However, Congress, in 1939, did not raise the tax to pay for the "premiums," nor did it fund SI separately. It did, however, cut the lump sum death benefit (which had served, in part, as survivors' insurance), and has reduced it over the years so that it is now a nominal $255.

It will be recalled that the original act did not ignore dependent children. It provided for them in the means-tested assistance program, then called Aid to Dependent Children. SI shifted a portion of this population to the non-means-tested social insurance part of the law by making it available to wives with dependent children whose husbands died after at least six quarters of coverage in the preceding twelve quarters (since changed to six of the preceding thirteen quarters. In addition, male surviving spouses are now eligible.) The benefit was set relatively higher than the retirement benefit. The widow received 75 percent of the Primary Insurance Amount (that is, 75 percent of the benefit based on the worker's average monthly earnings had he survived, at those earnings, to retirement age) plus 50 percent of the PIA for each dependent child, up to a family maximum. Benefits stopped when the last dependent child reached eighteen (now twenty-two if the child is in college, with 75 percent of the PIA for each child).[53]

Survivors' Insurance also had an impact of Aid to Dependent Children. Beneficiaries were primarily white (as blacks were concentrated in the agricultural sector, which was not then covered) and respectable—they were properly married wives rearing the children of husbands who had proved their attachment to the labor force. This left ADC with a higher proportion of nonwhites, unmarried mothers, and those whose husbands had deserted and were not easily found. Such persons had less political power and sympathy.[54] Not surprisingly, discussions of welfare reform are characterized by more rage and racial animosity than discussions of social security reforms.

One more 1939 change is worth noting, although it seemed small at the time. The 1935 act had imposed a strict retirement test for the explicit purpose of inducing older workers to leave the labor market. Seeing that payments were not to start until 1942, Congress in 1935 must have viewed the Depression's high unemployment rate as a permanent phenomenon. Fears were also expressed that payment of benefits to the working aged would act as a wage subsidy and serve to reduce wage standards. Additionally, the cost to the system would be lower to the extent that some post-sixty-five workers continued to work in lieu of accepting benefits. For those reasons the 1936 act prohibited benefits entirely in any month during which the beneficiary had any earned income.

The 1939 act permitted earnings of up to $14.99 per month without loss of benefits for the month. The next penny of earnings, however, wiped out all benefits for that month. Like other provisions of the law, this was to be liberalized over time. It will assume importance in our analysis when we deal with the question: Should people be induced or compelled to leave the labor market simply because they are sixty-five years old? The word "compelled" is not too strong, since the act helped to institutionalize employers' practices of compulsory retirement at sixty-five.[55]

All in all, the 1939 amendments encouraged the incrementalist position. Thereafter, for the next decades, the act would be broadened. More people would be covered, benefits increased, and new programs added toward the goal of a comprehensive economic security system. For the incrementalists, it seemed easier to accomplish change in bits and pieces, amendment by amendment, depending on the mood of any particular session of Congress. In the meantime, U.S. entry into World War II took the lawmakers' minds off Social Security, and they did not return to the subject until 1950 (except for the extension of SI to railroad workers in 1946).

It will not be necessary to detail the fourteen or so amendments that were made (as of 1978) since 1939, and I shall stay with the highlights. In terms of coverage, a series of amendments extended coverage to many of the people excluded in earlier years, including the self-employed, regularly employed farm workers, members of the armed forces, and clergy. In some cases, coverage was elective, which brought in most employees of nonprofit institutions and most state and local employees (states and localities are free to withdraw from the system on two years' notice). Generally, the newly covered workers were "blanketed in," that is, those close to retirement were made eligible on the basis of very few quarters of coverage. This was of considerable help to many poorer workers who had been excluded, but it also provided windfalls of considerable value to many who were not in need. Indeed, in the case of the poorest who would be relying on Old Age Assistance, some found themselves no better off, as local welfare authorities deducted their Social Security benefits from their public assistance benefits. In such cases, the Trust Fund provided fiscal relief to the states rather than individuals, which was certainly not the intent of such extension.

Except in a few minor cases, the Social Security taxpayers financed the blanketing in. Exceptions to the principle of self-sustainment were made by transfers from general revenues to the Trust Fund for wage credits on behalf of World War II and Korean War veterans, persons of Japanese ancestry interred during World War II, and persons who reached the age of seventy-two before 1969. Although self-sustainment is still the rule, the fact that it has been breached in the past provides precedent to those who favor subsidy from general revenues.

One of the broad omissions from the social insurance aspects of the act were the disabled whose disabilities were not caused by work-related accident or illnesses. For those with work-related disabilities, state Workers' Compensation laws provided income support (as well as medical care) during the period of disability, partial or total. Others were excluded from social insurance except in the five states that enacted Temporary Disability Insurance on bases similar to Unemployment Compensation.[56] Public Assistance was available, on a means test basis, in all states except Nevada since 1950, and public assistance to the blind (blindness is, of course, one of many possible disabilities) goes back to the original act.

The omission was corrected in several steps. In 1956 the totally disabled aged fifty or over were added, provided that they were covered in twenty of the preceding forty quarters. Children over eighteen who were disabled before eighteen also received coverage for dependents' and survivors' benefits. Two years later coverage was extended to dependents of disabled workers, and the age restriction was abolished in 1960. Unlike Survivors' Insurance, Disability Insurance was funded by an increase in the tax, payable into a separate fund.

The year 1956 also saw a breach in the magic age of sixty-five. Wives of retired workers became eligible at age sixty-two at an actuarily reduced benefit, as were dependent mothers. Later amendments extended this privilege to all covered workers, and widows can claim reduced benefits at age sixty.[57]

The next important breakthrough occurred in 1965 with the amendments that provided hospital and health insurance for the aged, later extended to Disability Insurance recipients and to those who require treatment for certain kidney diseases. The United States had long been one of the few industrial nations without a national health service or national health insurance law. It will be recalled that health coverage was one of the Bismarckian reforms in the nineteenth century, and over the years health coverage developed in most of the Western world.

In the United States opposition to national health insurance was strong enough to remove such a provision from the 1935 proposals for Social Security. Blue Cross and Blue Shield plans, as voluntary private insurance, were organized in the 1930s by the health care industry in an attempt to defuse the issue, and the post–World War II period saw a growth in employer-financed health and welfare plans.

Many of these were collectively bargained and used either private insurance carriers or a self-insurance basis to provide benefits.

This growth had two consequences. One is that it helped increase the demand for medical services (pushed up further by the sharp population growth of the postwar period) and thus drove up the price of health care. As a result, it made individual self-insurance (saving for illness) increasingly expensive. This led to the second consequence. Many of the aged were not covered by employer plans, since coverage commonly terminated with severance from the job. Private carriers were loath to take on new older cases because of the high risks. Where insurance was available to the aged, the premiums were prohibitively high for most of the population at risk.

The American Medical Association fought the proposal for Medicare, but it found that many of its members no longer shared its views. At the same time, the demand for health insurance for the aged came not only from the older population but also from their adult children. As is the case with many income transfers, the benefits would accrue not only to the recipients but also to those who would otherwise bear the financial burden.

Finally, 1965 was a peak year in the Great Society programs. Lyndon B. Johnson had just been elected by a sweeping majority with a mandate to carry out the liberal reforms promised by his predecessor. The nation was moving into a period of high prosperity. Experts and laymen alike had cause to believe that the nation could afford social experimentation—afford even to end poverty. The war in Vietnam had not yet reached the period of escalation that was to engender so much domestic bitterness and economic havoc. The amendment, together with its public assistance parallel (Medicaid, described above), easily passed the Congress.

There are two parts to Medicare: Hospital Insurance (Part A) and Supplementary Medical Insurance (Part B). Hospital Insurance (HI) was available, without cost, to all Social Security and Railroad Retirement beneficiaries, and to all aged who reached sixty-five before 1967, regardless of whether they qualified for Social Security. Thereafter, a small number of quarters of coverage are required, growing over time until fully insured status will be needed.

In short, HI was available to virtually all of the aged as of 1967, and practically everyone else of that status thereafter. The few who are left out could join by paying a monthly premium. Like private insurance, HI covers certain specified hospital and posthospital services and contains deductible and coinsurance features. As noted earlier, it does not cover extended nursing home services.

Financing was provided by an increase in the Social Security tax placed in a separate Hospital Insurance Trust Fund. Since payment of the tax is made by those currently employed, HI is a clear intergenerational transfer.

Part B, Supplementary Medical Insurance (SMI), is a voluntary medical insurance program, financed by a monthly premium. Like HI, it resembles private insurance, including deductibles and coinsurance. It is open to all aged, regardless of Social Security coverage. States are permitted to "buy in" on behalf of public assistance recipients. Premiums are based on experience but subsidized on a matching basis out of federal general revenues. The income transfer aspects of SMI stems from (1) the fact that the program accepts all risks, unlike a private insurance company, which can be choosy—the palpably good risks finance the palpably poor risks—and (2) the subsidy from general revenues.[58]

In terms of coverage, the changes since 1965 include the extension, in 1966, of retirement coverage to persons aged seventy-two who did not qualify for benefits and had reached seventy-two before 1968 or had three quarters of coverage for each year after 1966 and before seventy-two. Also, as mentioned earlier, Medicare was extended to recipients of Disability Insurance by the 1972 amendments.

No attempt has been made here to enter into all of the details of Social Security. Instead, I have tried to trace the developments of the main parts of the social insurance structure that emerged from the original 1936 act. From a limited individual retirement program, more or less fully funded and restricted to about 60 percent of the labor force, the system has moved to a pay-as-you go basis with wide-ranging cash benefits for survivors, dependents, and the disabled and medical benefits for the aged and disabled. About 90 percent of the labor force is covered, and a large portion of those not covered are in federal employment and state and local employment, where similar benefits can be found. Attachment to the labor force is the *sine qua non* of coverage, and this has kept the poverty population at minimum or no coverage.

The growth of the system, both in numbers and in benefits, has required increasing taxes. Beginning with a joint tax rate of 2 percent on payrolls up to $3,000, the tax rate has risen to 12.1 percent of $17,700 (in 1978). As maximum taxable earnings have risen (the wage base), so have maximum cash benefits, since some relation between earnings and benefits has been preserved. This, in turn, has led to more complex formulae to compute the recipient's cash benefit. Benefits are generally progressive, with a relatively high minimum for low-wage workers. The original act had three brackets for calculating the Primary Insurance Amount (PIA) on which cash benefits are based. These were increased from time to time and tended to increase minimum benefits.

In 1956 the number of brackets was increased to four. In 1977 there were eight, all but one of which, after the first, were declining percentages of the next amount of average monthly earnings (AME). The 1977 amendments have returned to a structure of three benefit brackets.

In 1972 Congress decided to forgo the periodic changes in benefits and to index both the cash benefit and the computational formula for the PIA by changes in the Consumer Price Index (that is, the percentages in the brackets were raised by inflation. The wage base was subject to adjustments based on changes in average annual earnings. This generated higher maximum benefits and overcompensated for inflation. In the inflation of the 1970s, this developed into a mechanism for driving up benefit payments so greatly that something drastic needed to be done. This, together with revenue losses from high unemployment, pointed toward the early exhaustion of the Trust Fund.

A primary purpose of the 1977 amendments was to "decouple" the benefit structure in order to prevent future benefits from rising faster than real wages. The details of decoupling are discussed later in the book, but it should be noted here that the effect is a relative decrease in future benefits. The amendments also provided for higher payroll taxes needed to finance the system, at least until the end of the century. Other changes include (1) an increase in the amount of wages that retired beneficiaries can earn before loss of benefits and a reduction of the age at which no benefits are lost through earnings to seventy beginning in 1982, (2) an increase in benefits for those who retire past sixty-five, (3) freezing the minimum benefit, and (4) increasing the special minimum benefit for long-term low-wage earners. All benefits continue to be adjusted for price changes after the point of retirement.

## SOCIAL INSURANCE AND PUBLIC ASSISTANCE: A COMBINED VIEW

Having traced the development of the two types of programs, it is necessary now to consider them as parts of one public income maintenance structure. Some programs were separately conceived, with no thought given to integration or interactions among them. Others were intended to be transitional or supplementary. Together they represent the growth in the American welfare state that was accelerated in the 1930s and again in the 1960s. Some of this growth was intentional and represented a conscious legislative effort to improve economic security for Americans (similar to the growth of European welfare states). Part of the growth was unintentional, such as the enormous rise in the AFDC, SSI, DI, and medical programs.

Furthermore, the distinction between social insurance and public assistance has not always remained clear and is offered here more for its heuristic purpose than as a hard and fast set of definitions. From the very beginning of social security, the system incorporated two somewhat conflicting goals. One, derived from the older assistance tradition, was the goal of social adequacy of benefits. The second, derived from popular notions of insurance, was that benefits should be related to the wage earnings record of the claimant: The higher the earnings and hence the tax contribution, the greater the benefits.

The initial compromise between these goals, which has been broadened over the years, was to set a minimum benefit for anyone who qualified at all, and to create a benefit structure by which incrementally higher average earnings records yield relatively diminishing incremental benefits. Although this violates the strict principles of a private annuity contract, it is in conformity with some generally accepted notions of vertical equity as reflected in the personal income tax system, which, at least on its face, established a progressive rate structure and exempts very low-income earners from any tax liability.

The fact that social insurance differs from private individual insurance in having a redistributive or "welfare" component need not distract us here (it will be explored in another chapter). Social insurance is inherently different from private insurance (among other things, it is compulsory) and has been different since its Bismarckian origins. For that matter, private industry pensions also have redistributive components, since many such plans tie fixed benefits to length of service rather than earnings and often provide credit for service rendered before the plan was inaugurated. A more important consideration is whether the extent of the welfare component exceeds commonly accepted notions of what is fair. The high minimum benefit, about $121 per month, is a case in point. A second consideration is whether any or all of the welfare component should be financed through Social Security or through a transfer of funds from general revenues to the Trust Fund, or be hived off entirely into the public assistance system.

The argument in favor of a strong welfare component in Social Security is weakened by the development of a parallel structure of public assistance. Although most public assistance programs were shaped by the Social Security Act, legislators have tended to view the two systems as separate. One, Social Security, provides basic protection upon which workers can build during their productive years. The second serves as the safety net for those who, for some untoward reason, were not covered by Social Security, or those whose Social Security benefits are below what is considered a social minimum standard of living.

Although the two systems appear to be separate, they can be viewed as one two-tier structure, both from a fiscal point of view and from the viewpoint of a potential claimant who is either ready to apply for benefits or is planning his pattern of savings in anticipation of future benefits. The fiscal aspect is no small matter, if Social Security is to be self-sustaining and must finance itself, including the welfare component, out of a limited tax base. However, since Social Security taxes are currently spent, and since both taxes and benefits appear in the consolidated federal budget, it is reasonable to look at both parts of the consolidated budget and to state and local budgets.

These can be viewed as bookkeeping devices, and one can examine the consequences of shifting part or all of the welfare component from one part of the budget to the other. Such shifting would not diminish beneficiaries' claim on the public purse but might enable us, in a subsequent chapter, to look into policy options that are needed to maintain Social Security as self-sustaining, or to question whether a self-sustaining system is optimal for our needs.

From the claimants' point of view, the structure is unified because claimants may be eligible for benefits from both systems. In a larger sense, it does not matter from whom the benefit checks come, but how much they add up to. (It should be kept in mind, however, that means-tested benefits occasion psychic costs because of the stigma attached to them).[59] Of course, claimants may not always have the information they need to find out what package of benefits is available to them. Food stamps are a good example, since it appears that they are underutilized.

Where benefits interact, those who receive multiple benefits may find that a change in one benefit affects the others. Thus, legislative generosity in improving one benefit may reduce another, leaving the claimant no better off or, in some cases, worse off (as when higher Social Security benefits lead to loss of Medicaid eligibility). Similarly, if a state moves to improve Workers' Compensation benefits, many of which have lagged behind inflation, it will find that a marginal number of DI recipients lose the portion of DI benefits that would otherwise bring them over 80 percent of previous average earnings. In the first example, a transfer has occurred from one part of the combined government budgets to another, as Social Security payments out of the Trust Fund increase, and Medicaid payments (out of general federal and state revenues) decrease. In the second example, the transfer is from employers who pay Workers' Compensation insurance premiums to the Disability Insurance Trust Fund. In short, bookkeeping transfers have occurred, either within the federal budget, across federal–state budgetary lines, or (in the last case) from the private to the public sectors. Such transfers are rarely intentional. They are the side effects of other social policies.

The unitary nature of the system may shape plans for employment, savings, and even family formation. In this respect, benefits behave like taxes, and benefit losses from earnings can be treated like taxes. In the secondary labor market, where segments of the poverty population find employment, little or nothing may be gained for a worker by coverage under Social Security. For example, enforcement of Social Security coverage for part-time domestics is notoriously difficult, even though coverage extends to persons who receive $250 in wages in any one year. Such workers may prefer to avoid the Social Security tax and the income tax (if applicable) because they are covered by the parallel public assistance program. On retirement, their SSI benefits may be as good as their Social Security benefits. Those who are female heads of households can treat AFDC as a substitute for Survivors' Insurance and Unemployment Insurance. And Medicaid is a more than adequate substitute for Medicare.

Persons planning for their old age may, if they are not wealthy, find it easy to divest themselves of their assets so as to qualify for Medicaid in the eventuality that they may need nursing home care in their final years. Divestiture may be through dissaving—why not enjoy your money while you can—or by transfers to children (licit or illicit). Why spend one's savings on the nursing home operator when Medicaid is willing to pay in any event?

In view of the incredible complexity of the unitary system, there may be an infinite number of ways in which the system distorts individual and family behavior. As noted earlier, it may lead to divorces where one spouse's medical expenses are too burdensome for the other to bear, and Medicaid becomes available. One can imagine the reverse: since Old Age Insurance benefits for divorced dependent spouses require ten years of marriage, couples planning to break up near such a time may postpone the divorce until after the ten years have elapsed. As divorce rates rise, pressures may develop to shorten the period, which, in turn, will reduce the cost of divorce.

Some of these distortions may be trivial. Others may be profound. Any benefit system will create distortions. When the two systems are viewed as one, it can be seen that the possibilities for distortion of labor market and family behavior are multiplied.

In the foregoing pages, I have traced the development of public income maintenance in its two parts, social insurance and private assistance. Focus has been on provisions for the aged, and no attempt was made to go into all finer details. I have also tried to show that the distinction between social insurance and public assistance is not always clear, and that the two parts of the system can be treated together, both from a public finance viewpoint and from the viewpoint of actual and potential claimants for benefits.

In the chapter that follows, employment-related pensions will be analyzed. These, plus private savings, constitute an important part of income for the aged. Indeed, as will be seen, their importance has received legislative recognition with the passage of laws that protect private pension plans and tax law provisions that encourage private savings.

# CHAPTER THREE

# Employer-related Pensions

## PRIVATE SECTOR

UP TO NOW, the primary concern of this book has been with public measures to provide income and services to the aged, disabled, and survivors. The decades since World War II have seen an enormous growth in the number of people covered by the third, or top, tier of the income maintenance structure. Pension plans and associated health and welfare plans are now commonly found in both the private and the public sector. About 46.2 percent of private sector employees are covered by pension plans, and coverage for public sector workers is estimated at almost 100 percent.[1] Not all such workers who survive to retirement will receive partial or full benefits, but the number will grow as the more recent plans mature and because, in the private sector, the Pension Reform Act of 1974 (Employee Retirement Income Security Act, or ERISA) requires degrees of vesting and participation that were absent in many earlier plans.

A brief digression on terminology may be useful before proceeding, as the language of pensions can be arcane to the layman. When we speak of *vesting*, we refer to the property rights that an employee acquires after he has completed the term of service required by his plan. Generally, he cannot sell his interest or draw against it before the retirement age specified by his plan, but he has a legal right to whatever benefits may accrue upon his retirement, from the portion of the contributions that have become vested. If he moves to an employer whose plan has a reciprocal agreement with his previous employer's plan, he may *roll-over* (transfer) the vested portion of his employer's contributions. Plans may be *contributory* or *noncontrib-*

*utory*. In the former case (a minority of all private plans), the employee contributes along with the employer. Commonly, employee contributions always remain the employee's property, in the sense that they are vested. In a noncontributory plan, the employer makes all the contributions in behalf of the employee.

*Funding* pertains to the building of actuarially adequate reserves to finance future pensions. A plan is *underfunded* if its assumptions about the life expectancy of its beneficiaries or about the future returns on its investments, or even its expectations about future benefit levels, are incorrect. An underfunded plan may pose the threat of insolvency as it matures. Two other funding measures are useful. One is *unfunded total liabilities,* which are the extent to which all future pension liabilities exceed assets. A second, more narrow, measure is *unfunded vested liabilities.* This pertains to the shortfall, if any, between assets and the vested portion of pensions. In the event a pension plan fails or is terminated, employers are liable only for unfunded vested liabilities, up to a maximum of 30 percent of an employer's net worth. The issue of underfunding applies largely to defined benefit plans (see below). For private and nonfederal public plans, a substantial portion of the reserve is invested in private sector securities. Persons responsible for the fund have a *fiduciary* responsibility, at least in the private sector. This means that they are personally liable for actions that are not reasonable and prudent.

The term *past-service liabilities* refers to claims against the fund by persons who were covered when the plan began, even though no contributions were made on their behalf before the plan began. Such retroactive coverage is common. By the same reasoning, any decision to increase benefits creates new past-service liabilities. In the private sector, ERISA requires that such liabilities be funded over a period of years.

*Portability* refers to the employee's ability to move his pension rights from one employer to another. Multiemployer plans, those in which a group of employers participate, are more likely to have this feature. Social Security, of course, is fully portable except into the remaining uncovered sectors, principally the federal government.

Plans can also be defined in terms of *defined contributions* and *defined benefits.* In the former, the employer pays a specific amount (usually a percentage of wages) into the fund; benefits are then a function of the amount contributed per employee, the earnings of the fund, and its actuarial experience. *Defined benefit plans* are the reverse: The benefit level and structure are defined in advance, and a sufficient reserve needs to be built to fund them. The latter are more common, with benefits defined in various ways, such as length of service, age, combinations thereof, or even as flat amounts.

Finally, funds may be *insured* or *self-insured*. In the former case, the contributions essentially purchase an annuity guaranteed by an insurance carrier who does the investing and bears some of the risks associated with fluctuations on the return of the investments. *Self-insured* plans bear this risk themselves, although they may entrust the investment function to the trust department of a bank or seek investment advice from the outside.[2]

As the foregoing discussion suggests, there is an almost infinite number of combinations and permutations possible, including features not mentioned here, such as profit-sharing, thrift plans, and Employee Stock Ownership Plans (ESOPs). The diversity of the plans is at once both a strength and a weakness. The strength comes from the ability to experiment and from the adaptability of plans to diverse types of employers and unions. Lack of uniformity, however, not only creates inequities but may impede the movement of labor from employer to employer. It also provides incentives for underfunding and, occasionally, for maladministration and even the looting of the funds.

Two more types of funds are worth mentioning, inasmuch as they will grow in importance in the years ahead. One is for self-employed individuals, who may set up a Keogh Plan trust fund for themselves and contribute up to 15 percent of net profits (before taxes) with a maximum of $7,500 per year. The second is the Individual Retirement Account (IRA) for employees not covered by employer pension plans. Such employees may contribute 15 percent of wages (before taxes) into a qualified trust fund (usually a savings account) with a maximum of $1,500 per year. In both cases, premature withdrawals are subject to a penalty plus income tax.

Unlike Social Security or SSI, pension benefits are subject to income tax upon receipt (except to the extent that employees have already paid taxes on their contributions in contributory plans). In this sense they serve as tax shelters. To the employer, contributions are tax deductible as part of his labor costs. Because retired employees are likely to be in a lower income tax bracket than those who are working, their tax liability during their lifetime is lower than it would have been if employers made payments directly to them. Both Keogh Plans and IRAs show the tax shelter in a more obvious form: Individual participants file annual forms with the Internal Revenue Service and make the appropriate tax calculations on their tax returns.

Tax shelters are not confined to retirement systems. Leaving aside the shelters that are primarily for corporate managers and for wealthy persons, there are two other shelters of importance to middle-income employees. These are the deductibility from taxable income of interest and property tax payments. They provide an incentive for private home ownership, which, aside from consumer durables, is the principal tangible wealth holding of middle-income families. Payment of the principal on a mortgage is a form of saving to the family, subsidized by the deductible feature of interest and property taxes.

Because nothing is free, tax policy to encourage saving, either through pensions or through home ownership, means that someone makes up the shortfall. If the federal budget is preset in terms of politically perceived needs, then (1) general taxes must be higher than they would otherwise be, and/or (2) there is a transfer of income from those without a tax shelter to those with a tax shelter. The latter are likely to be more affluent, insofar as pension plans and home ownership are more frequent among well-paid than among poorly paid workers,[3] although the advantage is offset, in part, by the progressive rates of the income tax. If government budgets are not preset by need, then more services and income transfers could be offered with a given structure of tax rates, or overall taxes could be lower. The issue of public policy to encourage private saving, including saving for old age, will be further developed in a subsequent discussion of capital formation.

#### Historical Development

As noted earlier, pensions are a relatively new development. There had always been the occasional employer who took care of an old and faithful retainer who reached an age beyond which he was of no further use to the employer. In the private sector such pensions were rare in the ninetheenth century. Here and there an employer might reward a meritorious long-service worker with a pension. Such pensions generally were not funded but paid out of the employer's current revenues. The notion that the employer was somehow responsible for the welfare of his employees contravened both the individualistic philosophy of the nineteenth century and the common law of the employer–employee relationship.

The point is worth stressing. The employer's obligation under the common law was to provide a reasonably safe work place (subject to exceptions that need not detain us here) and to pay for work actually rendered at the wage agreed upon. Because the employment contract was "at will," the employer could change wages and working conditions as he saw fit and could terminate the relationship without notice. The employee had a similar freedom to seek work elsewhere if he was dissatisfied with the terms, or possibly to bargain with the employer. The two owed each other little more than a fair day's pay for a fair day's work, however defined. Even where unions existed, largely among the skilled crafts, written agreements were rare until the end of the nineteenth century and were not, in any event, enforceable at law. Either party could break them at will and accept the resultant conflict.

The pioneer industry to establish something like coherent pension plans was the railroad industry, although in the United States pride of place goes to the American Express Company in 1875, which provided pensions for permanently disabled workers with twenty years of continuous service.[4] The Baltimore and Ohio Railroad, which had always prided itself on its enlightened labor policy, organized a contributory plan in 1888,[5] followed by the Pennsylvania Railroad's noncontributory plan in 1900,[6] which served as a model for other railways. Coverage reached 50 percent of railway workers by World War I, when the railways were temporarily nationalized, and rose to 80 percent by the end of the 1920s.[7]

In hindsight, railways were an obvious place to start. Railway workers were well organized into unions, sufficiently so that given the disruptive nature of railroad strikes, a federal law covering their labor relations dates back to 1926. Perhaps more to the point, the industry was the first to undergo federal regulation, which prevented a price competition, through the Interstate Commerce Act of 1887. So long as railroads were protected from competition among themselves, and in the absence of serious competition from other forms of transportation, they were in a good position to pass increased labor costs forward to the users of their services.[8]

The first decade of the twentieth century also saw a growth of pensions in public utilities. Although less subject to union organization, public utility prices were regulated at state levels on the same general principle as railroads, and thus with the same ability to pass costs forward to users. This growth continued through the 1910s and 1920s, joined by such industries as iron and steel, oil, and machinery manufacturing. Steel (including iron) and oil were concentrated industries, with traditions of nonprice competition established (but not always maintained) by U.S. Steel and Standard Oil.

The main features of the early pensions were that they were noncontributory, were based on age and length of continuous service, and were paid out of current income. Payment was not a legal obligation and was entirely discretionary for the employer.[9] A few were funded as trusts, although with few precautions regarding actuarial soundness, and some life insurance companies began to enter the field with the sale of group annuities.

By the end of 1929 there were 397 plans in existence, of which 77 percent were noncontributory.[10] Such plans offered employers a number of advantages. By reducing the employer's labor turnover, they reduced his costs of searching for and training new workers, insofar as pensions based on length of service induced workers to remain. They also provided a means of industrial discipline, as payment was discretionary in most cases. Finally, they did not necessarily engage the employer in a long-range commitment that he might later regret, for workers had no legally vested interest in their pensions, and the plans could be abolished. From time to time, plans died with the demise of an enterprise or when an employer believed that he need not or could not continue them.

A small number of trade unions also developed pension plans. There had always been a tradition among some unions to engage in mutual benefit activity for survivors, sickness, and disability. However, the first union old age pension plan with some degree of funding, established by the Granitecutters, did not appear until 1905. A number of other small unions, such as the Cigarmakers, developed welfare plans, and the first large union in the field, the Typographers, established a pension plan in 1906–7 to take care of older workers who were unemployed as a result of a series of strikes. Three railroad unions established old age benefit plans as a matter of right; most union plans, in contrast, depended on the state of union treasuries and their abilities to assess members.

Although the end of the 1920s saw 40 percent of union membership (about 1.5 million workers) covered by some type of old age and disability plan, all the plans were weak. Like many employer plans, they succumbed under the impact of the Great Depression.

The above indicates that the beginning of the twentieth century saw a trend toward private pension plans, mostly employer-sponsored, a few union-sponsored, and virtually all noncollectively bargained. The trend was interrupted in the 1930s, and the resultant disillusionment with the experience helped turn the minds of the larger employers and the (now growing) labor movement toward public retirement plans. Unions at that time disliked employer-sponsored plans. The next development in private sector plans was to come in the 1940s and 1950s, with a strong emphasis on collectively bargained plans.[11]

During World War II, the federal tax code was changed to clarify the tax position of pension and welfare funds. At the same time, the War Labor Board, which regulated wages, adopted a policy that favored fringe benefits over wage increases on the theory that fringe benefits were less inflationary. Although this stimulated some interest, the principal breakthroughs came after the war. A series of strikes by the United Mine Workers in 1946 led to an agreement to establish a welfare and pension fund financed on a pay-as-you-go basis by a royalty per ton of coal mined. The Mine Workers, led by John L. Lewis, insisted that the union be the sole administrator, following a pattern established in a few other trades. The Taft–Hartley Act of 1947 settled this issue for the future by requiring joint or tripartite administration of multiemployer benefit funds.[12]

The main push occurred when the Inland Steel Corporation disputed a Steelworkers demand for pensions on the ground that pensions were not a bargainable issue under the National Labor Relations Act. The National Labor Relations Board rejected this argument and was sustained in the Court of Appeals. When the Supreme Court refused to review the decision of the lower court, the effect was that unionized employers were therafter required to bargain with their unions over benefit plans.[13]

As a result, unions began to take a lively interest in pensions. The 1949 steel strike hinged on this issue, and a pension plan was finally negotiated.

About the same time, the United Auto Workers made a similar demand and won it, although at Chrysler this required a strike that lasted 104 days. The two unions set the pattern for the organized sector of large industry. Thereafter, unions representing employees in small-employer industries set a corresponding trend to multiemployer plans. In both cases, the plans were set up to be (or at least appear to be) actuarially sound.

Thus, the 1950s saw the beginning of what can be called the pension movement. Private pension coverage expanded rapidly—almost explosively—not only via collective bargaining but also in nonunion firms. The growth in coverage is shown in Figure 3-1. In 1950, some 9.8 million workers were covered. Coverage nearly doubled by 1960, reaching 18.7 million workers. By 1970, 26.1 million workers were covered, a growth of 40% over the previous decade. In 1975 (latest data available), 30.3 million workers had coverage.

The number of beneficiaries has also grown substantially, as shown in Figure 3-1. In 1950, a mere 450,000 workers were retired on private pensions. By 1975, the number had grown to 7.1 million, and it will continue to grow as workers who were covered in the last few decades reach retirement age. It must be remembered, however, that not all covered workers will receive benefits and that some benefits are and will be low. This results primarily from the fact that the system discriminates against job-changers.

Of equal interest is the growth in the reserves of pension plans, as illustrated in Figure 3-2. The practice of funding private pensions, in contrast to Social Security, has given pension plans a leading role in American capital markets. Thus, in 1975 the book value of reserves grew by $20.9 billion.[14] These monies went in search of investment opportunities, mostly in the market for private equities.

What is especially noteworthy is that the system, along with the other benefit plans, relentlessly spews out a flood of funds in search

**FIGURE 3-1** Private Pension and Deferred Profit-Sharing Plans: Number of Covered Workers and Number of Beneficiaries, 1950-75

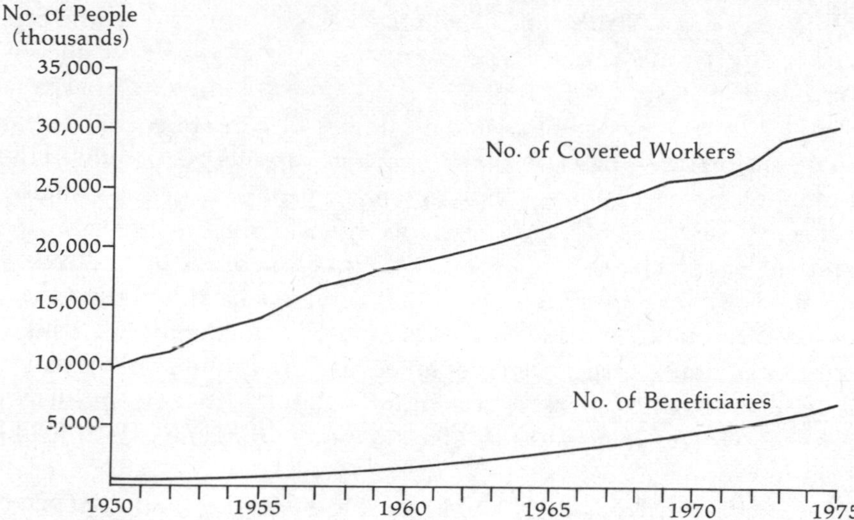


Sources: Alfred M. Skolnik, "Private Pension Plans 1950-74," *Social Security Bulletin*, 39, No. 6 (June 1976): 4, and Martha Remy Yohalem, "Employee-Benefit Plans, 1975," *Social Security Bulletin*, 40, No. 11 (November 1977): 20-26.

**FIGURE 3-2** Private Pension and Deferred Profit-Sharing Plans: Reserves, Book Value, 1950-75

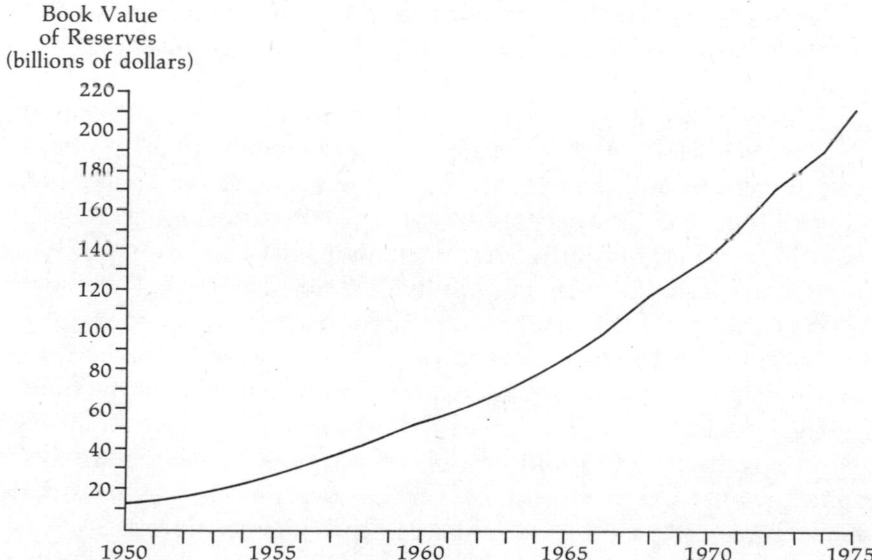


Sources: Same as Figure 3-1.

of investment instruments. The relative amounts, however, will change over time as benefit payments become a greater proportion of contributions.

This flow of savings has had a number of consequences. One is that pension funds have become important suppliers of capital to the economy. Some of this is simply a replacement of private saving by collective saving, but, on net balance, pensions have increased the amount of saving available for capital investment. A second consequence is a change in the structure of capital markets. Investment decisions are made or guided by a relatively small number of banks, trust companies, insurance companies, and investment advisers. As a result, securities markets are more volatile. Any one portfolio change involves huge sums, unlike the portfolio change of an ordinary investor.

A third consequence is a shift in the ownership and control of American industry. This has been highlighted in a provocative book by Peter Drucker,[15] who refers to the advent of pension fund socialism. Drucker calculated that as of 1974, American workers were the beneficial owners of 35 percent of the equity capital of American business. By 1985 the proportion should be between 50 percent and 60 percent. A decade later, two-thirds of equity capital, and perhaps 40 percent debt capital (bonds, notes, etc.) should be in pension fund hands.[16]

The implications of this phenomenon are not clear. Drucker argues that the essence of socialism is worker ownership of the means of production, and that this is now being achieved. It is, however, *control* that really matters, and neither workers nor unions exercise control over corporations. Those who manage the pension funds do not control the management of individual corporations. The law requires sufficient diversification of any fund's portfolio[17] so that control is unlikely. Nor is such control sought. The legal responsibility of a pension fund fiduciary is the prudent management of the fund's assets, not of a corporation's business.

In any event, the rapid growth of pensions in the 1950s led to some problems. Toward the end of that decade scandals regarding maladministration and occasional embezzlement surfaced. Some of the worst cases, which caught the public's attention, were found in multiemployer plans. In this sector, union control is dominant,[18] notwithstanding the provisions of the Taft–Hartley Act that required joint administration.

Although the scandals pertained to some "worst cases" covering a minority of workers, there was sufficient agitation to induce Congress to legislate. The Welfare and Pension Plans Disclosure Act was passed in 1958, requiring all plans to file detailed reports with the Labor Department. The law's effectiveness was questionable, at best. The information collected under the law was limited, and there was no provision for audits. Mere disclosure did not prove to be a strong tool of enforcement.

Another issue began to develop in the 1960s. This was the fear that many pension plans were unsound or, even where sound, might not provide pensions for many covered workers. Again, it was the worst cases that were discussed. These were the pension plans with excessively rigorous participation requirements, little or no vesting of benefits, inadequate provisions for termination, rather imaginative actuarial standards that meant poor funding, and investment practices that were open to suspicion.

Many, perhaps most, of the problems were found among small plans and multiemployer plans. Most large single-employer plans met the standards that were subsequently legislated.[19] Even there, however, the occasional horror story was found. An example was the collapse of the Studebaker–Packard Corporation. Its pension fund was not mismanaged. The problem was that the fund simply could not meet its obligations and left its participants poorly provided for.

It took Congress no less than seven years to pass a new law. The Javits bill was first introduced in 1967. By then, pensions were a big business. Unions, employers, financial institutions, consulting firms, and government agencies had a deep interest in the proposed legislation. They lobbied extensively in behalf of their interests. In 1974 an elaborate compromise was enacted, entitled the Employee Retirement Security Act and affectionately known as ERISA. This law, which will be discussed in a later section of this chapter, established standards in all areas of funding and administration and created a Pension Benefit Guarantee Corporation to insure plans in the event of termination. Church-related and public employer plans are excluded.

### Current Issues in Private Sector Pensions

**Extent of Coverage.** As of 1975 about 30,300,000 workers were covered by private pension plans, and 7,050,000 were drawing benefits. Average benefits were $2,204 per year, a figure that must be treated with care, for many beneficiaries received more and many less than the average. Total reserves in the private pension system amounted to $212.6 billion (book value), an impressive sum in the nation's capital markets.[20] Growth in coverage has been declining from an average annual rate of 6.7 percent in 1950–60 to 3.4 percent per year since then.[21]

Growth in coverage of firms can be expected to decline as the target population reaches saturation (although the number of beneficiaries will continue to grow as plans mature). Labor organization, which was a prime stimulus for the growth of the pension movement, has been in a period of relative decline in the private sector. Most unionized firms, and many large firms that might be prone to labor organization, now have some kind of pension plan. Hence, unless union organization resumes its growth—perhaps as the Sun Belt becomes more industrialized—the saturation point will soon be reached. This is an important point to keep in mind. Even if part-time and sporadic workers are excluded from consideration, and even if we exclude the self-employed and younger workers who will ultimately move into covered jobs, the private pension system cannot be expected to provide coverage for 100 percent of its regular full-time labor force. The excluded workers are likely to be concentrated in low-wage service trades and small manufacturing and will then be dependent on Social Security, public assistance, intrafamily transfer payments, and whatever resources they will have managed to accumulate. Many will be poor.

The Pension Reform Act of 1974 has made some provision for workers whose employers do not provide pensions. Such workers may set aside up to 15 percent of wages, with a maximum of $1,500 per year, in a tax-deferred trusteed account of their own, the IRA, referred to earlier. This is of little help to persons who are at present nearing retirement age, because they will have little time left to accumulate any sizable sums. It will be recalled that Social Security made provision for workers who entered the system late. Some private pension plans do likewise, as do most public sector pension plans.

IRA participants are on their own. A worker who puts away $1,000 per year at, say, 6 percent compounded annually will need twenty-five years to accumulate $50,000. Since $1,000 is 15 percent of $6,667 per year, it is unlikely that a low-wage primary earner can save at that rate, although the IRA may be a useful savings vehicle for a low-wage secondary worker married to someone covered by a pension plan. Nonworking spouses can obtain some protection if the working spouse divides his IRA contribution into two accounts to a maximum of $875 each. If the marriage terminates, the nonworking spouse retains a property interest in the funds accumulated in his or her behalf, but the total sum is not likely to be great ($25,000 if we use the above calculation). Thus, IRAs favor higher-paid workers who can set aside the full $1,500. To a $25,000-a-year earner, this is only 6 percent of his or her salary. It is likely therefore that IRAs will be used more heavily by higher-salaried workers than by lower-wage workers in the covered group.

An exception may be where employers (usually small ones) would like to offer a pension plan but cannot or do not choose to meet the complex requirements of the Pension Reform Act. Such employers may sponsor IRAs for their employees under simpler rules than those that apply to ordinary pension plans. Moreover, the contribution limits are more generous than those for individually sponsored IRAs: 15 percent of compensation, with a maximum of $7,500 per year.

### Restructuring Because of ERISA

*Description of the law.* The Pension Reform Act (ERISA), passed in 1974, is still in the process of making large changes in the structure of the nation's private sector pension system. The extent of this restructuring is difficult to predict as of now (1978) for several reasons. One is the extreme—almost excruciating—complexity of the law, so that some years of experience will be necessary to see how employers and trustees will adjust. A second is the wide degree of rule-making and administrative discretion possessed by the two administering agencies, the Labor Department and the Treasury. As of early 1977, the rule-making process was not yet complete, even though the law was in effect, thereby creating considerable confusion among those responsible for the administration of pensions. As new problems arise, rules will change and a body of interpretative case law will develop. In addition, the act will probably be amended, at least in incremental fashion, from time to time.

Although a detailed explanation of the law is beyond the scope of this book,[22] the major points will be sketched here, so the reader can get a sense of the law and its probable impact. It should be kept in mind that the law does not require an employer to establish a plan and, indeed, permits him to terminate an existing plan (subject to some safeguards).

1. *Vesting.* One of the most important reforms of ERISA is the establishment of minimum requirements for vesting. Because vesting is expensive, it had long been common practice to minimize it. In this way, employees who left or died before retirement subsidized the pensions of those who survived. This created an incentive to some employers (and sometimes to union leaders) to promise relatively high benefits at low cost.

A 1972 survey made by the Bureau of the Census had shown that one-third of the then 23 million workers in private pension plans had vesting of sorts. However, the vesting rate of older workers was surprisingly low, considering that they were more likely to have long service than younger workers. Of workers aged fifty or older with ten or more years of service, only half had vested pensions.[23] Although vesting provisions were, in general, liberalized between 1965 and 1975,[24] Congress was not willing to rely on the generalized trend and decided to legislate standards.

ERISA provides pension plans with a choice of one of three minimum vesting standards, although plans may be more liberal if they so choose. They are:

1. the ten-year rule: full vesting in the tenth year of an employee's service
2. the five to fifteen years rule: 25 percent vesting after five years of service progressing steadily to 100 perccent after fifteen years
3. the rule of forty-five: if the employee has been a plan participant for five years, and the sum of age and service

equal forty-five, then vesting at 50 percent, rising to 100 percent in equal steps of 10 percent over the next five years

There are some important provisos. The vesting plan chosen may not discriminate in favor of corporate officers or highly paid officials. The government may impose stricter standards if the employer shows a pattern of firing people before their benefits become vested. However, plans may lawfully include forfeiture of vested benefits upon the death of a participant (unless the plan provides a survivor's annuity).

2. *Participation and Coverage.* In general, ERISA preserved the earlier principle of the tax code that employees be covered on a nondiscriminatory basis. Employers may require a waiting period of one year, or until age twenty-five, whichever comes later. In order to reduce discrimination against hiring older employees, workers hired within five years of the plan's normal retirement age may also be excluded. The cost of covering them in a defined benefit would be too great.

Coverage of employees will be enlarged, however, because a year of service is defined as a twelve-month period with not less than 1,000 hours of service. This will provide vesting for many regular part-time employees. Furthermore, previous service with an employer counts as service toward vesting. Finally, special rules will cover seasonal and maritime workers.

3. *Funding.* Standards of funding have been tightened to minimize the problem of underfunded plans. Old plans must amortize past service liabilities over a forty-year period, and post-ERISA plans must do this over a thirty-year period. (Fully insured plans may be exempt from this.)

The reason for allowing a lengthy transition is that immediate funding would have required contributions to be so great that many employers would be forced to terminate their plans to avoid bankruptcy. As the system matures, most past service liabilities will diminish, thus strengthening the financial bases of the plans.

Similarly, gains and losses from changes in experience (for example, experience losses from the unanticipated aging of the work force in a declining industry) must be funded or amortized over a fifteen-year period for single employer plans and a twenty-year period for multiemployer plans. Poor experience has been an important cause of underfunding.

Other highlights pertaining to funding include the use of reasonable actuarial assumptions and a more realistic method of valuing the assets of the fund. There were too many horror stories of actuarial assumptions and valuation of assets that were exercises in fantasy, and Congress sought to correct such abuses. Among other reports, periodical actuarial reports must now be filed with the administering agencies. Standards of fiduciary behavior have been tightened, and fiduciaries are personally liable for imprudent losses.

4. *Guarantee of Benefits.* A high priority for Congress was to guarantee benefits of defined benefit plans (the majority) where plans are terminated. To accomplish this end, ERISA created the Pension Benefit Guarantee Corporation (PBGC) in the Labor Department. All plans must purchase insurance from the PBGC, which guarantees the payment of vested benefit rights. The guarantee at age sixty-five is limited to $750 per month or the participant's average wage during his highest five years of coverage, whichever is less. It is actuarially reduced for persons below age sixty-five. The limit will rise with increases in the Social Security wage base, reaching $1,688 in 1981 and then rising with changes in national average annual wages.

This provision introduced something entirely new in private pensions: liability of employers for underfunding of terminated plans. Until ERISA, liability was limited to the assets of the pension plan itself, as a separate entity. Now the PBGC can attempt to recoup losses on a terminated but underfunded plan by holding the employer liable. Although liability is ostensibly 100 percent, the PBGC cannot recoup more than 30 percent of the employer's net worth.

5. *Joint and Survivor's Option.* One of the goals of Congress was to make some provision for the spouses of deceased beneficiaries. Although many large corporate plans had a variety of provisions for postretirement death benefits,[25] many small plans have avoided this for cost reasons. Under ERISA, a defined benefit plan automatically provides 50 percent of benefits to a surviving spouse who has been married at least one year before the employee's retirement. It can do so by an actuarial reduction of benefits to cover spouses' joint life-

times. The participating employee is free, however, to waive this in order to get a higher monthly benefit in his own lifetime.

The same protection is afforded if the employee dies while still at work but was eligible to retire at the time of his death. In this case, the survivor's annuity need not be paid unless coverage was specifically requested by the employee. Such election can be made within ten years of normal retirement age.

Congress, it will be noted, gave employees some freedom in covering their spouses (where their plans had no such provisions). Presumably, this allows employees to choose what best fits their needs. It is interesting to note, however, that in the first instance the employee must opt *out* if he or she does not want to cover a surviving spouse. In the second instance, he or she must opt *in*.

It was Congress's expectation that the joint and survivors' options would be costless, inasmuch as pension plans may lawfully offer actuarially reduced pensions to cover the option. Some actuaries, however, believe that in practice increased costs will be unavoidable.[26] Another source of increased costs, for both joint and survivors' options (and, in some cases, for pensions earned by working women), may come about from changes in the actuarial treatment of women. Until now, women have been treated as having a longer life expectancy than men, and actuarially determined survivors' options often take this into consideration in calculating the monthly benefit by lowering it below what the benefit would be if women were assumed to live as long as men. In the event that the courts treat this as illegal sex discrimination (or if Congress legislates accordingly), then the cost of joint and survivor's options will rise, because women, on average, live longer than men.[27]

6. *Reporting Requirements.* Reporting requirements are too extensive for examination here, although it may be noted that the sheer volume of paper work may discourage smaller employers and pension plans. Basically, reports must be filed with the Labor Department (Labor Management Services Administration and the PBGC) and the Treasury (Internal Revenue Service). In addition, certain information must be furnished to plan participants and beneficiaries.

Since many workers change jobs, it may be easy for them to lose track of vested benefit rights accumulated with various employers.

In the event an employee is separated, the Internal Revenue Service (IRS) must be notified of the vesting status of such an employee, and it transmits this information to the Social Security Administration. Thus, when retired workers file for Social Security benefits they will be informed of the vested benefit rights they have accumulated.

7. *Rights of Participants and Beneficiaries.* In addition to a right to receive plan descriptions and certain reports, there are two types of rights afforded to employees. The first is the right of an employee or group (not necessarily the union) to intervene in IRS proceedings on whether or not their pension plan legally qualifies under IRS rules. In the past such determinations were solely a question between the employer and the IRS.

A second right deals with disputes over benefit claims between employees and the pension plan. ERISA broadens the right of access to the courts, and both the Secretary of Labor and the Treasury Secretary may intervene. In addition to claims, private suits may seek to compel enforcement of the substantive provisions of the law. The Labor Department has interpreted this to mean that arbitration, which is cheaper and quicker than litigation, may be used in lieu of the courts. In the process of drafting the rules, the words "final and binding" were dropped as modifiers to arbitration. Accordingly, it is not clear whether the loser in an arbitration case can appeal to the courts. Obviously, extended litigation can be difficult for beneficiaries who are badly in need of a pension that has been denied to them. Equally, if beneficiaries, individually or in groups, become litigious, they will impose legal costs on the plans.[28]

9. *Integration with Social Security.* Plans that pay a flat dollar of benefits per year of service (about 58 percent of all plans) are less likely to be integrated with Social Security than plans that are based in whole or in part on average compensation. The former type is more prevalent among collective-bargained plans than the latter.[29] ERISA permits the integration of plans with Social Security where the targeted or defined benefit is composed of both pension and Social Security benefits. This is permissible with respect to contributions into a pension plan, so that a rise in Social Security tax payments can be offset, wholly or in part, by a reduction in contributions. However, once retired, beneficiaries are protected from a

decrease in their pensions resulting from a further increase in Social Security benefits.

*Analysis of the Impact of ERISA.* It is too early to assess the full impact of ERISA on the private pension system, and it would be foolish to estimate the numbers of firms, plans, employees, and retirees who will be affected or the quantitative changes in fund sizes, investments, or benefits that will occur. Pension plans change of their own accord, through either collective bargaining or employer responses to labor market pressures and threats of unionization. As of 1978, employers and unions were still in a state of confusion. Interpretive rules are still being written and will be amended. Litigation in the courts can be expected, which will modify or alter the effective provisions of the law. Actuaries and lawyers will be kept profitably busy for a long time.

However, a general analysis of the law is possible, along with an assessment of the probable direction of trends. The law has been in effect for some years now, and practically all pre-ERISA plans have undergone modification. Some plans, especially the ones in the largest industries, needed fewer modifications, because in many cases they were in substantial compliance with the important aspects of the law. Some others required a complete overhaul. Still others were terminated. The option of providing IRAs may become more attractive to smaller employers.[30] Defined contribution plans may also become more attractive, for they escape some of the strictures of the law. Unions, however, prefer defined benefit plans, because these enable them to tell their members more precisely what has been won at the bargaining table.

The vesting standards will probably increase the number of workers who will receive at least some pension at retirement. Workers who change jobs are less likely to do as well as those who stay put, except where job changes are made within firms belonging to a multiemployer plan. This is especially true in defined contribution plans, where length of service counts heavily and waiting periods can be applied.

The standards of participation and coverage will also add to the number of pensioners, including those in regular part-time work. Greater economic security for workers will result from the improved standards of funding, which will reduce the number of plans now headed for doom. Similarly, the government guarantee of vested benefits will afford some protection to workers whose plans are terminated.

Stricter standards of reporting, with provision for audit, and tighter fiduciary standards will, one hopes, not only increase security but reduce the amount of looting and maladministration found in shadier sectors of the private economy. However, much of what is outlawed in this regard has always been illegal. We hardly needed new laws against embezzlement, but rather a willingness and capability to enforce them. The fiduciary standards will probably induce plan administrators to make more conservative investments—not an unmitigated blessing, because the economy benefits from the availability of venture capital.

Many plans now provide for survivors of beneficiaries, including some that provide a greater-than-actuarial equivalent joint and survivors' provision. Plans that do not provide at least actuarial equivalents have been revised. It is impossible to predict how participants will respond to the option. The rising incidence of divorce among older persons may tempt some married workers to opt out in contemplation of divorce. An educated guess would be that, on net balance, more protection for spouses of retired workers will be afforded. This will enable them to supplement their Social Security benefits. The price to be paid will be lower monthly benefits. For those whose combined pension and Social Security benefits are low, the choice may be difficult, and the availability of SSI may tempt some among them to opt out if, after their own demise, the surviving spouse can meet the means test. It should make for some interesting family discussions at the point where the choice must be made.

Greater ability for workers to dispute claims, together with the plan information provided to them, will be especially helpful in those egregious cases where plans have unjustly denied claims. It will add an element of security for thousands of workers but will probably not affect the bulk of the target population. It may be noted that the social and public assistance systems provide quicker and cheaper avenues of appeal.

Not long after the passage of ERISA, it was observed that an increasing number of plans were being terminated and that the IRS was receiving fewer applications for tax qualification of new plans. In 1973, and again in 1974, some 59,000 new plans were approved and about 4,300 were terminated. In 1975 approvals dropped to 30,039 and terminations rose to 8,108. The Social Security Administration estimated that less than 1 percent of covered workers in 1975 were affected by plan terminations.[31]

Some of the terminations may have been the result of business conditions, and the issue was of such concern that Congress asked the General Accounting Office (GAO) to study the effect of ERISA on the termination of pension plans. The GAO sampled 10 percent of the 7,310 single-employer defined benefit plans that decided to terminate during the period between September 1974 and June 1976. A questionnaire was used.[32]

The study found that only 17.3 percent of the plans were terminated solely because of ERISA, and ERISA played a role in the termination of 35.3 percent more. Thus, ERISA had an effect on the termination decision in 52.6 percent of the cases.

Forty-one percent of the respondents indicated that they provided alternative coverage.[33] The most commonly cited alternative was profit sharing. About 10 percent changed to employer-sponsored IRAs, the balance being about evenly distributed among money purchase (i.e., defined contribution) plans, other defined benefit plans, and a category simply labeled as "other."[34]

Perhaps the most interesting finding was that most terminating plans did not meet the ERISA standards for participation and vesting.[35] If this is the case, then the ERISA-induced terminations were not necessarily a bad thing. They represented promises that would probably not have been kept, and it is precisely the purpose of ERISA that such promises should not be made in the first place.

To summarize so far, ERISA is shaking out the worst of the plans. The administrative costs imposed by the law are high, both to the plans and to the government. The cost of vesting and amortizing of unfunded liabilities will compel some plans to require higher contributions. This may lead to relatively lower wages, although the trend has not been noticeable so far. As pension plans are a form of forced savings to employees, the higher contributions will increase such "savings," a matter of importance when we discuss savings and capital formation.

**Are Private Pensions Underfunded?** Despite the enactment of ERISA, the financial standards of pension plans remain an area of controversy. This is a matter of interest not only to employees but also to stockholders and bondholders, because unfunded liabilities are a potential charge against the assets of a firm. In a devastating critique published in *Fortune*,[36] A. F. Ehrbar pointed out that ten of the top hundred companies in the list of the Fortune 500 have unfunded vested liabilities equal to one-third or more of their net worth. In seven of the ten cases, the liability was greater than the market value of the companies' shares. The author warned that stockholders had better watch out, because ERISA had transferred the risk from employees to them.

There are no statistics available on the magnitude of unfunded liabilities in defined benefit plans. Based on corporate annual reports. Ehrbar estimated $50 billion in unfunded vested liabilities. The actual figure, he thought, might be considerably higher.

Worse yet, unfunded liabilities cannot really be compared among companies, because each pension plan uses its own assumptions about future wage levels and the future earnings of the plan's investments. Although these assumptions might all be reasonable by actuarial standards, Ehrbar observed some behavior that struck him as odd. One example was a company that first negotiated a pension increase with its union, and then reported a decline in pension costs and unfunded liabilities. The major reason for this "saving" was a change in the assumption regarding the future earnings of the fund.

In addition to criticizing such actuarial behavior, Ehrbar noted that the Pension Benefit Insurance system might work perversely. An important aspect of ERISA is the provision that "reinsures" vested benefits through the PBGC. In effect, the plans in operation contribute toward payment of the liabilities of the plans that fail. This spreads the risk among all defined benefit plans.

No one can insure against a catastrophic decline in securities prices. Pension fund assets are heavily invested in common stocks. A stock market crash would push some—perhaps many—into default. In turn, surviving plans would be assessed heavily to pay for the defaulted liabilities, at the very time that such plans, and the employers behind them, were confronting hard times.

The picture may not be as bleak as it looks. In a survey of 461 of America's largest corporations, Kenneth H. Keene and Sandra M. Kazinetz reported that of 336 respondents, only 5.4 percent had unfunded liabilities of 30 percent or more of net worth (the maximum liability). Indeed, 30.7 percent reported no unfunded liabilities, and 46 percent reported liabilities of less than 10 percent. They concluded that the total picture is sound. The measure of unfunded liabilities is relevant only when a plan is terminated, and few, if any, of the plans could be expected to terminate.[37]

Whatever the case may be, some troublesome issues remain. Retirement systems, whether private or public, can only deliver from what the economy produces. There is no way in which the risk of economic fluctuations can be averted. The mechanisms that we have adopted can only shift the risks among different members of the community.

In defined contribution plans, the risk is borne by employees and by beneficiaries—in the latter case, risks may fall on insurance companies if the benefits are insured annuities. But even insurance companies have been known to default. In defined benefit plans, the risk is borne by all of the participating employers, subject to the limits imposed by ERISA. The balance of the risk falls on employees. Although each defined benefit plan is funded on the assumption that termination is possible, the collective system is essentially on a pay-as-you-go basis, like Social Security.

Cutting through the legal and actuarial jargon of our pension system, we see its ultimate economic reality. Pensions are paid from current output. The real question is not whether a foolproof pension system can be devised. That is not possible. Instead we must ask whether the mechanism created by ERISA (and by the Social Security system) is optimal in two essential ways: (1) Does it avoid dysfunctional behavior, and (2) does it distribute risks in some socially acceptable fashion?

**Contribution to Capital Formation.** A major difference between Social Security and private pension plans is that the latter are at least partially funded and that contributions flow into the capital markets. Such contributions are savings in a sense that is more real than Social Security "savings." As in Social Security, there are some intergenerational transfer payments from younger to older workers, to the extent that unfunded past service liabilities must be amortized. There are also transfers from workers who never reach vesting status to workers who do.[38] Nonetheless, the characteristic of funding and the fact that most assets are held in private sector securities make such pensions conceptually different from Social Security.

According to Munnell, guaranteed retirement systems have two effects on savings behavior. One is the benefit effect (that is, the expectation of future benefits), which leads workers to reduce voluntary savings over their life cycle. The second is the retirement effect: The possibility of earlier retirement can induce increased saving because the length of time of wage income is shorter and the length of time without it is longer. Munnell's studies indicate that the benefit effect is dominant for Social Security.[39]

The question here is what the impact of pensions may be on savings and therefore on capital accumulation. Until recently, the conventional wisdom had been that pension plans increase voluntary individual savings. These findings were reported in the 1960s by Philip Cagan and George Katona in separate surveys of saving behavior.[40] Cagan hypothesized that pension coverage calls attention to retirement needs, thus creating a "recognition effect." Katona explained his results by the hypothesis that as people get older, their savings efforts grow as they recognize the possibility of achieving a standard of living acceptable to them (his "goal feasibility effect"). Both findings appeared to contradict the standard economic theory (life-cycle theory), which posits that consumers try to arrange their consumption and savings in such a way as to maintain a level flow of consumption over their lifetimes.

In a more recent study, Munnell re-examined the impact of private pension plans on voluntary saving. Her results indicate that private pensions, on net balance, tend to reduce individual voluntary saving, thus contradicting the Cagan and Katona studies and helping to confirm the validity of the standard life-cycle theory. However, the reduction in private saving appears to be smaller than total contributions to pension plans. Thus, for 1973 Munnell estimated a reduction of $13 billion in voluntary personal saving due to the existence of private pensions. In that year contributions to pension plans came to $21.1 billion, thus adding an increase of $8.1 billion toward capital accumulation for the country as a whole.[41]

The impact of ERISA is likely to increase contributions in order to provide for more rapid vesting and the amortization of past service liabilities. Accordingly, the effect of the law will be to increase total amount of savings and therefore of capital accumulation—always assuming, of course, that higher savings, in the long run, always lead to more real capital. Some offset to this may occur to the extent that higher pension contributions will lead to a relative decrease in money wages, reducing workers' ability to increase their individual saving.

If the above is true, then the fear that pensions will diminish capital accumulation (and therefore future incomes of workers and/or retirees) appear to be groundless. From a capital accumulation point of view, private pensions are adding to the stock of capital, and the same is generally true of state and local public employee pensions.

However, this is not an immutable law. Conceivably, as pension plan participants become more informed about vesting and more secure in their pension expectations, the benefit effect may become greater and lead to a decline in savings. Alternatively, if the trend toward early retirement continues, the retirement effect may become greater and increase savings. At present, the trend in private pension plans is to provide greater options for early retirement and benefits higher than their actuarial equivalents,[42] and it remains to be seen whether the higher costs imposed by ERISA will reduce this trend. Social Security is available at age sixty-two, and some private plans provide "bridging" benefits between actual retirement and eligibility for Social Security. To the extent that these plans are collectively bargained, we may be witnessing a shift in collective preference away from present income and toward future income.

Finally, the motives for savings are more complex than can commonly be accommodated in econometric studies. Workers may prefer the forced savings of pension plans and may allocate their current expenditures in accordance with the bottom line of their pay slips. Periods of uncertainty can affect savings behavior—witness the rise of personal savings during the inflation of 1974.[43]

Demographic changes may also play a role. These include the rising labor force participation of women and the higher incidences of divorce and single-headed families. If capital accumulation is an important policy consideration, then savings behavior will have to be monitored on a continuing basis, so that trend changes can be detected early and policy changes can be made accordingly. In pensions, as in Social Security, it cannot be assumed that a system that is optimal now will be optimal for the indefinite future.

**Social Security and Private Pensions**

It has been argued that the Depression of the 1930s created the popular desire for security that led to the enactment of Social Security.[44] Undoubtedly the Depression played an important role by creating a political climate for reform, as embodied in the New Deal.

However, the desire for income security has deeper roots than one historical incident. Most urbanized and industrial nations had developed social insurance measures for income security before the first third of the twentieth century. The need for income security was generated by sociological forces associated with industrialization and (for retirement security) by the demographics of an aging population.

At some point in time, a sufficient number of persons would emerge who were outliving their ability to work or to find jobs. Industrialization and urbanization weakened the family and community support systems of the previous (if nonidyllic) agricultural society. Younger persons would have observed that old age meant destitution. Hence, the appearance of provisions for retirement income was only a matter of time. In the United States the time came in 1935.

Given the advantage of hindsight, one can see that widespread retirement pensions would have their birth in the shape of public programs. The private labor market was not creating pension programs, with the exception of the sporadic examples cited earlier. There are many reasons why employers might choose to institute pensions—reduction of turnover costs, better industrial discipline, greater employee loyalty—but these obviously were not compelling enough to induce many employers to provide pensions. Where such pensions existed, the Depression wreaked its havoc. The largest network of pension systems, found in the railroad industry, was rescued when Congress federalized it in 1934. Others were not so lucky.

In short, the private pensions were not viewed as an alternative to Social Security. Rather, they were viewed as an interesting, if insecure, anomaly. The suggestion that employers be permitted to opt out of Social Security if they provided secure pensions was given scant consideration. Its principal advocates were spokesmen for insurance companies, who saw a market for annuities that would be created by an optional Social Security System. They did not receive much support from employers.

The foundations of private pensions were laid, as shown earlier, by a change in the Tax Code that went into effect at a time when income taxes became a significant factor for most workers, and when the policies of the War Labor Board made fringe benefits rather than pay increases a recruiting device in a tight labor market.

Even this was not sufficient to lead to wide adoption of pensions. It was the lusty young labor movement that developed in the 1930s and 1940s that turned the trick. At a time when Social Security payments averaged $26 per month, pensions were an obvious issue, later to be followed by demands for other fringe benefits.

Thus, the two retirement systems entered a period of coexistence. For some time, both extended coverage and improved real benefits. Growth of pension coverage in the 1960s, however, came more from greater employment than from the introduction of new plans.

The relationship that emerged between the two systems was that Social Security provided basic benefits, and that pensions supplemented them up to some desired target. So long as total benefits were relatively low, both systems could grow and maintain a peaceful coexistence.

By the end of the 1960s Social Security benefits entered a period of dramatic increase, spurred on by ad hoc adjustments and the indexation that was enacted in 1972 and became effective in 1975. Between 1968 and 1975, benefits rose by 105 percent.[45] In view of such benefit levels, and the taxes needed to finance them, coexistence became uneasy. The relative roles of the two systems were changing. If the trend continued, Social Security would crowd out private pensions.

As early as 1970 Robert J. Myers, then Chief Actuary of the Social Security Administration, warned the pension community of an emerging expansionist philosophy that wanted virtually all preretirement income to be replaced by Social Security upon retirement. Such expansionists were found among the top staff of the Social Security Administration, people who influenced program design. Given their way, expansionists would change the role of Social Security as a floor of basic protection on which savings are built individually or collectively through pensions.[46]

The expansion of benefits certainly took place, as Myers feared it would. Some of it was inadvertent, resulting from the technical error in the indexation formula introduced by the 1972 amendments. However, the expansion has come to a halt as a result of the Social Security amendments of 1977. The floor of protection is now higher, but on this floor pensions have retained their role as supplements to public benefits.

This does not dispose of some other issues that can affect pensions and their relationship to Social Security. One of the most important of these is coverage of that half of the labor force not currently included in pension plans. A second issue is the protection of pension benefits from inflation. A third issue is the provision of better survivorship benefits.

Those who retire on pensions plus Social Security constitute a retirement elite. Many of the rest retire on benefits that result in a serious decline in their previous standards of living. This is because individual savings rates, over a lifetime, would have to be impossibly high to enable this group to acquire the equivalent of pension benefits.[47] Suggestions have therefore been made for mandatory minimum private pensions.

A variety of plans have been offered. Robert D. Paul recommends mandatory pensions in the form of defined contribution plans at 2 percent of payroll up to the Social Security wage base. Since the uncovered sector contains many small employers for whom the administrative burden would be great, he suggests that they be permitted to opt into a quasi-public system. Collection and administration would be handled by the Social Security Administration. Investments could be done through a consortium of private banks and insurance companies. A portion of the benefit should be indexed to consumer prices. This would require government issues of indexed bonds.[48]

A number of European countries have mandatory private pensions.[49] France has an extremely complex scheme consisting of two highly centralized systems. These are essentially pay-as-you-go systems, with risks pooled among all the employers in each system. Pensions are fully vested, portable, and inflation-proof.

The United Kingdom established a mandatory scheme, effective in 1978. It consists of two tiers. The lower tier is the flat-rate social security pension that previously existed. The upper tier is an earnings-related supplement, consisting of two optional devices. One is a government plan financed by payroll taxes levied on employers and employees. The second is an option to employers to opt out by providing a private plan that is at least as good as the public one. This means that pension credits must be revalued each year according to changes in average annual earnings. For a fee, the employer can limit the revaluation to 5 percent per year, shifting the risk to the public National Insurance system. There are provisions for vesting and portability, but credit for past service is not required. At the point of retirement, inflation-proofing is provided by the government.[50] Both the public and contracted-out plans will reach their targeted benefit levels (adjusted for changes in average annual wages) in twenty years.

Both Switzerland and the Netherlands are in the process of installing a mandatory layer of private pensions coordinated with their public social security programs. Their motives are interesting. In both countries, such mandatory pensions are seen as ways of providing more adequate retirement benefits without expanding the public system.[51]

If it is a social goal that the workers without pension coverage should receive better retirement benefits, and if further expansion of Social Security is undesirable, then some form of minimum mandatory coverage may be indicated. It would, however, present economic problems to the industries involved, since they are predominantly in the low-wage, labor-intensive, and competitive sectors.

How much of a problem is created depends on whether the additional costs of such pension contributions are passed forward in the form of higher prices, or backward as relatively lower wages. In the first case, which might exist where markets are predominantly domestic, the burden would fall on consumers. Some fall in sales would result, and thereby some loss of employment.[52] In the second case, the decline in relative wages would be felt by a group already noted for its low wages.[53]

The question of who would actually pay the pension contributions has not been explored in any systematic empirical manner. Hence, further discussion here is fruitless. However, some rough generalizations can be offered here regarding the proposal for mandatory minimum pensions.

1. If, on net balance, costs are passed backward, then the goal of universal coverage could be accomplished by compelling workers without pension coverage to contribute to IRAs. This is not likely to be a politically popular move. It could be sweetened by making a tax deduction (or a tax credit) worth more than the contribution, at least for low-wage workers. Such a subsidy would be akin to a tax reduction for low-wage workers.

2. Possibly, the element of compulsion might not be needed if the tax subsidy is sufficiently great. As now constituted, IRAs do little for low-wage workers. Some improvement even on a voluntary basis, can be useful. It would correct the present inequity by which low-wage workers without pensions subsidize their pensionable higher-wage colleagues.

3. Compelling employers to provide pensions, or at least to make pension contributions, would encounter strong political opposition from these employers. They would, quite naturally, view it as an externally imposed increase in their costs. Opposition might be reduced by permitting the added compensation to be included in minimum wage calculations, but most employers in this sector pay more than the minimum wage and would not see any benefit. A tax inducement might be helpful but would probably have little effect. However, compulsion plus a tax subsidy might be a workable option.

4. Mandatory pension supplements with past service credits are highly unlikely because of their costs. Therefore, mandatory pensions would most likely be in the nature of defined contribution plans, of little use to workers who are now in mid-career or later. Even a scheme with a future targeted benefit, like the new British plan, would run into opposition because of future cost uncertainties.

However, Social Security benefits are skewed to favor lower-wage workers. Less of a private pension supplement is therefore needed to maintain postretirement living standards at preretirement levels.

**Filling the Gaps.** Given the rise in the relative role of Social Security, pension planners may want to turn their attention to filling the gaps in existing pension plans. The joint and survivors' option required by ERISA goes some way toward helping survivors. Indeed, many pre-ERISA plans had provision for survivorship. However, the high incidence of poverty among aged women suggests that more could be done to maintain living standards of dependents.

The joint and survivors' option applies only to spouses, not to divorcees. Neither employers nor unions have any motivation to protect divorced spouses, and there will be increasing numbers of them as the divorce rate continues to rise. It is noteworthy that Social Security has reduced the length of marriage requirement for spouses' benefits from twenty years to ten years. Private plans are not likely to follow this example, unless compelled to do so by law.

Other gaps can be mentioned briefly, although a complete list would require an extensive essay. One is in the area of disability. Pension plan provisions here range from relative generosity to niggardliness. In the absence of disability provisions, vesting helps, but only when the disabled worker reaches the plan's retirement age. Another gap is unemployment at ages close to retirement. Again, vesting does not help until retirement age, unless provision for earlier benefits is made. Older workers have much greater difficulty in finding re-employment. One ironic reason is the prevalence of defined benefit plans based on final average pay, which makes the employment of older workers expensive.[54]

It may be argued that private pension plans are not the proper vehicle for social policy goals such as providing for divorced spouses. All that is suggested here is that pension planners may find it desirable to fill such gaps as may be in their interest. They are not, however, entirely beyond social control. The enactment of ERISA should be sufficient proof of this.

**Inflation-Proofing.** The advent of persistent inflation raises the issue of indexation. It is all very well to provide decent benefit levels at the point of retirement, but there is something tragic about the relentless deterioration of benefit values caused even by inflation rates as "low" as 5 percent to 8 percent per year.

Indexation of benefits at the point of retirement is virtually impossible for any one private pension plan. Defined contribution plans do not even try. Ad hoc increases have been known occasionally in defined benefit plans, and a very few have actually tried indexation. ERISA may discourage such attempts, because indexation in times of inflation would continuously create unfunded liabilities. So long as pension plans remain fragmented, each must strive toward the goal of full funding in order to remain sound. Only a centralized pension system, like the French, can afford to operate on a pay-as-you-go system, and thus to index benefits.

The usual proposals for indexation call for indexed government bonds as an investment medium. There is no special magic to indexed bonds. Like indexed Social Security benefits, such bonds would shift the burden of inflation primarily to the working generation, although the distribution of the burden would differ. They have the disadvantage of crowding out private sector investment. In addition, they constitute a further public subsidy to private pensions, one that is hardly warranted so long as private pensions cover less than half of the employed population.

The problem seems insoluble at this time, and it may be that it is best addressed by economic policies to combat inflation. The only solace is that Social Security *does* protect part of the retirement income of pension beneficiaries, and all of the income of those who subsist solely on Social Security. There is no ready solution to the problem, but solutions will have to be sought unless the pressures of inflation are abated.

**The Impact of the 1977 Social Security Amendments.** We turn now to a question that intrigues both pension planners and, presumably, future beneficiaries: What will be the effect of the 1977 Social Security amendments on occupational pensions? The discussion is necessarily speculative and will be confined mainly to private sector pensions. In many cases, it may be difficult to separate out the particular effects of ERISA and the new age discrimination law, since the three statutes will probably interact with one another. Nevertheless, a look into the future, however speculative it may be, can be useful as a guide to the possible roads that pensions can take.

*Higher payroll taxes.* Considerable concern has been expressed over the schedule of payroll taxes enacted in 1977 to finance Social Security. The much-quoted figure of $227 billion in the next ten years is said to make this the largest tax increase in our history. This point of view can be misleading. Congress was, after all, faced with the options of reducing benefits or finding additional sources of revenues. In point of fact, it somewhat reduced future benefits relative to preretirement earnings, but this course of action had some obvious political limits. Clearly, additional revenues were needed.

There were two sources of revenues available to Congress if it wished to maintain the traditional payroll tax. One was a further extension of the wage base subject to the payroll tax. By 1982 taxable payroll will rise from 85 percent to 91 percent of all payrolls, so that the scope for further expansion is now severely limited. The second source of revenues was an increase in the schedule of future payroll taxes above the schedule of increases that were previously in force.

It must be borne in mind that the tax on covered earnings was to rise in any event, even if the 1972 amendments had proved to be workable (they did not). Most American workers earn wages well below the maximum wage base, so that they and their employers are principally affected by the increase in the tax *rates*.

A glance at Table 3–1 shows that the increases in the new rates over the old ones, however onerous, are far from unbearable. The peak increases will occur in 1990, when the payroll tax levied on each side rises by 1.2 percentage points, or 18.6 percent, over what had previously been legislated. The real pain occurs from the increase in the wage base, which, as noted above, does not affect most workers.

Nonetheless, higher taxes will be perceived as higher costs by employers and as less take-home pay by workers. Hence, one can expect that an effect of higher taxes will be to stiffen employer resistance to greater pension contributions. This effect may be compounded by ERISA, especially among employers who are hit not only by increased administrative costs but also by cost increases due to the new participation and vesting requirements.

Robert J. Myers has pointed out that had the old law remained in effect, private pensions would have been dealt a catastrophic blow, since even higher taxes would have been needed to finance a system

**TABLE 3-1** Increases in Social Security Payroll Tax Rates Resulting From 1977 Amendments, Compared to Previously Scheduled Increases

| | Percentage Points | Percent |
|---|---|---|
| 1979–1980 | .08 | 1.3 |
| 1981 | .35 | 5.6 |
| 1982–1984 | .40 | 6.4 |
| 1985 | .75 | 11.9 |
| 1986–1989 | .70 | 10.9 |
| 1990–2010 | 1.20 | 18.6 |
| 2011 and after | .20 | 2.7 |

Source: Computed from Social Security Administration, *Legislative Report*, No. 17, December 16, 1977, Table 1.

that doubly compensated for inflation.[55] The new tax schedule is preferable to what might have happened in the absence of the 1977 revisions. It may retard increases in pension contributions for better benefits. But there are also counter-pressures, as will be seen below.

*Lower relative benefits.* A little-noticed but significant aspect of the 1977 Social Security amendments is the reduction in relative benefits that goes into effect for persons retiring after 1982. The reduction can be seen in terms of the percentage of final pay replaced by Social Security benefits. For most workers retiring at age sixty-five, the replacement rates will be about 10 percent lower than those the previous law would have yielded. The decline will be smaller for very low earners, most of whom are not covered by private pensions, and greater for those who are at the higher end of the earnings spectrum.

This rollback came about because the benefit computation formula under the 1972 amendment was oversensitive to inflation. It produced replacement rates that were higher than Congress had intended. The new law more or less returns the replacement rates to those in effect before the 1972 indexing formula was adopted. Still, a cut is a cut. At some point, workers will become aware of the change. Union bargainers will notice it sooner.

It is likely, therefore, that pressure will develop for pension increases to make up for the shortfall. The pressure will manifest itself first in the collective bargaining sector, since union spokesmen have access to professional pension expertise and are more knowledgeable than their constituents. The extent of the pressure will vary, depending on the age composition in various firms and industries. Young workers tend to prefer money in their paycheck, while workers past the age of forty-five tend to think about retirement.

At this time it is hard to estimate how early the pressure will be felt and how intensely it will manifest itself. The tail end of the baby boom generation is still working its way into the labor market and is too young to think about retirement. On the other hand, the average age of the total population continues its long-term upward trend. At some point, more pension benefits will be sought, and patterns will emerge from the collective bargaining process. Such patterns may spread to some nonunion employers, including those who traditionally match union gains for competitive reasons or because their policies are aimed at forestalling union organization.

As noted above, the decline in replacement rates will be greater for employees in the high-earnings brackets, such as supervisors, managers, and professional personnel. Most employees in these categories are nonunion. Nonetheless, there are reasons why pension improvements to correct the decline in their replacement rates may also develop.

Earnings for high-paid employees tend to reach a peak later in life than is the case for production and service personnel. Many enter the labor market later than most workers, having spent more time in school. Furthermore, they "build careers" on the basis of past performance and employer expectations of future performance. Thus, they reach their labor market primes at ages when pensions commonly enter into people's minds, and at salaries that make any tax shelter attractive. Since such persons sell their services in competitive labor markets, employers may need to improve pension coverage in order to attract or keep such employees.

It appears, then, that future employer resistance to pension improvements may be offset, in whole or in part, by pressures and needs to make up for the decline in the replacement rate of Social Security. It remains to be seen what the net effect will be.

*Stabilized replacement rates.* The decline in future replacement rates came from the 1977 provisions that "decoupled" the Social Security benefit formula in order to prevent benefits from rising faster than inflation. In addition to reducing future benefits in relative terms, the new formula stabilizes future replacement rates at levels that Congress has deemed proper.

This is a matter of considerable interest to the pension community, for it helps to define the role of pensions in the total retirement system. For many years this role was uncertain. When the pension movement entered its dramatic growth stage in the 1950s, Social Security benefits were considerably lower, in real terms, and pensions, although inadequate by themselves, were used to "top up" Social Security in order to provide a combined retirement income that approached adequacy. Not surprisingly, integration with Social Security was a common feature of the early plans.

In subsequent decades various *ad hoc* increases in Social Security sharply improved real benefits, and the indexation of benefits in the 1972 law drove real benefits higher. This served to reduce the scope for pensions in the retirement system, at least for workers who had adequate coverage. A number of observers began to despair of the future of pensions, for continuous growth in real Social Security benefits would ultimately eliminate the need for private pensions.

The upward march of real Social Security benefits has now been arrested. The role of pensions is now more clearly defined, as the secondary supplement, with pride of place in retirement going to Social Security. Nevertheless, pensions play an important role for the approximately 50 percent of workers who are covered by them. By stabilizing the replacement rate, Congress has eased the task of employers and unions who try to devise rational pension plans.

Now that the uncertainty about future Social Security replacement rates has been removed, it is easier to target defined benefit plans to achieve desirable retirement goals. Many defined benefit plans are based on average pay in the last few years of work. To the extent that future wage levels can reasonably be projected, compensation packages of wages and fringe benefits can be designed so as not to undershoot or overshoot a retirement income target that may be desired by employers or employees. Excessive retirement benefits are undesirable from both employer and employee points of view (except that the latter may like them as an inflation hedge). In short, it is now more feasible to allocate the total compensation package among wages and various benefits in a more optimal fashion.

This suggests that integrated plans may make something of a comeback. The pressure of higher payroll taxes make such plans more attractive to employers—this is part of the resistance to greater pensions that was referred to above. Unions have traditionally disliked integrated plans, because an external force (a change in Social Security) affects the size of the employer contribution. But the tradition is not an old one and may not be set in concrete.

It may be possible to persuade unions to change their negative attitudes if they see that savings from integration can be used for other purposes. For example, the joint and survivors' option now required by ERISA can be enriched in some plans by using a less than straight actuarial assumption. Alternatively, health and welfare benefits may be improved or better wages paid.

The nonunion employer, quite naturally, prefers integration for cost-saving reasons. ERISA and rising payroll taxes are tempting some employers away from defined benefit plans toward defined contribution plans, toward other pension instruments like Employee Stock Ownership Plans or group IRAs (both are really defined contribution plans), or simply toward termination. However, many employers need pension plans in order to keep a competitive stance in the labor market.

Defined benefit plans have an important advantage—they are easily understood by employees. Although the details of integration are sometimes arcane, the results are not. The employee understands that, on the date of retirement, he or she is entitled to an income that is a percentage of a computable number, be it final pay, final average pay for (say) three years, or career average pay. Thereafter, the Social Security portion becomes indexed to consumer price levels, and the pension plan benefit is protected from further changes due to integration. The latter benefit is not likely, however, to be protected from the ravages of inflation.

Integration will continue to have its opponents. Not the least of these is the Internal Revenue Service, which eyes them with justifiable suspicion. Congress has mandated that pension plans qualifying for tax deductions should not discriminate in favor of higher-paid employees, and the IRS has devised some intricate formulae to limit the extent of integration. Whether the present formula is proper is a matter of debate for actuaries and beyond the scope of this work. In the absence of some reasonable limit, plans that heavily favor high-level personnel would undoubtedly proliferate. There is no reason why the general taxpayer should subsidize excessively high pensions for persons who are able to save for themselves.

Other opponents of integration include those who view it as a device for taking away an earned benefit as a result of an increase in payroll taxes or Social Security benefits. Of the two basic methods of integration, the offset method is particularly irritating, for it places the reduction of employer contributions in sharp focus. The "excess" approach, which accomplishes much the same things, may strike employees as more reasonable.

This is not to say that integration is desirable under all circumstances. There may be good reasons why employers or employees might prefer pensions that are fully additive to Social Security. One example might be in plans where pension benefits are low. Another might be in the case of defined contribution plans, where uncertainty regarding the size of the final payout may create a desire for inflation protection during employees' working careers. The additive feature there removes a part of the uncertainty. It is, after all, the adaptability of private plans to particular industrial circumstances that makes them such a valuable part of the retirement system.

Although stabilized Social Security replacement rates make it easier to design rational pension plans, a troublesome issue remains. The issue is inflation. Perhaps future readers will find this problem of only historical interest, just as we today look back upon the mass unemployment of the 1930s as historical curiosity. At the moment, however, varying degrees of inflation appear to be evident in most economies, including ours. The subject is very much on the minds of the public, including those persons who expect pensions, those who now collect them, and those who devise and manage pension plans.

It is possible to upgrade pension credits during workers' careers to compensate for inflation at the point of retirement. It is difficult—perhaps impossible—to adjust benefits to price changes past the point of retirement. Unless ways are found to abate inflation well below present levels, private pension plans will not be able to deliver their promised benefits in terms of real purchasing power.

Social Security mitigates this problem. These benefits can be indexed because central government has the power to tax or—ultimately—the power to create money. No individual pension plan has such powers. Of course, the greater the proportion of the total retirement benefit that comes from Social Security, the less is the need for indexation of private pension plan benefits. The rise in the Social Security wage base, mandated in 1977, will increase this proportion somewhat for workers in the higher wage ranges. The cost is in higher payroll taxes, but any indexing scheme is necessarily costly.[56]

*The effect on existing integrated pension plans.* Many existing pension plans are integrated with Social Security.[57] These are affected by the new law not only in general terms but also with reference to their integration mechanisms. For broad purposes, it is useful here to distinguish between two principal types of defined benefit plans: (1) final average pay plans and (2) career average plans. In the former, benefits are related to earnings over a time period close to retirement. In the latter, the benefit is credited each year, based on that year's earnings, or a flat benefit of a monthly sum per year of service is given.

The offset technique is frequently used to integrate final average pay plans. In such cases the effect of the 1977 law depends on (1) changes in actual dollar amounts of Social Security benefits,[58] which vary with earnings levels below the wage base, and (2) the plan's actuarial assumptions regarding future Social Security benefit increases.

In the light of the new law, many plans will find that Social Security benefits will be smaller than anticipated. Hence, they need to revise their Social Security benefit assumptions, or else their offset will be greater and their plan benefit will be lower than called for. Social Security benefits, at points of retirement, will continually change through time, because they are now adjusted for changes in national average earnings levels. It is therefore necessary to make periodic revisions of the benefit assumption in order to avoid excessive offsets or plan benefits.

Career average plans are commonly integrated by the excess or step-rate method. This provides for relatively greater benefits above some breakpoint, usually the Social Security wage base. For employees below the wage base, the benefits from the pension plan remain unchanged. However, the Social Security benefit will be lower than was previously anticipated. Therefore, a need may develop to improve plan benefits in order to maintain the level of retirement benefits that was intended by the plan.

By 1983 fewer than 10 percent of employees will have salaries above the wage base. The effect of the new law on such employees is not clear. A large proportion of their retirement benefits will come from Social Security (thus, incidentally, protecting a larger proportion of their benefit from inflation, since Social Security benefits are indexed to the consumer price level). The higher wage base leads, in time, to a higher Social Security benefit. However, the benefit increase is not proportional to the increase in the wage base; it is less than proportional. The net effect, for many such employees, will be a relative reduction in retirement income. Adjustment of pension benefits to make up the shortfall is technically difficult, but not beyond the ingenuity of actuaries.

For either broad type of integrated plan, the new law requires changes in costing methods. The 1972 law had the effect of requiring actuaries to make reasonable assumptions regarding future levels of the Consumer Price Index (CPI) as well as future levels of average wages. The decoupling provision of the 1977 law removes the need to forecast changes in the CPI, since consumer prices no longer affect the wage base and, through it, future Social Security benefits.

*The delayed retirement credit.* The last two decades have witnessed a trend toward early retirement, stimulated by the early retirement options found both under Social Security and under many pension plans. Although this trend may continue further, there are forces at play that may reverse the trend, especially among nonmanual workers. One of these is the increase in the retirement credit for Social Security, from 1 percent to 3 percent for every year worked past age sixty-five. A second is the new age discrimination law that protects workers until age seventy instead of sixty-five. The third is the relative shortage of labor that will develop in the 1980s and thereafter, when the low birthrates of the 1960s and 1970s will be felt in the labor market.

Later retirement reduces the costs of private pensions, just as it reduces the burden on the Social Security system. Production workers with hard, repetitive tasks may not be greatly tempted to stay past age sixty-two or sixty-five, but these are a declining proportion of the labor force. Some of the workers whose tasks are more interesting or less onerous may prefer to stay at work for a few years past age sixty-five, depending on how they value the pecuniary and nonpecuniary rewards from work relative to leisure at lower income.

The 3 percent credit is well below the actuarial value of the additional Social Security benefit from staying at work. It may therefore not be a powerful inducement to stay on, especially if pension plans freeze benefits at age sixty-five. Apparently, pension plans will be permitted to do this. However, as a labor shortage begins to make itself felt, employers may be willing to increase pensions for service past sixty-five (defined contribution plans tend to have this effect anyway). Such increases will still reduce pension costs, provided that the increases in benefits are not greater than their actuarial value.

The net effect is difficult to predict. An educated guess is that the short-term impact may be minimal. Where the pension plan itself provides a powerful inducement to retire early, as in the automobile and steel industries, there may be no changes in retirement patterns. Over the longer run, however, both employers and workers may get used to the idea of later retirement. This will be strengthened by the long-term changes in the labor market. The relative reduction in labor supply will itself raise the compensation of workers. This will induce employers to hold on to experienced workers, and experienced workers will be tempted to work somewhat longer. Better health, over time, may add to this effect.

There has already been talk of gradually raising the normal Social Security retirement age from sixty-five to sixty-eight. This would constitute a further reduction in benefits relative to tax contributions and would hold workers longer in the labor market. Historically, pension plans have followed the Social Security retirement age. Should Congress enact such a provision—its motive would be to reduce the burden of Social Security—pension plans are likely to follow the example.

It has been said that Social Security benefits can never be lowered, but only raised. In 1977 Congress displayed a willingness to lower them for future beneficiaries. Faced with strong objections to high payroll taxes, it may be willing to do so again. A very gradual increase in the Social Security retirement age may be a convenient way of doing this, because the full effect will fall on a future generation of voters.

There is a demographic trend that may reduce popular objections to this course of action. Family formation now occurs later in life. This means that the peak consumption needs of people—housing, consumer durables, and child-raising costs—occur later. A social decision to exchange an extended future work obligation for a present reduction in taxes may be quite rational. But this is in the realm of political speculation.

*The easier retirement test.* A purpose of the original Social Security Act was to remove older workers from the labor market to make room for younger ones. To do this, benefits were reduced one-for-one for every dollar of work income. Over the years, this was modified. In 1977, before the new law, the first $3,000 of annual earnings, or $250 of any month, were exempt from the retirement test at age sixty-five (the amount was lower at age sixty-two), and benefits were reduced at a rate of fifty cents per dollar of earnings above the exempt level. The test did not apply past age seventy-two.

This provision was eased by the 1977 amendments. At age sixty-five, the annual exempt amount is being raised in steps to $6,000 in 1982 ($4,200 at age sixty-two). Thereafter, it will be adjusted upward by changes in average annual earnings. The test will, in 1982, cease to apply past age seventy. However, the *monthly* exempt amount has been eliminated, except for the first year of retirement.

The change in the retirement test will affect the part-time labor market. Firms will be able to retain older workers on a part-time basis, or to phase them out more gradually by offering reduced work schedules past age sixty-five. Some employers may find this course of action desirable.

With some ingenuity, it is possible to coordinate pension plan benefits with earnings in such a way that an older employee is better off if he works a shorter work year. Such an employee would receive the relevant wage income for time worked, plus reduced Social Security and reduced pension benefits. Although total income might be lower than from full-time work, the additional leisure would be worth it for some.

A partial retirement plan along the lines suggested above would be attractive to workers who do not put too great a value on leisure. Among these might be healthy persons, workers who derive some satisfaction from work, men with younger working wives, and widows with low Social Security (and possibly low pension) benefits.

There are undoubtedly workers who prefer a broader range of choice than the all-or-nothing options of complete retirement and full-time work. Not all employers can accommodate such choices, but some can. This is evidenced by the growing role of the part-time labor market. Note, however, that the elimination of the monthly retirement measure may make it impossible to recall high-paid workers for an occasional period. The benefit loss might be too great if earnings from such occasional employment exceed the Social Security annual maximum.

## PUBLIC SECTOR PENSION PLANS

As a result of the growth of the public sector since World War II, government employees now constitute 17 percent of all employed workers, or about twice the percentage that obtained in 1948.[59] Since most are covered by pension and other benefit plans, it is useful to trace the development of such plans.[60] Outside the federal sector, they display a diversity almost as great as the diversity in the private sector. In addition, public sector plans present a variety of important issues and problems, including underfunding of accrued liabilities.

### Historical Development

Aside from pensions for war veterans, the early pensions emerged in the latter part of the nineteenth century at municipal levels for special groups. Policemen were first, followed by firefighters and teachers. What is probably the first such plan was enacted for policemen in New York City in 1857, covering disability with a pension and a lump sum for death. Strictly speaking, it was not comparable with a full-fledged retirement pension. What is interesting about it was the rather casual nature of the financing. Funds came from such various sources as private donations and the sale of confiscated and surplus property. It was not until 1878 that retirement benefits were included, and employee contributions added as a source of finance.

A drive for teacher retirement plans began with voluntary associations in various cities (New York led in 1869), but the first compulsory funds did not make their appearance until the end of the century. The early plans depended entirely on contributions of covered employees, and financial soundness was provided by permitting the plans to decrease benefits whenever funds were insufficient.

Public employers, like their private counterparts, took little interest in providing retirement benefits for their employees. Presumably, they were bound by the same nineteenth-century ethic described earlier. Attitudes regarding the employer's responsibility to his superannuated workers began to change in the twentieth century. In 1911 Massachusetts pioneered with a law establishing a statewide contributory system for state nonteaching employees. A law *enabling* cities and towns to establish retirement systems had passed the previous year, and one for county employees passed in 1911. The systems were optional to the lower-level governments and found few takers in the first decade. In 1913, however, Massachusetts teachers became covered under a separate system.

Formal systems became more prevalent in the 1920s and followed the pattern that had developed earlier. They tended to be compulsory, contributory, fragmented among different levels of government, and separate for special groups such as teachers, police, and firefighters. Just as public utilities and railroads (before motor carriers appeared) had the power to "tax" the users of their services, governments have an explicit taxing power to pass costs along. Hence, they were in a better position than competitive employers to raise their costs by enacting pensions. Unlike the private sector, the contributory principle became well established.

In any event, growth continued. By the early 1940s about half of state and local employees were covered and, as noted above, the current figure is somewhere close to 100 percent. Most are now state-administered and cover large units, although many small units persist. The period after World War II saw both growth and liberalization of benefits, including coverage of more contingencies; benefits are increasingly based on final salary, and Social Security is usually additive.[61]

**Federal Pensions**

Retirement provisions for career armed forces personnel date back to 1861. In 1920 the federal government entered the pension field for its civilian employees with the enactment of the Civil Service Retirement System. Growth of the federal sector occurred in the 1930s and thereafter. Over the years, coverage was extended to all officers and employees of the executive, legislative, and judicial branches and to those employed by the District of Columbia. Special provisions exist for members of Congress, Congressional employees, hazardous duty employees, and air traffic controllers (who, in most cases, must retire at age fifty-six).

In addition, there are separate plans for the Tennessee Valley Authority, the Federal Reserve System, the Federal Reserve Banks, and some other miscellaneous groups. These, unlike the Civil Service retirement system, also participate in Social Security on an additive basis.[62]

From its beginning, the Civil Service retirement system was contributory. Ostensibly it is funded on a 50–50 basis, with employees and their agencies each contributing 7 percent of compensation. However, the actual ratio of contributions for retirement is 38 percent by employees and 62 percent by government because of certain direct appropriations in addition to the contributions.[63] A fund consisting of U.S. government obligations exists, somewhat parallel to the Social Security Trust Funds. As a practical matter, the fund would quickly run dry if it depended solely on these contributions and interest on the bonds. As a result of liberalized benefits, a large unfunded liability exists, and current law provides for annual contributions from general revenues to liquidate this over a thirty-year period. The liability is growing. In 1972 it stood at $75.7 billion, as compared with $28 billion in the Trust Fund.[64] By 1975 the liability had grown by $21.7 billion to $97.2 billion, while the Trust Fund had only increased by $10.6 billion to $38.6 billion.[65]

Furthermore, the unfunded liability does not include pension increases due to changes in the Consumer Price Index. Like Social Security, federal benefits rise with increases in the CPI, but unlike Social Security, benefits are adjusted twice a year instead of once a year. The Board of Actuaries does not consider liabilities resulting from cost of living increases as part of the "statutory" unfunded liabilities that are subject to liquidation. Inflation raises benefits two ways: (1) by raising salaries on which benefits are based (last three years' salaries) and (2) by the inflation adjustment for beneficiaries. The Board of Actuaries stressed this problem in its 1975 *Report* noting that "the present approach to funding the System will lead to spiralling costs in the future, no only in dollar amounts but as a percentage of covered payroll.[66]

The sums at issue are quite substantial. In 1976 retirement, disability, and survivors' benefits totaled $16.5 billion, paid to 2.6 million people. Beneficiaries and expenditures are about evenly divided between civilian and military personnel. Growth has been notable. Since 1966 the number of beneficiaries has increased by 153 percent, and total benefits by 295 percent. In the armed forces, the benefit growth has been astonishing. Although beneficiaries increased by 140 percent during 1966–76, total benefits grew by 351 percent.[67]

In the armed forces system, benefits are available after twenty years, at half of basic pay (exclusive of allowances) and at 75 percent of basic pay after thirty years. Subsequent employment in the civilian part of the federal government does not preclude collection of a military pension. This is a particularly valuable right for those officers who, upon retirement, find employment in the Defense Department. Military personnel, unlike their civil service counterparts, are covered by Social Security. Because early retirement from service is possible—and, in many cases, compulsory—there is time for a retired serviceman to establish rights to a second pension. If this is a federal pension, all of the person's retirement income is sheltered from inflation.

The military pension system is also noteworthy for being unfunded. One consequence of this is that the real cost of supporting a military establishment is greatly understated by its current operating statistics. To the extent that Civil Service pensions are underfunded, the same thing is true.[68]

Clearly a crisis of sorts is brewing in the federal retirement system. At the moment, the operating statistics of the total civilian federal employee benefit system are showing surpluses on most accounts, and the Trust Fund is growing. Accordingly, the problem lacks the immediacy associated with Social Security, but it will have to be faced at some time. Because members of Congress participate in a parallel system, they can be expected to have a personal interest in the problem when it becomes acute. So far, at least, no one has suggested that the principle of "self-sufficiency" be applied here, in contrast to Social Security.

**State and Local Retirement Systems**

More than 9 million state and local employees are covered by 2,394 retirement systems. In fiscal year 1975–1976, the systems had receipts of $21.6 billion, including employee contributions and earnings on assets. Benefits, exclusive of employees' withdrawals of their own contributions, amounted to $7.5 billion. Of these, $5.3 billion were paid by the 176 state-administered plans that dominate the system. Assets amounted to $112 billion.[69]

There are two rough measures of soundness that can be applied to these plans. One is the ratio of payments to receipts. The second is the ratio of payments to assets.[70] On both of these measures, the aggregated funds appear to be in good shape.

In 1975–76, the ratio of payments to receipts was a respectable 39.2 percent. This has shown little change over the previous two decades despite the fact that beneficiaries have grown faster than members. The reason for this good showing is that earnings on assets have risen even faster. Insofar as the relative number of beneficiaries will continue to grow, earnings must keep pace if this ratio is to be maintained.

The aggregate ratio of payments to assets, which fell in the 1960s, has returned to its earlier levels and now stands at a healthy 7.6 percent. This figure becomes meaningful when one considers that a pay-as-you go system, like Social Security, would have a ratio of payments to assets that is close to 100 percent. On the whole, the public retirement system looks sound.

Unfortunately, many of the parts do not look as good as the whole. Using the ratio of payments to receipts, the total of state and local plans in Maine have a ratio of 84.4 percent. The figure for Massachusetts is 66.2 percent, and 61.4 percent for West Virginia.[71] States and localities with payments-to-receipts ratios of this magnitude are facing trouble in the not too distant future, having little scope for the future asset accumulation and earnings increases that will be needed for the rising number of retired employees.

Some, but not all, of the problem lies in the local systems. These show a higher incidence of pay-as-you-go funding than do the states.[72] For example, many local police and fire pension systems in Kansas are unfunded. In 1977 the state ordered all unfunded systems to begin funding on actuarial bases or to join the state's pension system. For Kansas City, the cost of funding will be a staggering 73.9 percent of payroll, slightly less if it joins the state system. For other cities, the percent of payroll needed for funding will run from as low as 14 percent to as high as 73 percent.[73]

None of the above touches upon the actuarial assumptions of plans that are ostensibly funded. Where these are unsound, the current contributions to the plans are below future needs. The egregious case—but not the only one—is New York City. During the period 1914–1918, a commission developed an actuarial system for teachers and city employees other than police and fire. The assumptions were based on experience during 1908–1914. The system that was adopted served as a pattern for many other public pensions in the United States.

The assumptions were sound when they were made but were left unchanged. After five decades, including a period of liberalization that followed the advent of collective bargaining, the assumptions bore no relationship to reality. For example, the assumptions predicted sixty-five deaths among women teachers aged twenty-eight to thirty-two for the period 1962–1965. In fact, there were six deaths. Mortality after retirement was 73 percent of what the assumptions projected.[74]

Changes are now under way to improve the viability of New York's pension system. The changes are costly and come at a time when the city is in a poor financial condition. There is, undoubtedly, a lesson to be learned from this experience, as a rising proportion of state and local taxes will be used not for current services but for services rendered in the past.

### Comparing Public and Private Pensions

If we look for important points of comparison between private and public systems, the following similarities and differences emerge:

*Source of Revenues*: Because private systems are largely noncontributory (about 80 percent), employers are the principal sources of revenues into the pension plans. Given the dynamics of a market economy, some employers will prosper and others will fail. Only a few employers with great monopoly powers (e.g. private utilities) can "tax" their customers, and even this "taxing" power has its limits.

Public plans derive their revenues from the jurisdiction's taxing power. This gives them a certain advantage, because taxes are compulsory payments made by persons subject to the state's or locality's taxing power. However great this taxing power may be, it is not infinite and depends, in part, on the economic climate of the taxing jurisdiction. The narrower the jurisdiction, the easier it is for taxpayers to migrate beyond the reach of the local government's taxing powers.

It may take a long time for this fact to sink in, because political leaders are likely to have shorter time horizons than corporate managers. However, the current problems of the central cities, plus the advent of ERISA in the private sector, are stimulating an interest in public plans.[75] Indeed, ERISA itself provides that Congress will study public plans to see if certain standards of the law should be extended to them.[76]

*Funding*: Underfunding was one of the problems that led to reform in the private sector. It appears that many public sector plans have succumbed to the same temptation to defer problems into the future.[77] Arguably, there may less need for full funding, especially in statewide systems, but rising benefit costs that stem from rising salaries can create future problems, even in jurisdictions whose plans are currently well-funded. In part, the argument transcends the issue of "soundness." It concerns the relative responsibilities of present versus future taxpayers to meet obligations incurred today. If one believes that pensions are deferred compensation for services rendered today, then a move somewhat closer to full funding seems to be in order as a matter of equity between generations.

As in the private sector, any attempt to move rapidly to full funding is probably impossible. For example, Massachusetts, which is on a pay-as-you-go basis, has $11 billion in unfunded liabilities. Even to amortize this over forty years (the ERISA standard) would mean doubling the state's contributions at a fixed rate cost of 25 percent of wages for amortization alone. The farther the day of reckoning is put off, the greater the future costs will be.

*Assets*: Like private pension funds, the state and local funds keep their assets primarily in private sector securities. Indeed the proportion of their assets in the private sector is slightly higher than for private plans. In 1976 public funds held 90 percent of their assets this way, against 79 percent for private funds. However, their investment policies are more conservative (often prescribed by law), in that 52 percent of the assets were in corporate bonds and only 22 percent in stocks, compared to private plans investment of 59 percent in bonds and 25 percent in stocks.[79]

*Vesting*: The requirements for private plans have already been dealt with above. Public plans tend to vest on the basis of length of service. Most do so after ten years. The balance have varying age or age-plus-service requirements.

Unlike private plans, which often vest in stages, public plans tend to vest fully once the vesting point is achieved. Vesting, however, is generally contingent on the terminated employee's leaving his contribution in the system, and most public plans are contributory.[80]

*Portability*: Portability is a problem in private plans, except among employees belonging to multiemployer plans. In public plans, portability generally exists within one system. It is common to find reciprocity agreements among systems within a state (but not across state lines), but an employee's movement from one system to another within the state can lead to some benefit loss.[81] This is of particular importance to teachers, who are probably more mobile than other civil servants.

*Benefit Levels*: Retirement benefits for public employees are higher than those for private pension plan participants. Where combined with Social Security (in about 70 percent of plans), benefits are approximately twice as great as in private plans. Public plans that do not participate in Social Security can also have high benefits where the equivalent of the Social Security tax is contributed into the plan; on average, however, plans without Social Security pay about one-third more than private plans. Part, but not all, of the higher public benefits can be attributed to their contributory nature.[82]

*Coordination with Social Security*: As noted earlier, coordination is now vestigial, because public plans did not adjust to the rising Social Security wage base. Accordingly, most Social Security benefits are additive. The Bankers Trust survey of a sample of private plans shows that pattern plans (negotiated with unions) are not commonly coordinated, whereas conventional plans (mostly unilateral) tend to have some coordinating feature, although the offset is likely to be less than 100 percent.[83]

*Escalation of Retiree Benefits*: According to Rosow, half of state and local plans provide some increases to beneficiaries to compensate for inflation.[84] The most common method is on an *ad hoc* basis, that is, the relevant legislative body makes occasional adjustments.[85] In the private sector, automatic escalation is rare. About 11 percent of conventional (unilateral) plans have variable annuity components that adjust to variations in securities prices—a feature that may work in the long run but may not be helpful to retirees if securities prices are falling while the cost of living is rising. In general, larger companies tend to make some increases, either at the employer's initiative and at a time and by an amount he thinks appropriate, or else (in negotiated plans) by extending increases in defined benefits to retirees.[86]

*Costs*: As might be expected, public plans cost substantially more than private ones.[87] Private pension premiums in 1975 were estimated at 5.5 percent of payroll,[88] whereas state-local employer contributions stood at 11.8 percent, almost exactly twice as high as in the private sector.[89]

The preceding two chapters have described the main elements of our three-tiered retirement structure. The lowest tier, SSI, applies to the minority of the population that arrives at retirement in a state of poverty. This minority has been significantly diminished by the growth of Social Security and, to a far lesser extent, by the growth in pensions. The second tier, covering 90 percent of the working population and its dependents, is Social Security. The third tier consists of employer-related pensions that cover about half the working population but will significantly benefit a somewhat smaller proportion of the retired population.

The three chapters that follow will explore, in considerable depth, the issues that were raised in the overview. Accordingly, we now turn to the functioning of Social Security in a time of social and economic change.

CHAPTER FOUR

# Social Security in a Time of Change

THE PREVIOUS CHAPTERS have described an income maintenance system for the aged consisting of several parts, or tiers. The cornerstone—that is, the tier with the broadest coverage—is the Old Age Insurance aspect of the Social Security system, which covers about 90 percent of the labor force and provides for both retirees and dependents (mainly spouses). About 50–60 percent of the labor force can build on top of this foundation by participating in private and public sector pension plans, although somewhat fewer than this proportion will actually collect any significant pensions if they survive to retirement, unless the employer-related pension system grows significantly in coverage. This is because some workers now covered will move out of coverage during their working years, and some plans will fail. ERISA, it is hoped, will reduce private plan failure in the future and will protect the vested portions of benefit rights in the event of plan failure, so that the relative number of pensioners will rise. However, the higher cost of ERISA may inhibit the future growth in coverage of private pensions.

The present tax system also enables a substantial proportion of the labor force to accumulate assets in the form of home ownership by giving tax preference to homeowners in the form of itemized deductions for interest and property taxes, and by the nontaxability of imputed rents from owner-occupied homes. Individual Retirement Accounts and Keogh Plans also provide vehicles for asset accumulation, although the numbers involved are likely to be relatively small.

In addition, the tax preferences for the aged (double exemption, special treatment of retirement income, exclusion of Social Security benefits, and low income exclusion) preserve a greater proportion of retirement income than earned income, thus raising the real value of such income, and the progressive nature of the income tax lowers the tax rate on the taxable portion of retirement income.

Medicare can be viewed as an important component of the total system, since it sharply reduces the medical costs of the aged. The benefit, it should be remembered, is tax free. An equivalent insurance policy, if available, might cost about $2,000.

For the poor segment of the aged, the public assistance component of the income maintenance system provides some support in the form of Supplemental Security Income, benefits for indigent veterans, food stamps, and Medicaid for those who qualify and whose Medicare coverage is insufficient. Among the latter are persons in need of prolonged or indefinite nursing home care. As noted earlier, a growing proportion of this group is likely to consist of persons whose working years were spent in the middle-income ranges. Medicaid is, so to speak, the ultimate form of income maintenance for the aged.

Contributions from relatives are probably an insignificant source of income for the aged, although hard data on this are impossible to obtain. A survey of persons who were fifty-eight to sixty-three in 1969 showed 3 percent of men and 9 percent of women reporting contributions from children in 1973 (when the sample had aged to sixty-two to sixty-seven). The survey also shows family transfers running in the other direction, that is, from older parents to children. Thus, in 1973, 4 percent of men and 3 percent of women in the sample were contributing to their children.[1]

The figures probably understate the extent of intrafamily transfer payments;[2] they suggest very strongly that aged Americans (especially couples) do not look toward their adult children for help.[3]

## THE NEEDS TO BE COVERED BY THE RETIREMENT SYSTEM

### The Target Population and Its Needs Today

There are about 23 million persons aged sixty-five and over in the United States at this time (plus 5 million more between sixty-two and sixty-five). This group will grow over time. Growth will be slow at first, at a declining rate until the end of the century, when an over-sixty-five population of about 32 million can be expected. The growth rate will pick up sharply as the war babies begin to mature in 2010 (sixty-five years after the end of World War II), and the total will reach its peak in 2035 at 56 million, with small declines thereafter. After 2050, growth or decline will depend on where the fertility rate settles down. If the rate persists at 1.7 (about the rate in 1977), the aging population will continue to decline. If it returns to something like 2.1 (the rate needed to replace one couple), some growth will occur.[4]

It may be an exercise in science fiction to discuss the needs of the aged population in the year 2050, but it is perfectly rational to look to the present and to assume that our social values will not change drastically in the next few decades. The word "needs" may not be the most felicitous one where people believe, and have been led to believe, that their retirement incomes are a matter of entitlement based on taxes, pension fund contributions, savings, or—in a larger sense—their contribution to society during their productive years. I use it merely for want of a better word.

The discussion of needs, furthermore, must be confined to material needs in a work of this nature. The needs of the aged, like those of other people, are complex and encompass social and psychological variables that economists overlook (at least until they themselves become old). Whatever these variables may be, they are neither quantifiable nor generally thought of as within the scope of a retirement system's purposes. Therefore, I shall omit them from consideration here, with the *caveat* that the omission may, after all, be a serious one.

Even if we leave out the nonquantifiable variables, it is important to remember that income—especially money income—is not a perfect proxy for the welfare of the aged. The point was recently developed by Marilyn Moon, who created a measure of welfare that goes beyond money income to include transfers in kind, tax expenditures (that is, favorable income tax treatment), intrafamily transfers, leisure time, and net worth. Using this measure, she found that economic welfare was somewhat more evenly distributed among aged families than the distribution of income. Unfortunately, she was forced to use the statistics for 1965 and 1966, because later data for some of her variables were not available—a chronic problem for researchers in the economics of aging. Because of this, her empirical results cannot be directly applied here because of the many changes that have occurred since the data were collected.[5] Accordingly, income remains the most usable proxy for welfare, at least until Moon's study can be updated with new figures.[6]

There are many ways to describe quantifiable need, both absolutely and relatively. At the lower end of the income scale, we have come to accept the Social Security Administration's poverty threshold as a benchmark representing a minimum income below which people are in acute need—in poverty. Any poverty line defined in money presents conceptual problems, because poverty is also a relative and subjective phenomenon.[7]

Nonetheless, if we use the poverty line as a rough guideline, a number of phenomena become observable. One is that the aged are naturally prone to poverty, at least in the absence of transfer payments. Thus, almost 60 percent of families headed by a person over sixty-five had pretax/pretransfer incomes below the poverty threshold in 1976, compared to 19 percent of the rest of the population. Social Security benefits raised 64 percent of the aged poor over the poverty threshold, which demonstrates the importance of the program as a poverty preventer for the aged. Other transfers, in cash and kind (such as SSI and food stamps), further reduced the incidence of poverty. Excluding Medicare and Medicaid, about 14 percent of aged families were poor. If the medical transfers in kind are included, the incidence of poverty fell to about 6 percent, which would indicate considerable success in the war on poverty among the aged.[8]

Unfortunately, the 6 percent figure cannot be used with confidence. In addition to reporting errors and the omission of institutionalized persons, there is a problem concerning the inclusion of Medicare and Medicaid. The use of these services is unevenly distributed among the target population, and it is misleading to attribute an average cost to each household. Furthermore, the institutions of Medicare and Medicaid themselves helped to raise the cost of medical care and thus increased the size of the transfer. In short, the "true" poverty rate among the aged probably lies somewhere between 6 percent and 14 percent. It is hard to pinpoint it with greater precision.[9]

That age is a predictor of poverty is also shown in a five-year study of five thousand families conducted by the Institute for Social Research at the University of Michigan. Using a slightly more sophisticated definition of income, Morgan and his colleagues found that the chance of being poor one year out of five (about 30 percent between ages twenty-five and fifty-five) rose sharply after ages fifty-five to sixty-four, to 40 percent for the sixty-five to seventy-four age group and over 60 percent beyond that. Indeed, the chances of being persistently poor (five years out of five) were 25 percent for the fifty-five to sixty-four age group, rising to 32 percent for the sixty-five to seventy-four group and 50 percent for those seventy-five or older.[10] Although the advent of SSI and the increases in the real value of Social Security benefits may have reduced the importance of age as a predictor of poverty, it remains clear that, left to themselves, the aged would be far poorer in the absence of transfer payments.

A second way to look at needs, once we get past the poverty line, is by estimating the cost of a market basket of goods and services. The Bureau of Labor Statistics computes annual budgets for three standards of living for a retired couple. The annual averages for urban couples in 1975 and 1976 were:

| | Lower Budget | Intermediate Budget | Higher Budget |
|---|---|---|---|
| 1975 | $4,501 | $6,465 | $ 9,598 |
| 1976 | 4,695 | 6,735 | 10,048 |

The figures are "after tax," that is, they do not cover the need for payment of personal income taxes. The figures would be considerably higher if it were not for Medicare, because only out-of-pocket costs for medical care (about $575) are counted. Also, there is considerable variation by region and specific metropolitan areas, running up to 20 percent above and 15 percent below the national average for metropolitan areas.[11]

All attempts to construct market baskets necessarily contain an element of arbitrariness. The choice of the items by the Bureau of Labor Statistics was made in the mid-1960s, was last priced in 1969, and has been updated since by use of the main components of the Consumer Price Index. To the extent that spending patterns have changed or may deviate from the patterns assumed by the Consumer Price Index (for urban wage earners), the figures for the three levels of living must be treated as approximations or guidelines. If a policy goal is built on the figures—for example, that a retired couple's income should reach at least the lower budget level—then such a goal is feasible if the figures "make sense" or represent some social consensus of adequacy.

Looking at the 1975 income distribution for families over sixty-five (latest available), it is possible to see what proportion of older couples fall into the three BLS categories. The comparison is rough, because not all couples over sixty-five are retired and some contain additional household members (mean family size is 2.3). Additionally, some of their incomes are taxable. Of the 6.7 million husband-and-wife families (a little more than half the aged population), 21.4 percent had incomes below $5,000 (about the lower level), 17.1 percent fell into the intermediate stage, and another 17.1 percent fell between the intermediate and upper levels. This left 44.4 percent at or above the upper level.[12]

Since the BLS does not construct budgets for the aged who are not retired couples, it is not possible to calculate a similar distribution, at least from official figures, for the rest of the aged population. However, we know in general that multiple-person families tend to have higher incomes than single-person households. In the case of the aged, the absence of a spouse means lower Social Security benefits and, in many cases, lower pensions.

**The Replacement Rate.** A number of writers have begun to use the replacement rate as a measure of the adequacy of retirement income. On the assumption that older persons wish to maintain their preretirement standards of living, the empirical question posed is: To what extent do Social Security, pensions and other transfers replace preretirement income? Obviously, the replacement rate need not be equal to 100 percent of the pretax preretirement income. It is the posttax, posttransfer rate that matters. This captures some of the variables that Moon used in her analysis, but it omits such things as net worth (principally in the form of owner-occupied housing) and the value of leisure. The last, incidentally, is an elusive concept, since income and leisure are, to a certain extent, complementary goods—the higher one's income, the more enjoyment can be derived from leisure.[13]

As defined by Peter Henle, the replacement rate is the relation between a person's benefit upon retirement and his preretirement earnings.[14] Henle recognizes that this presents some conceptual difficulties on both sides of the ratio. Any attempt to arrive at a rate (or set of rates) must make certain assumptions about the retiree's work experience, length of service, and retirement age. Furthermore a choice must be made as to whether to focus on the individual or on the family, because both Social Security and many private pension benefits may vary in size with the number of dependents. To complicate matters still further, the situation will differ as between families with two-earner and one-earner histories. Finally, a decision must be made as to whether to base the replacement rate on the retiree's career earnings, earnings at or under the Social Security wage base over a work career, the last few years' earnings, or earnings in the last year.

In the pages that follow, replacement rates will be examined for workers who retired on January 1, 1977, and for those who will retire ten years later. This will make it possible to assess the changes resulting from the 1977 amendments, which, in effect, reduced replacement rates for future retirees. Because there is an almost infinite set of combinations and permutations of the variables listed above, replacement rates are estimated for only a few of the possible assumptions.

**Replacement Rates in 1977.** Following Henle, hypothetical earnings histories were constructed for low-earnings workers and for workers in retailing, services, manufacturing, and construction.[15] (see Appendix to this chapter, Table 4-10). This, in turn, was used to calculate the Social Security benefits for workers with continuous earnings histories beginning in 1951 who retired on January 1, 1977 (earnings before 1951 are not counted for persons claiming benefits in 1977). Average annual earnings were calculated for the five categories and are presented in Table 4-1. In addition, Table 4-1 gives the Primary Insurance Amount (PIA), which is used to calculate family benefits and also represents the benefit for a single worker retiring at

**TABLE 4–1** Average Annual Earnings and Social Security Benefits for 1977 (Under the pre-1977 Law)

| INDUSTRY | WORKER RETIRED AT AGE 65 | | | | WORKER RETIRED AT AGE 62 | | |
|---|---|---|---|---|---|---|---|
| | | | With Spouse Claiming | | | | |
| | Average Annual Earnings | PIA | At Age 65 | At Age 62 | Average Annual Earnings | Worker Alone | With Spouse Claiming at Age 62 |
| Low earnings model | $3079 | $236.40 | $354.60 | $325.05 | $2948 | $185.00 | $273.50 |
| Retail trade | 4047 | 278.10 | 417.15 | 382.50 | 3856 | 218.56 | 322.44 |
| Services | 5526 | 343.50 | 515.25 | 472.31 | 5179 | 263.68 | 388.00 |
| Manufacturing | 6613 | 387.60 | 581.40 | 532.95 | 6264 | 299.00 | 439.14 |
| Construction | 7743 | 443.20 | 664.80 | 609.40 | 7237 | 335.00 | 492.01 |

Sources: Appendix, Table 4–10, Benefit levels from Social Security Administration.

age sixty-five. The table also gives Social Security benefits for the following characteristics: retired worker, age sixty-five, with dependent spouse claiming benefits at sixty-five and at sixty-two; single worker, age sixty-two; and married worker age sixty-two with spouse claiming benefits at age sixty-two.

Constraints of time, space, and the reader's patience led us to omit two-earner spouses, other combinations of retirement ages, and households with more than two people. The reader will also note that the use of a continuous work history implies no unemployment, which may strike one as unlikely. However, it should be borne in mind that the benefit calculation allows the claimant to drop the five lowest years of earnings, which should roughly compensate for occasional spells of unemployment that would introduce low-earnings years into a worker's history.

For the purpose of calculating replacement rates, it was necessary to decide on a base. Should average career earnings be used as a base? This notion was rejected because nominal earnings were driven up by inflation, and a career average would be unduly low, both from the individual worker's perception and for meaningful policy purposes. Adjusting average career earnings by the Consumer Price Index would understate the changes in real earnings that occurred and became part of the individual's and the community's perception of living standards. A more sensible approach, it was decided, was to use as a base the highest few years of earnings before retirement. This most clearly illustrates the impact of the retirement decision on income at or near retirement, when most workers have achieved the real income levels to which they have become accustomed at that juncture.

The methodology of constructing our hypothetical earnings histories necessarily gives the last year as the highest year, and this was chosen as the base. The reader is reminded that for actual earnings histories in contrast to hypothetical ones, an average of the highest three, four, five years might serve as a sensible base, depending on what social goal the retirement system is supposed to achieve.

Table 4-2 presents the annual Social Security benefits for workers retiring at sixty-five[16] in the categories given above, together with the rate at which pretax earnings are replaced by tax-free benefits. The progressive nature of the benefit structure becomes apparent

**TABLE 4–2** Social Security Replacement Rates[a]: Male Workers Retiring in January 1977

| Retirement Circumstances | Low-Earnings Model | Retail Trade | Services | Manufacturing | Construction |
|---|---|---|---|---|---|
| Worker retired at age 65: | | | | | |
| Single | | | | | |
| Annual benefit | $2836.80 | $3337.20 | $4122.00 | $4651.20 | $5318.40 |
| Replacement rate | 62.27% | 55.71% | 45.30% | 43.09% | 35.90% |
| With spouse claiming: | | | | | |
| At age 65 and over | | | | | |
| Annual benefit | 4255.20 | 5005.80 | 6183.00 | 6976.80 | 7977.60 |
| Replacement rate | 93.41 | 83.57 | 67.95 | 64.63 | 53.84 |
| At age 62 | | | | | |
| Annual benefit | 3900.60 | 4590.00 | 5667.72 | 6395.40 | 7312.80 |
| Replacement rate | 85.63 | 76.63 | 62.28 | 59.24 | 49.36 |

[a]Replacement rates calculated as percentage of annual benefits to 1976 earnings.

Sources: Appendix, Table 4–10, and Table 4–1.

from the calculations. In absolute terms, benefits rise with previous earnings. In relative terms, they decline. At the polar extremes, the decline can be quite sharp. For example, the low-earnings worker retiring at sixty-five with spouse claiming benefits at sixty-five has 93 percent of his earnings replaced by Social Security, whereas our hypothetical construction worker (a high-wage trade) in the same situation has a replacement rate of 54 percent. For the same pair of workers choosing to retire at sixty-two with dependent wives at sixty-two, the replacement rate (not shown on Table 4-2) varies from 72 percent for the low-earner family to 40 percent for the construction worker.

Since many workers can look forward to pensions, it is useful to examine the impact of Social Security plus pensions on the income of retiring workers. Workers in the low-earnings model were assumed to be largely excluded from the pension system, and calculations are confined to workers in four industries with average wages above the low-earnings model. Four pension plans that are more or less representative were chosen and are presented in the Appendix, Table 4-11. The choice was restricted by the nature of the latest available data as of the time of this writing, and an effort was made to find plans for employees whose 1976 average earnings roughly corresponded to the figures in the Appendix, Table 4-10.

Benefits inclusive of Social Security and pensions for the selected plans are shown in Table 4-3, together with the combined replacement rate. A glance at the table shows that the variation in replacement rates is considerably lower when pensions are included and that progressivity is reduced. Thus, the relatively low-wage retail worker retiring at sixty-five with spouse claiming benefits at sixty-five enjoys a replacement rate of 120 percent. At the polar extreme, the same pairing gives a replacement rate of 85 percent to the similarly situated construction worker. For the same pairing at age sixty-two (again, not shown on Table 4-3), the replacement rate is 100 percent for the retail worker and 71 percent for the construction worker.[17]

The introduction of inflation alters replacement rates. This is because pension benefits remain fixed for most beneficiaries, while Social Security benefits are adjusted for Consumer Price Index changes that are equal to or greater than 3 percent between the first quarter

**TABLE 4–3** Replacement Rates[a] for Social Security Beneficiaries Who Also Receive Private Pensions, Selected Pension Plans, Workers Retiring in January 1977

| Retirement circumstances | Retail Trade (Distributive Workers of America, District 65) | Services (Bronx Realty Advisory Board, Inc.) | Manufacturing (Pfizer, Inc.) | Construction (Boilermakers; National Plan) |
|---|---|---|---|---|
| Worker retired at age 65: | | | | |
| Single | | | | |
| Annual benefits | $5,521.20 | $5,742.00 | $7,447.20 | $ 9,866.40 |
| Replacement rate | 92.17% | 63.10% | 68.99% | 66.59% |
| With spouse claiming: | | | | |
| At age 65 and over | | | | |
| Annual benefits | 7,189.80 | 7,803.00 | 9,772.80 | 12,525.60 |
| Replacement rate | 120.03 | 85.75 | 90.53 | 84.54 |
| At age 62 | | | | |
| Annual benefits | 6,774.00 | 7,287.72 | 9,191.40 | 11,860.80 |
| Replacement rate | 113.09 | 80.08 | 85.14 | 80.05 |

[a]Replacement rates calculated as percentage of annual total benefits to 1976 earnings.

Sources: Tables 4–1 and 4–2.

of the current year and the first quarter of the previous year (unless altered directly by legislation.) This is illustrated in Table 4-4. For the sake of argument, a 6 percent annual rate of inflation is assumed, and a replacement rate for 1987 is calculated on the base of 1976 earnings inflated by the CPI. The purpose of the exercise is to show how much the standard of living attained at retirement is affected by inflation—in other words, a *real* replacement rate instead of a nominal one is shown.

Our retail worker who retired at sixty-five with spouse claiming benefits at sixty-five began in 1977 with an apparently anomalous replacement rate of 120 percent (Table 4-3)—that is, he and his wife were better off after he left work. Much is made of such a phenomenon in public discussion and in the literature, but, as can be seen from Table 4-4, after ten years he is back to his preretirement gross earnings, with a replacement rate of 104 percent. Should his spouse die in the interim, his replacement rate drops to 76 percent. Our construction worker with the same characteristics begins retirement with a replacement rate of 85 percent. Ten years of inflation reduce his replacement rate to 70 percent. The death of a spouse brings him down to 52 percent.

The lower-paid worker is in a better position to sustain his standard of living, because Social Security benefits, which are progressive, form a larger component of his postretirement income. It is, of course, a lower standard of living that he maintains. The calculations omit the probability that the higher-paid worker has income or assets from accumulated savings—most probably in the form of an owner-occupied house from which he derives an implicit (and untaxed) rental income, or which can be sold if smaller quarters are desired.

At least with respect to the combined Social Security and pension income, the fact that the real replacement rate for the higher-paid worker drops relative to his low-paid colleague is noteworthy. Whether or not this presents a problem in vertical equity is judgmental. However, as workers begin to perceive this, it may create both political and collective bargaining issues. In the political arena, it might lead to demands for attenuation of the progressive structure of the Social Security benefit, especially when continued increases in

**TABLE 4-4** Replacement Rates[a] in 1987 for Social Security Beneficiaries Retiring in January 1977 Who Also Receive Fixed Private Pensions, as CPI Rises 6 Percent per Year (Compounded)

| Retirement Circumstances | Retail Trade (Distributive Workers of America, District 65) | Services (Bronx Realty Advisory Board, Inc.) | Manufacturing (Pfizer, Inc.) | Construction (Boilermakers; National Plan) |
|---|---|---|---|---|
| 1976 Inflated Earnings | $10,727.13 | $16,296.69 | $19,332.51 | $26,837.89 |
| Worker retired at age 65 | | | | |
| Single | | | | |
| Annual benefits | 8,160.43 | 9,001.87 | 11,125.59 | 14,072.44 |
| Replacement rate | 76.07% | 55.24% | 57.55% | 52.43% |
| With spouse claiming: | | | | |
| At age 65 and over | | | | |
| Annual benefits | 11,148.62 | $12,692.81 | 15,290.38 | 18,870.48 |
| Replacement rate | 103.93 | 77.89 | 79.09 | 70.31 |
| At age 62 | | | | |
| Annual benefits | 6,880.20 | 7,286.04 | 9,221.56 | 11,747.21 |
| Replacement rate | 96.99 | 68.70 | 73.71 | 65.74 |

[a]Replacement rates calculated as percentage of annual total benefit to 1976 earnings inflated by 6 percent per year (compounded).

Sources: Appendix, Table 4-10, and Table 4-3.

the wage base change the Social Security tax from a regressive one closer to a proportional one.

On the collective bargaining side, pressures may develop to achieve indexation of pension benefits. Very few such plans already exist in the private sector. It may be that very large employers can envision their enterprises as having perpetual life, like government. For many employers, however, the continuing accretion of unfunded liabilities that would result from indexation would present an actuarial nightmare. How can an employer estimate future costs, especially when any one enterprise cannot expect that its prices and profits necessarily rise in line with the Consumer Price Index?

Another way of looking at replacement rates is to calculate them net of taxes. Table 4-5 presents such a calculation for comparison with Table 4-3. In Table 4-5, the base is 1976 wage income after payment of federal income and Social Security taxes. The benefits in 1977, the year of retirement, are computed after payment of income taxes—if any—on the pension. In the illustrative examples used for these tables, the only people with tax liabilities on their pensions were construction workers, except for those aged sixty-five with spouse claiming benefits at age sixty-five. None had incomes high enough to benefit from the retirement income credit, but the double exemption available at age sixty-five helped to bring most of our hypothetical retirees beyond the reach of the tax collectors.

As is shown by comparing the two tables, replacement rates are higher when calculated on this basis. Social Security benefits are tax-free; only the pension portion of retirement benefits is liable to taxation. Thus, the replacement rate in 1977 for our retail worker aged sixty-five with spouse aged sixty-five rises from 120 percent to 136 percent. The rate for our similarly situated construction worker goes from 85 percent to 105 percent.

The impact on the replacement rate of this type of after-tax calculation obviously varies with the age structure of the retired family, because the double exemption plays an important role. For retail and construction pairings, at sixty-five with spouses at age sixty-five, the relative impact is 13.3 percent for the retail worker and 23.5 percent for the construction worker. Workers in the intermediate categories fall between these figures. Thus, similarly situated couples in the manufacturing and service classifications find their rates changing

**TABLE 4–5** Replacement Rates[a] for Social Security Beneficiaries Who Also Receive Private Pensions, Based on After-Tax Income[b] and After-Tax Benefits, Retiring in January 1977

| Retirement Circumstances | Retail Trade (Distributive Workers of America, District 65) | Services (Bronx Realty Advisory Board, Inc.) | Manufacturing (Pfizer, Inc.) | Construction (Boilermakers; National Plan) |
|---|---|---|---|---|
| Net income 1976—single | $5,049.58 | $7,295.65 | $8,492.68 | $11,407.61 |
| Net income 1976—joint | 5,287.58 | 7,657.65 | 8,940.68 | 11,925.64 |
| Worker retired at age 65 | | | | |
| Single | | | | |
| Net annual benefits (1977) | 5,521.20 | 5,742.00 | 7,447.20 | 9,817.40 |
| Replacement rates | 109.34% | 78.70% | 87.69% | 86.06% |
| With spouse claiming: | | | | |
| At age 65 or over | | | | |
| Net annual benefits | 7,189.80 | 7,803.00 | 9,772.80 | 12,525.60 |
| Replacement rates | 135.98 | 101.90 | 109.30 | 105.03 |
| At age 62 | | | | |
| Net annual benefits | 6,774.00 | 7,287.22 | 9,191.40 | 11,860.80 |
| Replacement rates | 128.11 | 95.16 | 102.80 | 99.46 |

[a]Replacement rates calculated on percentage of Net Annual Benefits to Net Income.
[b]Temporary Credit for 1976 not included in income after tax calculation.

Sources: Appendix, Tables 4–10 and 4–11, and Table 4–3.

by 19.8 percent and 18.6 percent, respectively. The relative improvement for the higher-paid workers stems from the progressivity of the income tax. The higher their previous income at the point of retirement, the greater the benefit of a move from taxable to tax-free or tax-reduced status.

Because future tax laws are even less predictable than future Social Security laws, no attempt is made here to estimate after-tax replacement rates computed in constant dollars. The numbers would be different, but the pattern would be the same in the absence of tax changes. Variations in replacement rates would also be occasioned by the death of a spouse and would depend, *inter alia*, on whether the survivor is entitled to her own benefits, whether the deceased spouse chose the joint and survivor's option that ERISA requires in any pension plan, and the size of the option (ERISA requires a minimum of 50 percent and permits a correspondingly actuarial reduction in benefits.) Hence, readers are warned that the replacement rates calculated above are generalizations and do not necessarily apply to any particular person or family.

Tables 4-2 and 4-5 can also tell us where retired couples (aged sixty-five) in our example fall relative to the Bureau of Labor Statistics' (BLS) three standards of living. These, it will be recalled, are estimated after tax and reflect prices in autumn of 1976. Since we assumed retirement in January 1977, the slight increase in prices during the last quarter of 1976 can be ignored. Annual benefits for a couple in the low-earnings model (see Table 4-2) were $4,255, or about 9 percent below the lower budget. With after-tax benefits of $7,190, the retail trade couple did slightly better than the intermediate level (by 7 percent). The service trades couple did somewhat better than the intermediate level (by 7 percent). The service trades couple did somewhat better than the intermediate level, by 16 percent. The high-pay construction couple managed to surpass the higher budget of $10,048 by 25 percent.

**Replacement Rates in 1987.** For purposes of comparison, benefits and replacement rates were examined for workers who retire after the transition period of the 1977 law—that is, when the new benefit structure has been fully phased in. Indexed earnings histories were constructed for workers retiring at age sixty-five (Appendix, Table 4-12) on January 1, 1987. Except where otherwise indicated on the tables, earnings, prices, and the benefit formula were projected by the assumptions used by the Social Security Administration and the Department of Labor (see Appendix, Table 4-10).

Table 4-6 presents Average Indexed Monthly Earnings (AIME) and Social Security benefits for five categories of workers. Comparison with Table 4-1 shows that AIMEs are higher than the old Average Monthly Earnings (AME). The reasons, of course, lie in the new indexing technique, which adjusts each year's Average Monthly Earnings by changes in average annual earnings, and in the projected growth in nominal earnings after 1977. The higher benefits reflect higher nominal earnings.

Although absolute benefits rise with increases in annual earnings, they do not rise as rapidly under the new law as they did before. This can be seen by comparing Social Security replacement rates for our selected workers in 1977 and 1987. As shown in Table 4–7, the drop is minimal for very low earners but runs in the 10 percent range for others. It is apparent, therefore, that Congress finally managed to do what was once thought to be impossible. It reduced benefits relative to final pay for people who retire ten years after the passage of the 1977 amendments.

The calculations for persons retiring at age sixty-two generate some anomalous results. For many workers, the decline in the replacement rate at age sixty-two is less than at age sixty-five. If this is the typical pattern, then early retirement may continue to be encouraged.

The presence of occupational pensions cushions the decline in replacement rates, as seen in Table 4-8. Predictably, the larger the proportion of retirement income that comes from the pension, the smaller is the decline in the replacement rate. Thus, the loss for our manufacturing and construction workers is smaller than the loss suffered by our retail and service workers.

The above findings must be qualified. It should be remembered that the replacement rates were calculated by constructing hypothetical earnings histories, projecting them forward, making assumptions about future price levels, and assuming that pensions would

**TABLE 4-6** Average Annual Indexed Earnings and Social Security Benefits, Projected 1987

| | WORKER RETIRED AT AGE 65 | | WITH SPOUSE CLAIMING | |
|---|---|---|---|---|
| Industry | Average Annual Indexed Earnings and AIME | PIA[a] | At Age 65 and Over | At Age 62 |
| Low-earnings model | $ 8,404.17<br>AIME=$ 700 | $442.80 | $ 664.20 | $ 609.00 |
| Retail trade | 10,744.33<br>AIME=$ 897 | 517.10 | 775.70 | 711.10 |
| Services | 14,310.74<br>AIME=$1192 | 627.90 | 941.90 | 863.40 |
| Manufacturing | 17,397.29<br>AIME=$1841 | 724.40 | 1086.60 | 996.10 |
| Construction | 22,100.87<br>AIME=$1841 | 821.80 | 1232.70 | 1130.00 |

[a]Formula estimated to be in 1984
90% of $264
32% of next $1327
15% in excess of $1591
assumed that CPI increases by 5.5% annually from 1984 to 1987.

Sources: Appendix, Tables 4-10 and 4-12; Stephen F. McKay, "Computing a Social Security Benefit Under PL 95-216," Social Security Administration, Baltimore, January 23-24, 1978; and "Projected Workers with Taxable Earnings 1973-83," Social Security Administration (processed, 1978).

rise by the projected increase in average earnings. The last assumption is particularly open to challenge if Social Security and ERISA will lead to changes in pensions.

The average decline in the Social Security replacement rate for all workers may be less than the 10 percent range shown in Table 4-7. However, just as few workers have the hypothetical wage histories that were constructed for the analysis, so are there also few workers who fit an average. Actual changes in individuals' replacement rates will depend on actual earnings, price changes, pensions (where applicable), and the circumstances of retirement. But they will, in most cases, be lower.[18]

**TABLE 4-7** Changes in Social Security Replacement Rates from 1977 to 1987

| Retirement Circumstances | Low-Earnings Model | Retail | Services | Manufacturing | Construction |
|---|---|---|---|---|---|
| Worker retired at age 65: | | | | | |
| Single | −2.04% | −10.16% | −11.68% | −9.67% | −10.42% |
| With spouse claiming: | | | | | |
| At age 65 and over | −2.04 | −10.15 | −11.67 | −9.69 | −10.38 |
| At age 62 | −2.03 | −10.17 | −11.66 | −9.67 | −10.39 |
| Worker retired at age 62: | | | | | |
| Single | −4.14 | − 6.56 | − 8.43 | −4.45 | − 4.39 |
| With spouse claiming: | | | | | |
| At age 62 | −3.47 | − 6.98 | − 8.50 | −4.44 | − 4.52 |

Source: Computed from Table 4-1 and Appendix. Table 4-10.

**TABLE 4-8** Changes in Replacement Rates (with Pensions) from 1977 to 1987

| Retirement Circumstances | Retail | Services | Manufacturing | Construction |
|---|---|---|---|---|
| Worker retired at age 65: | | | | |
| Single | −8.93% | −8.51% | −6.31% | −5.92% |
| With spouse claiming: | | | | |
| At age 65 and over | −9.21 | −9.34 | −7.10 | −6.82 |
| At age 62 | −9.17 | −9.18 | −6.93 | −6.67 |
| Worker retired at age 62: | | | | |
| Single | −6.79 | −5.74 | −2.79 | −2.42 |
| With spouse claiming: | | | | |
| At age 62 | −7.05 | −6.45 | −3.13 | −2.84 |

Source: Computed from Tables 4-3 and 4-6, and Appendix, Tables 4-10 and 4-13.

### Changing Needs

The foregoing discussion of replacement rates implicitly assumes a certain amount of stability in patterns of need. Thus, the couples illustrated in the tables have been together for ten years, as (taking the law at the end of 1977) a dependent spouse who was divorced before the completion of ten years of marriage forfeits dependent's benefits. At the same time, patterns of expenditures and tastes in saving and consumption are assumed to be given. Additionally, the present practice in private pensions of distinguishing between the shorter average life expectancy of men and the longer average life expectancy of women has been assumed. If this actuarial practice is changed by the courts or by legislation, then policymakers must consider such changes in any reconstruction of the retirement system.

**Changes in the Family Unit.** There is little doubt that the nuclear family is undergoing change, although what we are observing may be the accumulation of a long-term trend. The national divorce rate in 1975 (latest data available) was 20.3 per 1,000 married women, slightly higher than the previous peak of 17.9 in 1946, when hasty wartime marriages broke up. The rate was relatively stable between 1950 and 1965 at about 10 per 1,000 married women, but has shown persistent increases since then (actually, since 1963). The median duration of marriage in 1975 was 6½ years.[19]

Divorce rates vary by age (as well as by region). Glick and Norton have estimated that one-third of all those now entering marriage can expect divorce, in contrast to one-sixth who enter marriage at mature ages. According to this study, half of the divorces occur within about eight years of the first marriage.[20]

Also of interest is the changing trend in the marital status of older women, as they constitute the main pool from which persons eligible for spouse's benefits are drawn. The data are shown on Table 4-9. As can be seen, the proportion of older women who are married has been rising (especially in the fifty-five to sixty-four age group), and the proportion of widows has declined. This probably reflects both longer life spans for men and rising rates of remarriage. However, the proportion divorced has also been rising, and the rise is a relatively large one, particularly in the fifty-five-to sixty-four-year-old

**TABLE 4-9** Marital Status of Women (Rate) 1930–70, Ages 55–64 and 65-plus

| Year and Age | % Single | % Married | % Widowed | % Divorced |
|---|---|---|---|---|
| *1970* | | | | |
| 55–64 | 6.8% | 67.95% | 20.23% | 5% |
| 65 and over | 8.12 | 36.46 | 52.21 | 3.18 |
| *1960* | | | | |
| 55–64 | 7.96 | 66.04 | 22.35 | 3.63 |
| 65 and over | 8.46 | 37.43 | 52.06 | 2.03 |
| *1950* | | | | |
| 55–64 | 7.92 | 64.97 | 24.67 | 2.42 |
| 65 and over | 8.92 | 35.68 | 54.27 | 1.12 |
| *1940* | | | | |
| 55–64 | 8.95 | 63.03 | 26.43 | 1.56 |
| 65 and over | 9.30 | 34.33 | 55.63 | .72 |
| *1930* | | | | |
| 55–64 | 8.93 | 62.02 | 27.79 | 1.13 |
| 65 and over | 8.11 | 34.67 | 56.49 | .05 |

Source: U.S. Bureau of the Census, "Historical Statistics of the United States, Colonial Times to 1970, Bicentennial Edition, Part 2," Table A160–171: Marital Status of the Population, by Age and Sex: 1890 to 1970 (Washington: U.S. Government Printing Office, 1975), pp. 20–21.

cohort. Presumably, the rise will continue as divorces increase among persons now younger.

The rapid rise in the divorce rate and concurrent shortening of the average length of marriage suggests that, over time, an increasing number of dependent spouses—mainly women—will find themselves excluded from dependents' benefits. This effect will be offset —but to an unpredictable degree—by the rising labor force participation of women. The latter will lead to greater use by women of Social Security benefits earned on their own account and to greater access to private pensions. Although divorced dependent wives may seek remedies in the form of alimony, it is notorious that alimony payments are difficult to collect over long periods of time and must be extremely difficult to extract from retired husbands. In any event, alimony payments cease with the death of the liable spouse, and women tend to outlive men.

The reduction, in 1977, of the required length of marriage helps to accommodate this situation. It raises the cost of Social Security by multiplying the number of persons drawing dependents' benefits based on one earner's account. Again, the labor force participation of women will be an offset, at least in part, against this cost.

There is no simple way of dealing with this problem, especially inasmuch as the very existence of the dependent spouse's benefits creates troublesome inequities of its own. Ultimately some resolution of the problem will have to be found. The logical direction in which the solution lies is in attaching benefit rights to persons rather than to families. A variety of devices can be used for this, including combining a family's earning records and attributing part of the benefit rights to the low-earning or nonearning spouse, or taxing the imputed value of a nonearning spouse's homemaking activities. The latter, of course, could lead to some very high tax rates on single-earner couples, something that might be equitable on the one hand but extremely burdensome on the other hand, especially in the lower income brackets.[21]

**Sex Discrimination.** Discriminatory treatment of the sexes is disappearing in Social Security, although aspects remain in employment-related pensions. In the former, a series of legislative changes and judicial decisions has eliminated discriminatory treatment. For example, the widow of a fully insured worker may claim widow's insurance benefits at age sixty (at a reduced rate of 71.5 percent of benefits at fifty if she is disabled). Until recently, a similarly situated widower had to show that he received half of his support from a fully insured deceased wife to claim widower's benefits, but this requirement is now gone.

As an aside, it may be noted that, until 1978, remarriage could have led to a reduction in a widow's or widower's benefits unless remarriage was to another person entitled to widow's or widower's benefits. Although this made sense in limiting the joint benefits of the newlyweds to 150 percent of the Primary Insurance Amount, the loss of benefit may have served as a deterrent to remarriage, especially for persons whose principal income was Social Security and who would have felt the loss keenly. Only anecdotal evidence exists as to the number of elderly couples who lived in sin or forwent their marital possibilities. It may not have been much of a social problem, but it is a further indication of how social policies can interfere with family formation.[22]

The question of sex discrimination in pensions is currently a burning issue, one on which legislation or judicial action is bound to occur. The different life expectancies of men and women are commonly taken into account in the determination of contributions of benefits. Thus in some plans, especially defined contribution plans, the monthly benefit to women who retire is lower than that for men with the same pay and length of service. Alternatively, if benefits are defined equally for both sexes, the employer's contribution is higher for women than for men in order to maintain actuarial soundness.[23]

It can be argued that unequal pensions do not constitute sex discrimination because, on average, the total benefit payments of any given plan will be the same for similarly situated men and women in the same age group. It is undoubtedly difficult to persuade women of this point of view. Furthermore, life expectancies differ among other groups: blacks and whites, for example, or smokers and nonsmokers. Accordingly, it has been suggested that unisex actuarial tables be used in lieu of separate tables; these tables average the life expectancies of the two sexes. Such a move would decrease relative benefits, or increase relative contributions, for men. It would be easy to do this prospectively for persons now entering the labor market. To do it retrospectively would raise problems and inequities, because workers planning for retirement have established saving and consumption patterns with an eye toward their retirement benefits. A sudden change would catch men (and their dependent spouses) unprepared for the lower benefits. The impact on employers would depend on the employer's mix of the sexes in his work place.

## INTERACTIONS

One of the purposes of including retirement benefits other than Social Security in this book was to test for interactions between Social Security and the rest of the benefit system. Some of the interaction that occurs is intentional in the sense that those who drafted the law intended these interactions to occur. Others are unintentional, the product of separately conceived policies that interact at the margin because they have overlapping constituencies. Unintentional interactions cause the system to behave differently from the expectations of its planners. They also cause clienteles to behave differently by presenting them with incentives that were not considered when the act was passed.

### Social Security, Pensions, and Other Benefits

From its inception, Social Security was intended to serve as the foundation upon which individuals and families could build more generous retirement programs for themselves. It was not intended to be the sole source of retirement income for workers, although many lower-wage workers with continuous work histories can sustain all or most of their low standards of living on Social Security payments alone. The absence of a means test meant that private savings, transfers from relatives, and pensions could be used to supplement Social Security benefits.[24]

Whatever the case may be, the last two decades have seen the rise of employer-related pension plans. Those in the private and nonfederal public sectors constitute compulsory savings that are available for capital formation. It can even be argued that federal pensions, to the extent that they are properly funded, behave likewise, even though their holdings consist of government securities. Such holdings reduce the U.S. Treasury's need to borrow in private capital markets, leaving private and corporate savings available for capital investment.

Interaction occurs where pensions are integrated with Social Security in the form of offset plans. In such plans, rising Social Security taxes or future benefits enable employers to reduce their contributions. This, at least in part, violates the goal of Social Security as a foundation for further retirement benefits, because the addition of a foundation stone by Social Security leads to the subtraction of at least part of a stone by the employer. Although integrated plans waned in frequency during the 1960s, the specter of continual increases in Social Security taxes is bound to revive an interest in offset plans. This will be the case not only for defined benefit plans that are prevalent in unionized labor markets but also in defined contribution plans that are more likely to be found in the nonunion sector. Employers in nonprofit institutions will be especially hard hit, because they are not in a position to treat Social Security taxes and pension contributions as tax-deductible costs.

In short, if the Social Security system is to remain self-sufficient, the need for even higher taxes will attenuate its role as a foundation. Workers may respond by reducing their savings, and employers will respond to the pressure by integrating their plans so as to reduce their contributions. Some may also respond by passing the tax increases backward to employees in the form of relatively lower wages. Others, who have market power, may try to pass the tax forward to consumers, reducing consumers' real incomes and hence their ability to save. Notwithstanding the beliefs by economists that workers bear the full burden of the tax (a proposition that would leave employers indifferent to the tax except as it may reduce the supply of labor), employers will behave *as if* their costs are increased by the net impact of their share of the tax.[25]

The exclusion of federal employees (and some state and local employees) from the system creates an unintentional interaction because of the progressive nature of the benefit structure. Such employees can easily pick up coverage by moonlighting in covered work or by early retirement coupled with a transfer to covered employment. As a result, an estimated 40 percent of civil service retirees are also collecting Social Security, many at the relatively high minimum benefit.[26] Although such persons paid Social Security taxes on their moonlight earnings, this relatively affluent group receives the benefit of a feature designed to help low-wage workers. Accordingly, they receive transfers from workers whose careers are in covered employment, a matter that raises issues of equity and of the efficiency of a feature designed to help the poorer segment of the population. The interaction was probably unintentional, but it appears to be politically difficult to correct, as by integrating federal pensions into Social Security and levying the tax on federal civil servants and members of Congress. A proposal to extend Social Security to the federal civilian sector was easily defeated in 1977.

Interactions between SSI and Social Security were noted in Chapter 1. At the low end of the income scale there are persons who qualify for both, provided they satisfy the means test for SSI. The rule is that Social Security benefits, except for the first $20, are deductible from SSI benefits. The federal minimum SSI benefit is indexed to the Consumer Price Index, but mandatory state supplements to SSI are not required to be indexed. Accordingly, such persons living in states with mandatory supplements may find that they do not get the full increase in benefits when the Consumer Price Index rises above 3 percent. The greater the proportion of their SSI benefit that consists of the mandatory supplement, the less will be their percentage increase in benefit, unless the state chooses to make voluntary adjustments for its elderly (and disabled) indigents.

The relative loss is not very great, but it can compound over time unless states make adjustments. For example, a New York couple receiving SSI who also qualify for the minimum Social Security benefit received $380.04 per month in 1978. This was only 4.8 percent more than their 1977 benefits of $362.64, despite the fact that their Social Security benefit had been raised by 6.8 percent (from $171 to $182.70) to compensate for inflation, and the federal portion of SSI was similarly raised by 6.5 percent. The failure of such a couple to keep up with inflation is due to the stability of the state supplement to SSI. Persistent inflation can therefore lead to a steady deterioration in their standard of living.

The situation is complicated by Medicaid. Double recipients also qualify for Medicaid if their income (depending on the state) is low enough. Those double recipients whose Social Security component is high relative to the SSI component may find that the indexing feature of Social Security not only reduces their SSI but, at the margin, may remove their Medicaid eligibility. This can be a considerable hardship to those who need to spend heavily on prescription drugs.

The hypothetical New York State couple above are also caught by both the Social Security and the SSI earnings tests, which differ. Suppose that one of them gets a steady job at $400 per month. Their Social Security benefit is reduced to $148.70; and SSI falls to $63.84. This adds up to a combined benefit loss of $167.50. In addition, the earner is liable to a Social Security tax of $24.20. The arithmetic shows that the $400 in monthly earnings increased family income by a mere $208.30, or 52 percent. In this example, the family faces an implicit marginal tax rate of 48 percent, exclusive of the possible loss of Medicaid. Note that this is just about equal to the 50 percent maximum marginal tax rate on earned income under federal income taxes. Since implicit tax rates for the two benefit systems differ, they will vary in any particular case depending on the relative proportions of Social Security and SSI in the combined benefit.[27]

Pensions affect SSI but not Social Security. If the pension benefit combined with Social Security is just high enough to remove a Medicaid recipient from eligibility, he or she might have been better off without it unless the pension is greater than the value of Medicaid.

Food stamps are additive to Social Security and to SSI (except in a very few states whose supplements "cash out" the food stamps). Food stamps are available only to households whose assets and incomes are low enough to enable them to qualify. The bonus value of food stamps is indexed to food prices and depends on a measure of net household income, including other benefits.

The use of a different index for stamps does not appear to present much of a problem. Conceivably, a rise in food prices accompanied by a rise in all other prices might overcompensate multiple beneficiaries, inasmuch as the Consumer Price Index used to adjust Social Security and SSI has a food component in it already, based on the market basket of an urban worker's family with *more* than two persons. The rate of benefit loss per dollar of added income is about 30 percent, and the benefit drops to zero when earnings are sufficiently high. Although this serves as a work incentive to the working poor, it adds to the work disincentives faced by the retired poor, who are already subject to the retirement test of Social Security and/or the implicit marginal tax rate imposed by SSI.

In the case of our New York couple, they were eligible for a bonus value of food stamps of about $240 per year if the head of the household did not work. Thus, their total benefits, including food stamps, came to $382.64. The additional gross earnings of $300 knocked them out of food stamp eligibility. By this calculation, the marginal tax rate on net earnings of $282.45 rises to 58 percent.

## EQUITY AMONG BENEFICIARIES

The literature on Social Security is replete with references to equity. Economists are particularly fond of the concepts of horizontal and vertical equity as measures of the fairness of particular tax and transfer programs.[28]

Legislators have somewhat different notions of equity, all too often based on the political pressures that they perceive as well as the personal biases they may bring to the examination of any given issue. Indeed, individual concepts of equity may differ depending on whether the individual looks at an issue in his role as worker, homeowner, consumer, investor, or disinterested citizen. Still, the subject cannot be dismissed. Economic notions of equity may serve as a useful measuring rod, even if no perfect concept of equity exists—and especially where the goal of equity conflicts with such other social goals as social adequacy. This conflict has been inherent in the Social Security system from its inception, especially since the 1939 amendments established spouses' benefits and, at the same time, made the benefit structure much more progressive.

#### Horizontal Equity

Perhaps the firmest idea of equity in the economic literature is horizontal equity: the equal treatment of equals for purposes of taxes and benefits. This, of course, raises the question of how equality is to be measured. The Social Security Administration bases its Primary Insurance Amount on the average indexed monthly taxable earnings history (AIME) of the worker, with the (social adequacy) proviso that the lowest five years are omitted from the calculation. Strictly speaking, the length of the work history for PIA calculations is not the worker's entire career, but earnings since 1951 or the attainment of age twenty-one and until age sixty-two, with the ultimate goal of a thirty-five-year averaging period.

If equality is measured by equal contributions to the Social Security system, then workers who began their careers at an early age will have paid taxes on which they receive no retirement benefits. Assume that two workers, Smith and Jones, have the same AIME at the point of retirement. For the sake of simplicity, assume that the thirty-five-year averaging period is now in effect. Say that Smith worked forty-five years in covered employment and that Jones worked thirty-five years. Smith will have paid taxes for ten years that do not count toward his retirement benefit. Not all of Smith's taxes in the first ten years would have gone for nought, since they entitled him to Survivors Benefits for his wife and children, if any, and possibly to Disability Benefits during part of this period. But no one ever told Smith that, in his first ten years, he was merely acquiring rights to Survivors and Disability benefits, two benefits for which Jones would qualify not long after the beginning of *his* shorter work career.

If the AIME is the proper measure of equality, then the structure of workers' earnings histories will lead to different AIMEs and therefore different PIAs. The indexing of AIMEs by wages complicates matters by raising the value of the long-term worker's early earnings, whereas the years of no earnings (or earnings in uncovered employment) are averaged in as zero. However fair or unfair this may be, indexing does not differentiate between the long-service worker who spent his years in covered employment at lower wages and the shorter-service worker with a shorter period of higher wages in covered work.[29]

Legislators have noted that many issues involving horizontal equity are of little interest to the electorate. Thus, there was little objection to the "blanketing in" of persons previously not covered by the act, such as the self-employed (whose total tax is, in any event, lower than the taxes paid jointly by employers and employees), workers in nonprofit institutions, and others. Such workers were not compelled to start at ground zero, with PIAs based on covered employment only. Instead, the formula for calculating their PIAs put them on par with other workers, even though their tax contributions were, in some cases, trivially small.[30] If this was unfair, it might have been equally unfair to treat such people differently from the way the early beneficiaries of Social Security were treated: The latter's benefits were, after all, also based on short earnings histories after the 1939 amendments.

It would appear from the foregoing discussion that even so simple a notion as horizontal equity becomes complex when considered on an operational basis, the more so when concepts of social adequacy are introduced. It may be noteworthy that the founders of the system did not intend to base it on any precise principle of equity, whether horizontal or vertical.[31]

The changing ratio of females to males in the labor force raises an issue of horizontal equity that may grow in political importance. It will be recalled that the taxing unit is the individual, whereas the benefit unit is the family. When the spouse's (and dependents') benefit was introduced in 1939, it was assumed that woman's place was in the home and that a predominantly male labor force would be paying the Social Security tax to obtain protection for its families—without an increase in the tax. The contributions of those females who were temporarily at work, pending marriage and childrearing, was a sort of bonus to the finances of the system, and even then it constituted an inequity. The relatively few women with a full work career ahead of them could, of course, earn benefits on their own account and be entitled to the greater of their own benefits or the spouse's, if any.

The rule is pretty much the same today, except that male and female spouses are treated equally. However, both the absolute number and the relative number of female workers have grown enormously. The number of employed single females increased by 2,345,000 (39.1 percent) between 1947 and 1977. The number of employed widows, divorcees, or separated women increased by 3,535,000 (107 percent) during the same period, and the number of employed married women rose by 14,352,000 (221 percent).[32] Furthermore, the length of time spent in the labor force by successive age cohorts of women has been increasing and can be expected to increase for the baby boom group, with fewer interruptions for childbearing or for other reasons.[33]

Two possible feelings of inequity may arise from this change. One is that the growing number of working wives will feel that they are subsidizing the leisure of their nonworking colleagues by lowering their cost of leisure. The nonworking spouses will, after all, be eligible for the spouses' benefits without having made a corresponding tax contribution.

The second possible type of inequity will stem from the fact that, at least for the foreseeable future, many wives will continue to be secondary earners. That is, they will be more concentrated in lower-wage jobs or part-time jobs and will have more interruptions in their working lives than men—although the length of the interruptions is decreasing. As a result, many will discover upon retirement that their spouse's benefit is greater than the benefit they earned on their own account. For this group the Social Security taxes that they paid "bought" no additional retirement benefits. It was simply a tax that reduced their earnings.[34] All taxes do this, of course, but the Social Security tax has an implied promise of a specific benefit, and this promise will be broken.

The horizontal inequity, in either case, is that two families with similar family earnings records and tax contributions can receive dissimilar benefits. The only equitable way out of this dilemma is to use a mechanism, such as those described earlier, that attaches benefits to individuals. This, however, conflicts with the proposition that social adequacy is a goal at least as important as equity. If, as many writers believe, social adequacy in Social Security is no longer important because of the advent of a more generous public assistance benefit for the indigent aged, then the spouse's benefit can be phased out over time, as poor aged families will, in any event, receive support from SSI with its broader financial base.

Finally, there is the obvious inequity between persons who were single throughout all or most of their working lives and those who were married but whose spouses become eligible for dependents' benefits upon retirement. For any given level of earnings, the singles will have paid the same taxes as these marrieds but will receive lower benefits (and the Survivor's Insurance would not have been of any use to them either). Again, the principle of social adequacy, which underlies this situation, conflicts with equity.[35]

It would seem that social adequacy, unlike equity, lends itself to some empirical measurement. If that is the case, then the question may be raised whether the 50 percent addition for the dependent spouse is, in some budgetary sense, adequate. To make a rough determination, I took the lower budget for retired couples and halved all items except housing. By this measure, admittedly very crude, a single aged person needs 67 percent of the income of an aged couple, which is precisely what happens in Social Security: The single beneficiary receives two-thirds of the benefits that accrue to a couple where the spouse claims dependents' benefits. A more refined estimate—one that reduces housing and transportation costs for a single person—might yield a slightly different result but would not change the order of magnitude. Thus, if the BLS budget is realistic, then the spouse's benefit more or less meets the test of social adequacy.[36]

As the above discussion indicates, even so well-defined a concept as horizontal equity—the equal treatment of equals—presents an almost infinite set of problems when attempts are made to apply it to Social Security. Equals are not easy to define. Are singles and marrieds really equal? Are families with the same earnings but different earnings patterns equals? A system that is strictly earnings-related might satisfy some consensus of welfare economists on grounds of equity, but what about the goal of social adequacy?

Nor will it do to argue, on equitable grounds, that SSI can deal with social adequacy because the net results might be the same. Shifting the burden of social adequacy might be more *efficient* in terms of the target efficiency of tax monies, but this is a somewhat different argument. Moreover, there is some loss of welfare (as economists define the term) in a means-tested system. For many recipients, the satisfaction gained from a means-tested dollar may be less than the satisfaction from an "earned" dollar, however attenuated the connection between past earnings and benefits may be. The tradeoffs between equity and adequacy, and among equity, adequacy, and efficiency, are ultimately political and social judgments.[37]

### Vertical Equity

Vertical equity refers to the structure of taxes and transfers that adjusts the relative positions of individuals or households.[38] In a utilitarian sense, vertical equity in benefits might be assured if the last dollar of benefits adds the same amount of satisfaction to each beneficiary.[39] Extreme difficulties arise from any attempt to make this concept operational. We do not know what the preferences of different people are unless we can read their minds or observe their behavior. As a general proposition, we accept the idea that the last dollar provides greater satisfaction to a poor household than to a rich one, or, given equal income, to a household with greater needs (e.g. medical or number of dependents) than to one with lesser needs.

If this is the case, then a tax or benefit structure does not need to leave the relative positions of persons or households undisturbed with respect to income. Indeed, this may be used to justify a progressive income tax or a progressive schedule of benefits. But how progressive? If, to use the economist's jargon, we do not have data on people's utility functions, then other notions must enter the picture. In other words, how progressive a tax or benefit should be becomes, pragmatically, a function of ethical preferences and political acceptability. As can be seen, vertical equity presents more theoretical problems than horizontal equity, and it may be impossible to discuss it without explicit reference to a theory of justice. Nonetheless, critics of Social Security frequently speak of vertical inequities, some relying on their own sense of justice and others on their perception of the polity's sense of justice.

The most obvious issue in vertical equity among beneficiaries is the progressivity of the benefit scale. The formula effective January

1979 for calculating the Primary Insurance Amount (PIA) from Average Indexed Monthly Earnings has three brackets, all in descending order. The brackets are:

90% of the first $180 of AIME
plus 32% of the next $905 of AIME
plus 15% of the balance of AIME until the maximum
taxable earnings are reached

As can be seen, the schedule is progressive. The higher the claimant's AIME record, the lower will be his replacement rate, except as modified by dependents' benefits. The intent of this redistributive schedule is ethical. It provides that low income earners will be relatively better off in retirement than their high-earner counterparts who have less absolute need in their declining years. The latter presumably benefit less from the additional dollar of benefits because their total benefit will be higher and because they were in a better position to accumulate savings or pensions for their old age.

Nonetheless, whether this schedule or some other schedule is equitable in a vertical sense eludes us. The politics of Social Security reveal an absence of conflict on this issue. This may indicate that the existing schedule of benefits is satisfactory both to present retirees and to present taxpayers, sufficiently at least to keep them politically passive. As noted elsewhere, there may well be an inequity with regard to federal employees and those state and local employees who have pension rights but are outside of Social Security. To the extent that they acquire Social Security rights through part-time or postretirement work, their actual civil service earnings are counted as zero. This pushes them into the higher benefit brackets, although they are more affluent than some lower-paid private sector workers who, at retirement, find themselves in the lower-benefit brackets.

Because the question of vertical equity is so troublesome, it tends to be resolved into other questions. Munnell, for example, discusses it in terms of target efficiency. She favors a proportional benefit schedule, one in which benefits are directly related to earnings, and supplementary aid to the needy through the SSI program.[40] This prevents the overspill of relatively high Social Security benefits to those who are not needy, such as retired civil servants, and targets benefits to the genuinely needy in an economical fashion. Thus, the canons of social adequacy are not violated, and the redistribution of income is less wasteful. This is a rational argument, but note that it hinges on efficiency, not on equity, which is not the same thing at all. It may be that pragmatic solutions to Social Security problems will have to rest heavily on efficiency, with popular notions of equity serving as a constraint upon efficiency. This, however, must be worked out in the political market place.

If social adequacy is seen as a dominating goal, then discussions of equity become sterile. J. Douglas Brown, who was among the pioneers of Social Security, points out that the Advisory Council of 1937–38 unanimously affirmed that "protection against hardship should be the fundamental guide in the establishment of the benefit structure." Although the council supported differentials in benefits related to previous earnings and contributions, it did not consider such differentials to be based *on any precise principle of equity* in the return of contributions as in private insurance.[41] To Brown, the declining benefit scale is a refinement of the principle of adequacy that can be justified in a social rather than a private insurance plan.[42]

### Intergenerational Equity

The fact that the Social Security tax is really a transfer payment from the working generation to the retired generation raises issues of fairness or equity among generations. The very establishment of the act and the extensions in coverage can be said to have been unfair to those born too early to achieve coverage. Indeed, if such persons saved for their old age, thus producing the capital stock for the next generation, then Social Security may have reduced the relative rate of return on their capital by reducing the labor supply available to the economy.[43] Further changes in benefits and taxes also altered the relative positions of the generations.

It is difficult—perhaps impossible—to define equity between generations, at least in financial terms. Should each generation be entitled to the same rate of return on contributions "invested" in the system? If so, in real terms (adjusted for price changes) or in nominal terms? Should each generation be entitled to the same replacement rate? For what tax payments and on what wage bases? Should the retired generation get the benefits of rising productivity incurred after its retirement, so that its living standards remain stable relative to those still at work?

To ask these questions is to see the futility of a scientific answer. The private sector cannot assure intergenerational equity, nor does it pretend to. Annuities available at one point in time may be better or worse than those available at another time. Perhaps more to the point, a growing economy makes succeeding generations better off, and a declining economy makes them worse off. We are less prone to quarrel with market outcomes than with social policies. Still, people *do* have a sense of fairness, and that sense may be violated as the system's financial problems have raised the public's consciousness. Although the mysteries of overindexing and decoupling are probably beyond the understanding of the lay public, the method of decoupling that was adopted in 1977 will have an impact on future taxes and benefits. At some point, the younger generation of workers may come to realize that they will pay more and benefit less than their predecessors. The inequities of the past cannot be undone.

Summarizing the question of equity, it should be clear that a scientific search for a system that is equitable in a horizontal, vertical, or intergenerational sense can only distract us from the pressing pragmatic problems. Even the economist's golden rule—let each generation save for the next as it would have liked its predecessor to have saved for it[44]—does not help. One is reminded of George Bernard Shaw's warning about the Christian golden rule: Do not do unto others as you would have them do unto you—their tastes may be different.

Equity problems will be faced politically, just as they are in matters of taxation, affirmative action, and other social policies. The willingness of future working generations to support their elders will depend on their acceptance of the Social Security system that is in place during their working years. We can expect that they will consider both their own interests and those of their elders, insofar as the latter will constitute a large voting bloc. The ability of future working generations to support their elders will, however, partly depend on the economy's performance at each point in time. The Social Security system's structure will play a role in this, but other factors that affect economic growth will be of equal or greater importance.

It is stressed throughout this book that retirees consume goods that are currently produced, not goods that have been saved up. Hence any redesign of Social Security—in the context of the total retirement structure—can be helpful if it removes aspects that tend to inhibit economic growth. One of these aspects is the impact of Social Security on the availability of human resources to the economy. A second aspect is the system's impact on the creation of capital, that is, the goods that are used to produce other goods and services. These two issues are discussed in the chapter that follows.

# CHAPTER FIVE

# Labor Markets and Capital Formation

## LABOR MARKET IMPACTS

THERE ARE TWO directions from which one can examine the labor market effects of Social Security. One is from the tax side and the other, more obvious direction is from the benefit side. On the tax side, the evidence is sparse. On *a priori* grounds, one would expect the payroll tax to influence the labor market behavior of workers, especially those who have some choice as to the amount of labor they can offer on the market. Unfortunately, there is little empirical work on the subject, and economic theory is not too helpful. Some workers may respond to the tax by increasing the amount of labor they offer in order to make up for the income lost by the tax; others may try to reduce it because the tax, by reducing current income, increases the relative value of leisure or homemaking. For a marginal group of workers, it may alter the choice between employment in covered and noncovered industry, but this choice has become narrow with the expansion of coverage. It can further be argued that the labor market decision is affected simultaneously by the tax and by the expected benefits.[1]

Similarly, if employers perceive themselves as bearing their share of the tax burden, they will respond to tax increases by treating them like any other increase in labor costs. Depending on their situation, they may depress their wage offers (at least relatively), which would shift the burden back to their workers; pass the tax forward to consumers; substitute capital for labor; or export capital to a country with lower net labor costs. The last two possibilities would shift the tax burden to the disemployed. Since these are more likely to receive social benefits than to pay taxes, the burden would be more broadly diffused through the economy among all taxpayers.

The state of knowledge on the topic is inconclusive. As the tax has risen from trivial to nontrivial levels, one would *intuitively* believe that it reduces labor supply, especially among secondary workers with a tenuous attachment to the labor market, and reduce labor demand by employers. Intuition, however, is not a substitute for facts. Empirically, the tax effect—if it exists—may be masked or overcome by other events. For example, on the supply side we see the rising labor force participation of women. If the tax is a deterrent, it is not a visible one. On the demand side, such variables as aggregate demand, fiscal and monetary policy, or events in the world economy may make it difficult to isolate the effects of the tax.

Unlike the issue of equity, the question of the tax effect on labor supply is not inherently unanswerable. Further research may cast light on this issue and determine its significance.

Evidence on the impact of benefits appears to be stronger. Eligibility for benefits and benefit rates, together with the retirement test, influence workers' choices to remain in the labor market. Social Security is not the sole factor in the retirement decision. Mandatory retirement, pensions and other sources of income, ill health, and unemployment all play a role, along with the simple desire to quit work.

Nonetheless, inferences about the impact Social Security benefit policies can be inferred from data about labor force participation rates. The overall trend in participation rates has been a substantial decline for older men. In 1940, 59.4 percent of men aged sixty-five to sixty-nine were in the labor force. By 1976 the rate for the sixty-five-plus group was 20.3 percent.[2] The labor force participation rate (LFPR) for elderly women has never been high (although this may change in the future) and does not show a similar long-term trend.

Figure 5-1 plots the rate of decline in LFPRs for men and women, by age, in the Census years 1940 (5-1a), 1950 (5-1b), 1960 (5-1c) and 1970 (5-1d). Census years were chosen because the data are given for each age rather than ten-year age cohorts. This permits inferences to be made about the behavior of sixty-two-year-olds, who became eligible for early retirement at reduced benefits, and seventy-two-year-olds, who are free of the retirement test. Since the LFPR has declined steadily for men, the rate of decline[3] is the significant figure, because the overall trend would otherwise mask the effects of the early retirement option and the freedom from the retirement test at age seventy-two.

Early retirement for men went into effect in 1961. Its impact can be inferred by comparing behavior over the years for men between the sixty-first and sixty-second birthdays. Figures 5-1a, 5-1b and 5-1c (for 1940, 1950, and 1960) show no peaks at sixty-two. However, Figure 5-1d (1970) shows a distinct peak at sixty-two, which suggests that men were taking advantage of the option. The trend has become stronger since 1970.[4]

Women were permitted early retirement in 1956. Again, the figures for 1940 and 1950 show no peak at 62, whereas a distinct peak appears in 1960 and 1970, showing an increase in the rate of withdrawal from the labor force for 62-year-old women in those years.

These peaks for men (and probably for women) may have been reenforced by the growth of early retirement provisions in pension plans which have helped this age cohort to achieve its financial retirement goals at sixty-two. These two factors are not necessarily unrelated, because pension plans may have been affected by the legislation. A further impetus might have come from the greater ability of the later cohorts to accumulate assets, principally housing, and the rise in the value of such assets. On the negative side, diminished job opportunities might also have played a role in the decision to opt for benefits at an early age, especially in 1970.

All four census years show the expected peak for men at age sixty-five, although the sixty-five peak for women does not appear until 1960. A possible explanation for the age sixty-six peaks for women in 1940 and 1950 was that coverage for women was narrower in the earlier years of the system. Possibly, some women were working longer to help support husbands who had retired when real benefits were relatively low. Since the number of women involved has been low, small changes in absolute numbers lead to large swings in the rate of change.

The peak at sixty-five cannot, of course, be attributed solely to Social Security, since the variables mentioned earlier played a part. Social Security probably helped to establish sixty-five as a "normal"

**FIGURE 5-1** Rate of Change in Labor Force Participation Rates, by Age, 1940, 1950, 1960, 1970

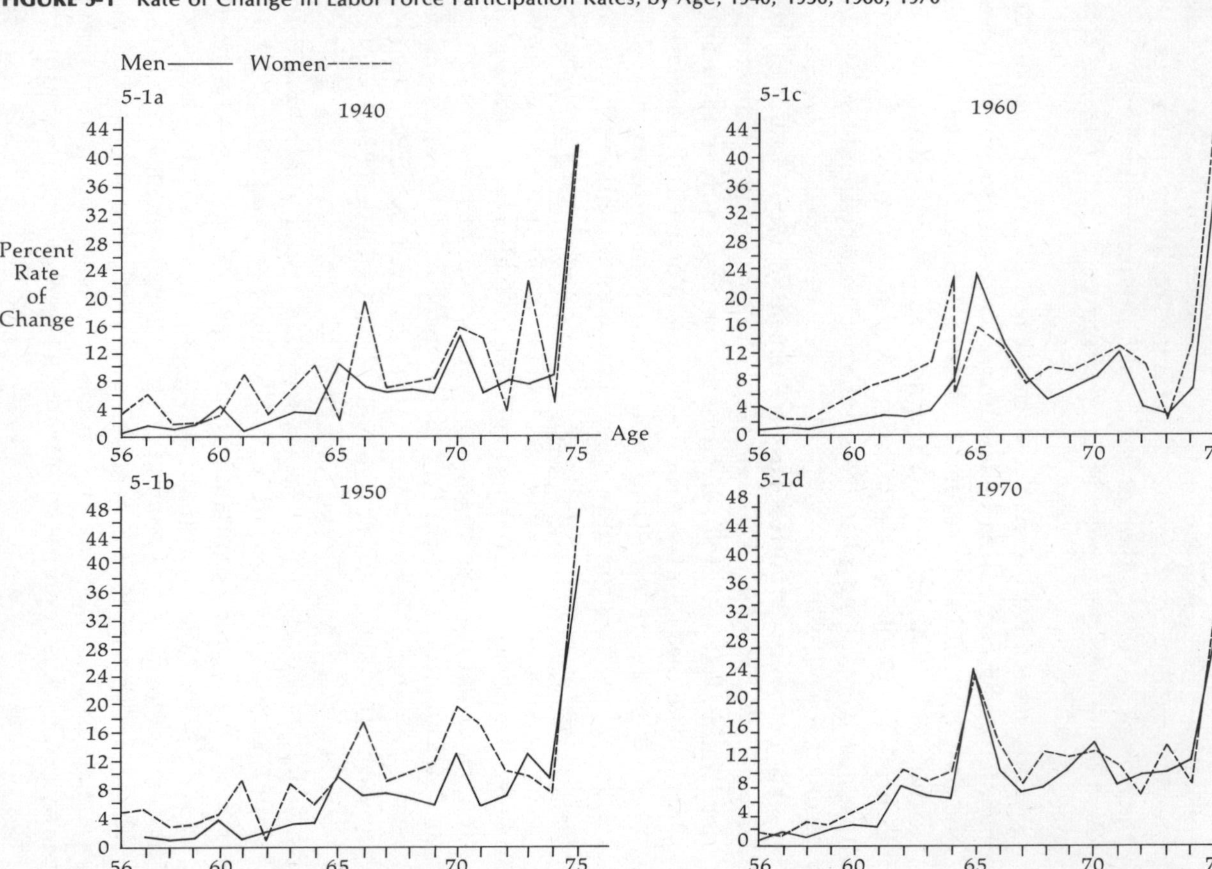


Source: Computed from the Census data cited in Colin D. Campbell and Rosemary G. Campbell, "Conflicting Views of the Effect of Old-Age Retirement," *Economic Inquiry*, 14, No. 3 (September 1976): 375, Table 2.

**TABLE 5-1** Data for Figure 5-1

| | Male Change in Rate (in %) | | | | | Female Change in Rate (in %) | | | |
|---|---|---|---|---|---|---|---|---|---|
| Age | 1940 | 1950 | 1960 | 1970 | Age | 1940 | 1950 | 1960 | 1970 |
| 56 | .446% | — | 1.00% | .674% | 56 | 3.51% | 4.30% | 4.23% | 1.81% |
| 57 | 1.45 | 1.25 | 1.34 | 1.81 | 57 | 6.25 | 4.86 | 2.45 | 1.43 |
| 58 | 1.02 | .692 | 1.25 | 1.03 | 58 | 1.66 | 2.36 | 2.77 | 3.12 |
| 59 | 1.49 | 1.16 | 1.84 | 2.44 | 59 | 1.69 | 2.82 | 4.14 | 3.01 |
| 60 | 4.32 | 3.52 | 2.23 | 2.86 | 60 | 3.44 | 4.14 | 6.21 | 4.87 |
| 61 | .610 | .852 | 3.00 | 2.58 | 61 | 8.92 | 9.09 | 7.49 | 6.29 |
| 62 | 2.08 | 1.71 | 2.60 | 8.20 | 62 | 2.61 | .476 | 8.72 | 10.69 |
| 63 | 3.51 | 3.00 | 3.68 | 7.15 | 63 | 7.38 | 8.61 | 10.92 | 9.19 |
| 64 | 3.25 | 3.09 | 7.52 | 6.51 | 64 | 10.14 | 5.75 | 6.89 | 10.12 |
| 65 | 10.08 | 9.97 | 23.42 | 25.35 | 65 | 3.22 | 9.44 | 16.46 | 24.91 |
| 66 | 7.32 | 7.09 | 14.36 | 11.04 | 66 | 20.00 | 17.79 | 13.30 | 14.54 |
| 67 | 6.77 | 7.47 | 8.71 | 7.87 | 67 | 7.29 | 8.95 | 7.95 | 9.57 |
| 68 | 5.01 | 6.87 | 5.72 | 8.29 | 68 | 7.86 | 6.55 | 9.87 | 13.52 |
| 69 | 6.37 | 5.53 | 7.34 | 11.01 | 69 | 8.53 | 11.40 | 9.58 | 12.24 |
| 70 | 14.39 | 13.08 | 9.28 | 14.60 | 70 | 16.00 | 19.80 | 11.36 | 13.95 |
| 71 | 7.27 | 5.61 | 12.65 | 8.55 | 71 | 14.28 | 17.28 | 12.82 | 11.71 |
| 72 | 8.33 | 7.14 | 4.13 | 10.16 | 72 | 3.70 | 10.44 | 11.76 | 7.14 |
| 73 | 7.75 | 12.82 | 3.23 | 10.40 | 73 | 23.07 | 10.00 | 2.22 | 14.28 |
| 74 | 8.98 | 9.41 | 6.69 | 12.12 | 74 | 2.50 | 7.40 | 13.63 | 8.97 |
| 75 and over | 42.03 | 39.28 | 37.84 | 30.45 | 75 and over | 41.02 | 48.00 | 43.42 | 33.80 |

Source: Colin D. Campbell and Rosemary G. Campbell, "Conflicting Views on the Effect of Old-Age and Survivor's Insurance on Retirement," *Economic Inquiry*, 14, No. 3 (September 1976): 375, Table 2.

retirement age, both in pensions and as a matter of status. It also may have helped to establish sixty-five as a mandatory age, thus relieving managers of the need to choose who, among their aging work force, was to go, and who might stay. In unionized firms such discretion would be intolerable, but even in nonunion firms the discretion might be unpleasant and lead to unrest among the upper-age work force. If this is the case, the impact of Social Security on the sharp rate of increase in withdrawal from work at sixty-five has been coupled with the retirement test.

The impact of the retirement test can also be seen from the peaks at age sixty-five, and the decline in withdrawal past that point. The liberalizations of the test (greater earnings permitted) are shown in Figures 5-1c and 5-1d for 1960 and 1970. In 1950 persons aged seventy-five or over were exempted from the test, and this was lowered to age seventy-two in 1954. (The 1977 amendments raise the earnings limit to $4,000, rising to $6,500 in 1982, at which time persons over seventy will be exempted from the test. Thereafter, the earnings limit will be adjusted by changes in average wages.)

Comparing the data on Figure 5-1, one sees peaks at seventy for males and females, which indicates the persistence of seventy as a normal retirement for a segment of the labor force (this has been a common retirement age in public service). However, the impact of the suspension of the test at age seventy-two can be inferred for male workers, at least by the change in the slope of the curve at age seventy-two in Figures 5-1c (1950) and 5-1d (1960). At that point, in both figures, the rate of decline diminishes visibly, which indicates a reduction in the rate of withdrawal from the labor force. Although a part of this may reflect re-entry, some of it constitutes the pool of workers who, having stayed in the labor market until age seventy-two, now leave it less rapidly, because they can keep all their earnings and collect all of their Social Security benefits.

Some of the conclusions reached above have been supported by other studies. On the early retirement option, an analysis of the Social Security Retirement History Study was made by Joseph F. Quinn. The Social Security Administration had always pointed to health status as the primary motive for early retirement.[5] Quinn found that *both* health and retirement benefit eligibility are important determinants and that they interact. Thus, while Social Security eligibility reduces the probabilities of labor force participation for both healthy and health-impaired individuals,[6] the effect of Social Security alone is eight times as great for health-impaired as compared to healthy workers. The effect of pension plans is similar, although less pronounced. The presence of income from other assets, including the imputed rent from owner-occupied homes, has a similar effect. Finally, local labor market conditions and job attributes also affect the retirement decision. Retirement probabilities are lower in tight labor markets and higher from jobs with undesirable attributes. The latter, Quinn noted, is especially true for men in poor health.[7]

Using a different sample and a somewhat different methodology, Michael J. Boskin came to somewhat similar conclusions regarding the retirement of the elderly. Over the time period of his study (1968 through 1972), he finds that increases in Social Security benefits and coverage, combined with the earnings test, were significant contributors to the rapid decline in the labor force participation of older persons. He found great sensitivity to the earnings test,[8] which induces a substantial distortion in the group's labor market decision.

Arguably, relaxation of the test would increase the systems's cost and thus possibly would create distortions on the tax side. Boskin suggests two provisos to this argument. One is that the additional real resource cost to the economy is likely to be less than the tax distortion, because the labor supply of older workers is more responsive to additional earnings than that of the general population. The second is that increased revenues and the decreased earnings tested rate would apply to a larger earnings base (presumably pushing some of them into the progressively lower benefit brackets at the point of retirement).[9]

It would appear, on the available evidence, that the retirement effect of Social Security (and other forms of nonretirement income) has led to a loss of human resources to the economy, with a corresponding loss of output and real income. How great has this loss been? One estimate is that if the LFPR of the elderly were the same today as it was in the 1930s, before the advent of Social Security, the increase in the labor force would be less than 3 percent.[10] It has been suggested that this may be matter of small magnitude for the economy as a whole and that it is probably offset by the increased efficiency of business enterprises that can be attributed to earlier retirement of workers.[11]

Whether or not this offset in efficiency really exists is a matter of some doubt, for there is no empirical evidence on the subject. However, the loss to the labor force can be expected to grow as the population ages, with a sharp effect in the second decade of the twenty-first century, when the post–World War II babies reach retirement age and need to be supported by the smaller age cohort that will then be at work.

So long as unemployment is sufficiently high, there may be no loss. The founders of Social Security, under the influence of the Great Depression, obviously believed that if some human resources were to be idle, it might as well be those of the elderly. They did not necessarily have efficiency in mind, but if younger workers are more efficient than older ones, then the use of their resources in lieu of older resources might offset the loss of output. If this is the case, the issue is resolved into a question of the distribution of earnings opportunities and income among gnerations. The younger workers pay a tax whose yield is used to bribe the older workers to leave the labor market—that is the carrot—and the earnings test, together with mandatory retirement, is the stick used to beat them out of the labor market.

To be sure, some of the older workers do better from this arrangement than others. Those with low earnings records have the highest replacement rates and, given some scope for earnings under the retirement test, may improve their living standards after retirement. Given one's taste in intergenerational equity, it may be argued that young workers should have priority for job opportunities and advancement. The old folks have had their day, and given the growing problem of providing opportunity for minorities and women, it can be said that these should receive preference over older workers.

This, of course, is a value judgment—and one that I do not share. Note that the need for a choice of favoring one generation over another in the labor market stems from the inability of the economy to use all of its human resources, and the choice problem would be diminished if the economy could function at substantially lower rates of unemployment. Thus, the design and functioning of an income maintenance system for the aged cannot be separated from the rest of the economy. An efficiently operating economy can take better care of all its people than a stagnant one, and redistributional problems in such an economy are likely to be less pronounced.

## THE IMPACT OF SOCIAL SECURITY ON SAVING AND CAPITAL FORMATION

In the early years of Social Security little attention was paid to the effect that the system might have on private saving and, thereby, on the nation's stock of real capital (that is, goods used to produce other goods, such as machinery). As shown in the historical chapter, the founders of the system gave the matter little thought. If anything, they believed that saving would be encouraged, inasmuch as workers would need to supplement relatively low benefits that were not high enough to support an adequate living standard. In the Depression, when so much capital was idle, no one contemplated the possibility of a shortage of capital. There was plenty of it, and it merely needed to be put to work.[12]

It was always believed that the Social Security tax was a form of compulsory saving, and in the 1950s and 1960s economists began to ask whether compulsory saving increased or decreased planned saving, that is, whether wage earners reduced the proportion of income they wanted to save as a result of their being forced to save, and as a consequence of their anticipating future benefits. The question was worth asking, because either yes or no was a plausible answer.

In 1957, Milton Friedman's theoretical work led him to the belief that the availability of assistance from the state would tend to reduce planned saving because it lessened the household's need for such saving. However, he concluded that more detailed analysis was needed to determine whether the net effect of Social Security was a decrease or an increase in saving.[13] Ten years later Henry J. Aaron found some empirical support for the reduced savings hypothesis in a transnational study of social security expenditures and savings rates. Strictly speaking, he found an inverse relationship between the two but warned his readers that the direction of causality was not clear. In other words, it could not be firmly decided whether higher social security expenditures were the result or the cause of lower saving.[14]

In the meantime, two studies of the saving behavior of persons covered by pension plans (a form of private compulsory saving) indicated that compulsory saving tended to increase planned saving. One reason was that having a pension plan caused households to "recognize" the need for making adequate provision for the future, whereas they might not otherwise worry about the future.[15] Another reason was the "goal gradient effect," whereby individuals make greater efforts to save the closer they get to their retirement goals.[16] These findings could be generalized from pensions to Social Security and entered the conventional wisdom on Social Security through the classic work of Pechman, Aaron, and Taussig.[17]

Conventional wisdom can have a short life. In 1974 Martin Feldstein published the first of a number of his studies on Social Security[18] that proposed a dramatically different view. The work was a sophisticated econometric study concluding that Social Security (1) drastically reduced saving, (2) thereby considerably reduced the nation's stock of capital, which in turn (3) reduced Gross National Product and (4) tended to depress wages and raise interest rates. This implies that the Social Security system, as now constituted, is in urgent need of reform, because it not only reduces national income but contributes to a maldistribution of income.

Almost simultaneously, Alicia Munnell published findings indicating that there was, indeed, a negative impact on saving, but of considerably smaller magnitude than that found by Feldstein.[19] These works were followed by a spate of further studies, some as yet unpublished, that came to still other conclusions. At this juncture, it appears that the conventional wisdom has been replaced by a raging controversy. Unfortunately, the importance of the subject and the stature of the authors of the various papers make it impossible to ignore the controversy or simply to await its outcome. The last shot is far from having been fired. If Feldstein is anywhere near correct, then changes are in order if we wish to achieve higher living standards in the future. As will be seen in Chapter 6, the reforms need not be those proposed by Feldstein.

I shall attempt in the paragraphs below to summarize the state of play and arrive at some very tentative conclusions, based on my analysis of the literature. Because much of this literature is written in economics rather than in English, it will be necessary to translate some of it; economics, like poetry, loses in the translation. Worse yet, economic writings that are clear to noneconomists may be incomprehensible to economists, and vice versa. With this *caveat*, we turn first to Feldstein.

Feldstein chose to explain consumption and saving behavior by using an extended life cycle model. In such a model, the consumer knows (or estimates) his permanent income through time and maximizes his utility (satisfaction or well-being) by allocating this income among various consumer goods. Feldstein extends this model by including a retirement decision. The consumer knows that he will retire at a point in time in the future. This motivates him to accumulate enough assets (save) in order to maintain his chosen level of consumption from the point of retirement to his death. In Feldstein's version of the model, there is no intention on the part of the consumer to leave any bequests to his children. Transfers made to children largely take place when the children are young and are part of the consumer's consumption pattern. Postdeath bequests may, of course, be inadvertent if the consumer dies before he expects to, but they are likely to be trivial in size for most of the population. Other economists, as will be seen below, add bequests as a motive for saving.

Social Security has two basic effects on private saving. The consumer knows that benefits will be available at the point of retirement. The benefits are an annuity, and the present value of this annuity constitutes an asset of Social Security wealth (SSW). This can be calculated as gross wealth or net of the present value of future Social Security taxes. The first effect, which Feldstein calls the asset-substitution effect, reduces saving as consumers substitute their expected SSW for the saving or private wealth accumulation that they would otherwise have engaged in. Note that the imposition of the Social Security tax not only substitutes for saving but, being compulsory, reduces the consumer's after-tax income.

The second effect, called the "induced retirement effect," stems from both the availability of benefits and the earnings limitations that confront Social Security beneficiaries. More persons would work past age sixty-five in the absence of Social Security. The system, however, induces them to retire earlier, thus shortening their working life and increasing their saving during their working lives in order to tide them over the longer retirement years. The decrease in income caused by retirement diminishes the ability to save in those years. Theoretically, the net impact of the retirement effect is indeterminate. It could, conceivably, be positive. This would increase saving and partially offset the asset-substitution effect.

Feldstein argues that 46 percent of all men over sixty-five were retired in 1930, a figure that rose to 75 percent by 1971. For the original 46 percent, only the asset-substitution effect operates. Only for the remaining 25 percent does Social Security have both a negative asset-substitution effect and a possibly positive induced-retirement effect. According to Feldstein's empirical estimates, any additional savings that result from the induced-retirement effect on the smaller group are outweighted by the asset-substitution effect that operates on all beneficiaries.

To understand Feldstein's empirical findings, it is helpful to divide asset-substitution into two categories: (1) the tax effect, which is the impact of Social Security taxes on disposable (after-tax) income, and (2) the wealth effect of the expected annuities. In 1971 Social Security taxes reduced disposable income by $51 billion.[20] This led to a reduction in personal savings of $18 billion.[21] In that year estimated gross SSW was $2,029 billion in 1971 prices. This led to an additional reduction of $43 billion in savings.[22] Thus, the wealth effect was twice as great as the tax effect. Adding the two puts the combined asset-substitution effect at a $61 billion reduction in savings.

Personal saving in 1971 amounted to $61 billion. It follows from this that the system's operation led to a 50 percent decline in savings. Feldstein then estimated that this meant a decline in private capital stock of 38 percent in 1971.[23] If asset-substitution had not taken place, Feldstein estimates that the long-run capital stock would have been 60 percent greater. For 1972 this means that Gross National Product would have been greater by 15 percent.[24] A more conservative assumption, according to Feldstein, would increase GNP by 40 percent. For 1972 this would have raised GNP by $127 billion.

As noted earlier, the system is also said to redistribute income in an unintentional fashion. This is because the reduction in capital stock makes capital scarce relative to labor. To a certain extent, this is offset by the reduction in labor supply caused by the inducement to retire, but Feldstein estimates this at an insignificant 3 percent. On net balance the effect is to raise the return to capital by 28 percent and to reduce wages by 15 percent.[25]

In Feldstein's model, the vice of the Social Secuirty system lies not in its existence but primarily in its financing and secondarily in the retirement test for beneficiaries. It is the pay-as-you-go method of financing that operates to reduce the stock of capital and the economy's ability to produce greater output. The Social Security wealth —the present value of future benefits—is a claim not on the output that can be produced by a stock of real capital goods but on the future ability of government to tax and borrow. The retirement test diminishes the ability of beneficiaries to enter the labor market and thus reduces their incomes and ability to consume. Thus, the income maintenance goal of the system is partly vitiated by the way it reduces the living standards of persons aged sixty-five.

Munnell credits Feldstein with discovery of the twofold effect of Social Security, which she calls the benefit effect and the retirement effect.[26]Although her methodology follows Feldstein, she introduces unemployment as a variable that reduces savings and constructs a retirement saving series to be used in place of aggregate saving.[27] Although she finds that the twofold effect does indeed operate, the two have up to now come close to canceling each other out. Thus, for 1969 her estimate is that the net reduction in saving was $3.6 billion, as compared to Feldstein's $38.2 billion for that year.

Munnell gives several reasons for the difference in their findings. One is that unemployment accounts for some loss of saving; by omitting unemployment, Feldstein's methodology leads to an overstatement of the negative effect of Social Security on saving. A second reason is that Social Security taxes do not reduce aggregate disposable income (Feldstein's tax effect) because, in a pay-as-you-go system, they are transferred from the taxpayers to the beneficiaries.[28]

In the third place, Feldstein underestimates the retirement effect. It does not enter his model directly. The benefit effect in Feldstein (his asset-substitution effect) is estimated net of the retirement effect, which he independently estimated as negligible. However, another work by Feldstein indicates that the effect is important.[29] Furthermore, surveys conducted by the Social Security Administration show that people retiring today have saved about the same proportion of their income as their predecessors who retired thirty years ago. This and other evidence suggest that private (i.e., non–Social Security) saving for retirement has not been sharply reduced by Social Security.[30]

It must be stressed, however, that Munnell does not claim to refute the essence of Feldstein's findings, but merely their historical magnitudes. She points out that the great decline in the LFPR of older persons is slowing down, a factor that attenuates the positive saving impact of the retirement effect. Benefit increases, however, have been accelerating, at least in the 1970s, which increases the negative saving impact of the benefit (or asset-substitution) effect. Thus the future net impact of Social Security may well be a decline in saving. Whether or not this is deleterious to the economy will depend on the extent of the nation's future need for capital. Should a greater need for saving emerge, the next question is whether it should be accomplished through higher payroll taxes that will shift the system from pay-as-you-go to full funding or through some less regressive mechanism.

This will be dealt with in the next chapter. At this point, I shall merely note that the 1977 amendments are intended to stabilize the proportion of previous earnings to be replaced by benefits, and that this will tend to limit future real inceases in benefits to changes in earnings. In turn, this will reduce the negative saving impact of the benefit or asset-substitution effect.

The third entry into the controversy comprises two works by Robert J. Barro. In the first Barro introduced a life cycle model of consumption and saving behavior and extended it to take account of bequests, that is, private transfer payments. He argued that an individual's sense of well-being (utility) depends not only on his own consumption but also on the well-being of future generations. Because Social Security is a transfer payment from the younger to the older generation, its advent created wealth for the older generation and a liability for the younger one. If people's sense of well-being encompasses the well-being of future generations, as Barro believes, then the present generation increases its savings sufficiently to leave bequests to its children. The purpose is to offset the liability created for the next generation, thus leaving it as well off as would otherwise be the case. Of course, young persons also make transfers to their elders. Increases in benefits to their elders would correspondingly reduce such transfers.[31]

Feldstein disagrees with this analysis for three reasons. The first is that the growth of benefits over time reduces the next generation's liability as its benefits improve. The second is that the implicit rate of return on Social Security tax payments may be equal to or greater than the real after-tax rate of return on the savings of the older generation of workers. They, accordingly, will have reason to believe that Social Security will be a gain to their heirs and will reduce their bequests (and saving) accordingly. The third reason is that, for most families, bequests are small. Most of the private intrafamily transfers are from parents to minor children and are therefore family consumption rather than transfers of capital.[32]

The reader may find it hard to believe that individuals plan their lives with the precision and economic rationality that are posited both by Barro and, in part, by Feldstein's critique. However, it is not necessary to treat all persons as ultra-rational. It suffices to believe that family members make transfer payments to each other and that members of an older generation derive statisfaction from leaving something to their children. With this in mind, we turn to Barro's empirical estimate of the impact of Social Security on private saving.[33]

Briefly, Barro was not able to test his hypothesis that the decrease in saving due to Social Security would just be offset by increases in private transfer payments. Data on private transfers are simply not available. However, he made econometric estimates of consumer expenditures for the period 1929 to 1974, excluding 1941 to 1946 for the main period of the analysis to avoid the distortions of World War II.

Although Barro followed Feldstein's model in many respects, he added some variables that Feldstein did not use[34] and changed the form of certain others. Two definitions of Social Security Wealth were used: Feldstein's Gross Social Security Wealth and his own narrow measure based on current benefit rates and current worker coverage. In both of these variations Social Security had no significant positive impact on consumer expenditures. This means it could not have had any effect on private savings, since the latter is merely the difference between disposable income and consumer expenditures.

The fourth important study that directly addresses Social Security and saving is a work by Michael R. Darby.[35] Like Barro's, Darby's world is one in which bequests are made. His econometric model combined two types of aggregate private savings: accumulation for retirement and accumulation for bequests. He was able to separate out saving for bequests by calculating consumption during the retirement period (income less increases in assets). Nonasset income and Social Security benefits were then subtracted, and the remainder was converted into an annuity at three different interest rates. This annuity constituted three estimates of life cycle wealth that was accumulated for bequest purposes, since it exceeded the wealth that would be needed to maintain the life cycle living standard. As noted below, the motive for bequest accumulation also has a precautionary element to provide for emergencies.

According to Darby, there are five ways in which Social Security can effect saving: (1) There is the dual effect of the expected benefit (or asset substitution) that decreases saving, together with the induced retirement effect that increases saving. Darby calls the net impact the Feldstein–Munnell effect. (2) The extent to which the system compels people to buy annuities (the benefits) that they would not otherwise purchase. This reduces the risk of outliving one's assets and thereby reduces the precautionary motive for saving toward expected bequests. (3) Since the amount of Social Security benefits is uncertain, savings are increased. (4) When the real interest rate that people use to make life cycle decisions is greater than the implicit yield of 3¼ percent on Social Security taxes, savings are increased by the expectation of the higher yield. (5) The reduction in labor supply tends to reduce both bequest saving and income proportionately.

The above suggest that there is no *a priori* theoretical conclusion possible regarding the net impact on savings made by Social Security, and that an empirical test of the historical evidence is in order. However, it is necessary to establish the notions that a model of consumer behavior over the life cycle is not viable if it denies the possibility of saving for bequests,[36] and that bequests play a role in decisions to consume and save. Darby shows this by relating changes in retirement and postretirement life expectations to the proportion of income saved, for the pre-Social Security years 1890–1930. During this period both life expectancy and retirement at sixty-five were rising, as was the ratio of expected retirement to expected life. The zero-bequest life cycle would predict a rise in the proprotion of income saved on the assumption that the chief motivation for saving is to provide for retirement. The data, however, do not show any relationship.[37]

It is possible that the lack of relationship between changes in retirement and saving behavior in 1890–1930 was caused by some fortuitous offsetting forces. Darby explores four such possibilities and rejects them. He concludes that life cycle saving (saving for retirement) was not the dominant share of saving for this period. If that is the case, there is no reason to believe that the substitution effect should be strong *after* the introduction of Social Security. In other words, bequests matter.

In his econometric estimates, using a model inclusive of both bequests and unemployment, Darby found that the plausible effect of Social Security on the proportion of income saved falls into a range of 0 percent to 10 percent, although a higher proportion cannot be ruled out. This suggests that the impact on capital stock[38] and on Gross National Product is considerably smaller than that envisioned by Feldstein, but possibly larger than Barro's. Roughly speaking, his range of results encompasses those found by Munnell.[39]

The principal conclusion that emerges from an examination of these studies is that the evidence is inconclusive. Estimates of a reduction in saving that range from zero to 50 percent are difficult to use as a basis for policy changes. Nevertheless, the weight of the evidence is that Social Security has *some* negative effect on saving, albeit probably small. Further studies are clearly needed in order to resolve the issue.[40]

To summarize, the operation of the Social Security System appears to reduce the amount of human resources available to the economy. It may also diminish the nation's capital stock. A relative reduction in the number of workers and of the tools that they work with means a relative reduction in the amount of goods and services that can be produced both for the young and for the old. While this is not an argument for the abolition of the system. it does indicate a problem. The problem will become acute as the cohort of war babies reaches retirement age early in the next century.

The chapter that follows addresses itself to the financing of Social Security. As will be seen, questions of financing need to take capital formation into account and, indeed, the functioning of the entire economy.

# CHAPTER SIX

# Financing Social Security

### IS IT REALLY INSURANCE?

Only by stretching the definition. If by insurance we mean acquiring financial protection against contingencies like loss of income, then the answer is yes. The worker who is in covered employment receives protection from loss of income resulting from retirement or total disability, and certain survivors receive it in the event of the worker's death. This is a very broad use of the word insurance, however. The protection is statutory, not contractual. It has been changed, and can be changed further, by legislation. Conceivably, it can be abolished without refunding the "contributions" paid by the worker, although this is a rather remote possibility.

In a similar sense, public assistance programs also offer protection. The difference is that eligibility does not depend on previous payment of an earmarked tax and that benefits are subject to a means test. The common perception of public assistance programs is that they are not insurance. In some countries they are included in the term social security, but they are never referred to as insurance.

Social insurance is a legitimate phrase so long as the modifying word "social" is kept in mind, for social insurance is quite different from its private counterpart. There is, of course, a certain resemblance. The tax, called a contribution, resembles an insurance premium. The benefits are paid when the prescribed contingency occurs. As in private insurance, actuarial considerations play a role. However, other considerations enter that make a crucial difference. Among these are the compulsory nature of participation, the provision for social adequacy in determining benefits, and the use of a pay-as-you-go method by which current tax collections are essentially transferred to current beneficiaries. Finally, benefits are indexed.

By the yardsticks of private insurance, social insurance is a substantially different animal. Clearly, few private insurance or annuity schemes can afford social adequacy provisions if they expect to sell policies in a competitive market. Compulsion is absent, except to the extent that workers covered by employer-sponsored insurance or pension plans have no choice except to seek employment elsewhere. Insurance carriers, on the other hand, are free to reject individuals or groups that present adverse risks.[1] No private insurance company is in a position to guarantee the real value of its benefits by indexing them, although it can offer variable annuities based on the prices of securities. Finally, pay-as-you-go annuities are unsound in the private sector because of the possibility that in-payments may stop before the obligation to make out-payments is complete. Only a government with taxing powers can engage in such a program.

In short, social insurance is quite different from private insurance and, for that matter, different from public-owned insurance schemes, like Veterans' Insurance, that are operated on actuarial bases. Thus, the use of the word insurance is unfortunate and misleading if it implies that the two types of insurance are comparable. The mythic value of the term is of considerable importance to the public's acceptance of the system. Beneficiaries need to believe that they have earned their benefits, and covered workers need to believe that they are earning future benefits. Together, the two groups constitute the system. In a moral sense, beneficiaries *have* earned benefits. One can only question whether this generation of retirees has earned all of the amount it receives, and whether present and future generations, who are and will be paying relatively higher taxes, can and should receive correspondingly higher benefits. The notion of a moral right to benefits based in some (imprecise) way to previous Social Security tax contributions is deeply embedded in our political ethos. And it is symbolized in the word "insurance."

## THE PAYROLL TAX AND ALTERNATIVE FINANCING METHODS

All social insurance systems in the Western industrial world rely on payroll taxes, but many do not rely upon them exclusively. As noted in an earlier chapter, the original Bismarckian model included contributions from the general revenues of government. The founders of the American system rejected contributions from general revenues and used a payroll tax, divided between employers and employees, to finance the system. This had a number of important political functions. One is that it reinforced the popular belief that Social Security was like an insurance and annuity policy whose benefits were earned (although the redistributive aspects, especially progressive benefit rates, have never been much of a secret). So one was being offered a handout.

In retrospect, one doubts whether American workers would have felt demeaned by a system that included some contributions from general revenues. European workers have never been troubled by this. Thus, a second political function of total reliance on equally divided payroll taxes may be more important. It creates a constituency of employers and workers who have an interest in limiting the financial cost of the system, because higher costs are transmitted directly back in terms of higher payroll taxes. This constitutency took forty years to develop, however. So long as economic growth and favorable demographics continued to raise revenues, Congress could afford to be generous in extending coverage and raising benefits. The dominating constituencies were beneficiaries and workers who, observing the benefits, were willing to pay ever rising taxes in order to get some of their benefits.

The strategy of creating a brake on costs did not work for a long time because the tax was not generally perceived to be an onerous burden. It was only in he 1960s that observers noted that the tax bore heavily on low-wage workers, and proposals were made to make the tax progressive. In effect, this was done by lowering the *income tax* liability of low-wage workers—the earned income credit is an example—which offset the burden of the Social Security tax, at least in part. This action represented an implicit recognition of the idea that it may not matter to the individual how his or her tax is divided between Fund A and Fund B. It is the total tax payment that matters. Note, however, that the sanctity of the Social Security payroll tax was left undisturbed. The special income tax reduction for certain low-wage earners is a subsidy from general revenues, and perhaps properly so, but this was less apparent when done through the income tax rather than through the Social Security tax.

In the late 1970s, however, the tax bite began to be felt more acutely. It will be recalled that the original rate was 1 percent each on employers and employees, on maximum taxable earnings of $3,000 (see Table 6-1). By 1966 the total tax rate (including Disability and Health Insurance) had reached 4.2 percent of maximum taxable earnings of $6,600. In 1978 the rate was 6.05 percent on a maximum of $17,700. The legislation enacted at the end of 1977 provided further increases in both tax rates and the maximum taxable earnings level (the wage base). The tax on employers and employees is scheduled to rise gradually from 6.13 percent in 1979 to 7.65 percent in 1990 and thereafter.[2] The wage base rise in 1979 is to $22,900, a 29 percent jump, rising by $3,000 to $25,900 in 1980, and is $29,700 in 1981. After 1981 the wage base will rise automatically with changes in average U.S. earnings. The changes are summarized in Table 6-2.

Table 6-1 provides more historical perspective. It can be seen that each change in the tax rate was not very painful when it occurred. The maximum impact was felt by persons affected by the change in the wage base, since a simultaneous change in the rate and the base catches them two ways. In the years when the base remained stable, the group at or above the base grew as a proportion of earners covered by the law. This presented a temptation to Congress to tap the growing pool of earnings past the wage base. Successive and later annual changes have reduced the relative size of this group to about 15 percent in 1977, and it will further diminish to 9 percent[3] in 1981 as the wage base rises faster than the nominal earnings of the group. After 1981 the relative size of the group will stabilize, as the wage base rise is limited by increases in average annual earnings.[4]

There are two consequences that stem from the reduction in the number of earners at the wage base. One is that Congress is reaching the limit from which significant additions to revenues can be gotten from major changes in the wage base. The second is that the group, albeit small, can be vocal and politically effective. High-paid employees are largely the highly skilled and educated. They write to Congressmen, and they vote. As it occurs to them that the progressive schedule of benefits works against them, they may become more agitated even though their absolute benefit levels will rise as a result of the higher wage base. Employers in industries with a high proportion of high wage earners will also feel the pinch, especially those in the public and nonprofit sectors who cannot reduce the impact of

**TABLE 6–1** Maximum Earnings and Wage Base and Tax Rate Changes

| Year | % of Total Covered Workers Reaching Maximum Earnings | Tax Rate, Employees and Employers, Each | Wage Base |
|---|---|---|---|
| 1937–39 | n.a. | 1.0% | $3,000 |
| 1940 | 5.39% | 1.0 | 3,000 |
| 1945 | 13.71 | 1.0 | 3,000 |
| 1950 | 28.86 | 1.5 | 3,000 |
| 1951–53 | n.a. | 1.5 | 3,600 |
| 1954 | n.a. | 2.0 | 3,600 |
| 1955 | 25.62 | 2.0 | 4,200 |
| 1956 | n.a. | 2.0 | 4,200 |
| 1957–58 | n.a. | 2.25[a] | 4,200 |
| 1959 | n.a. | 2.5 | 4,800 |
| 1960 | 28.00 | 3.0 | 4,800 |
| 1961 | 29.20 | 3.0 | 4,800 |
| 1962 | 31.17 | 3.125 | 4,800 |
| 1963 | 32.53 | 3.625 | 4,800 |
| 1964 | 34.50 | 3.625 | 4,800 |
| 1965 | 36.11 | 3.625 | 4,800 |
| 1966 | 24.23 | 4.2[b] | 6,600 |
| 1967 | 26.36 | 4.4 | 6,600 |
| 1968 | 21.39 | 4.4 | 7,800 |
| 1969 | 24.52 | 4.8 | 7,800 |
| 1970 | 26.02 | 4.8 | 7,800 |
| 1971 | 28.29 | 5.2 | 7,800 |
| 1972 | 25.01 | 5.2 | 9,000 |
| 1973 | 20.41 | 5.85 | 10,800 |
| 1974 | 15.14 | 5.85 | 13,200 |
| 1975 | 15.12 | 5.85 | 14,100 |

[a]From 1957 to 1966, tax rate includes disability insurance.
[b]From 1966 to 1975, tax rate includes disability insurance and health insurance.

Sources: *Social Security Bulletin* Table Q–2, December 1977, p. 73. Alicia H. Munnell, *The Future of Social Security*, Washington: Brookings Institution, 1977), Table A–12, p. 182.

their share of the tax (at least in the first iteration) by deducting it from taxable incomes.

The pinch for those who will continue to stay at the maximum is not inconsiderable. Under the pre-1977 law, the total tax on each side was scheduled to rise from $965.25 in 1977 to an estimated

**TABLE 6-2** Changes in Social Security Financing Under the Old Law and H.R. 9346 (1977)

**Changes in Tax Rates (in percent)**

| | Employees and Employers, Each | | | | | | Self-Employed | | | | | |
|---|---|---|---|---|---|---|---|---|---|---|---|---|
| | Old Law | | | H.R. 9346 | | | Old Law | | | H.R. 9346 | | |
| Years | *OASDI* | *HI* | *Total* | *OASDI* | *HI* | *Total* | *OASDI* | *HI* | *Total* | *OASDI* | *HI* | *Total* |
| 1977 | 4.95 | 0.90 | 5.85 | 4.95 | 0.90 | 5.85 | 7.00 | 0.90 | 7.90 | 7.00 | 0.90 | 7.90 |
| 1978 | 4.95 | 1.10 | 6.05 | 5.05 | 1.00 | 6.05 | 7.00 | 1.10 | 8.10 | 7.10 | 1.00 | 8.10 |
| 1979–80 | 4.95 | 1.10 | 6.05 | 5.08 | 1.05 | 6.13 | 7.00 | 1.10 | 8.10 | 7.05 | 1.05 | 8.10 |
| 1981 | 4.95 | 1.35 | 6.30 | 5.35 | 1.30 | 6.65 | 7.00 | 1.35 | 8.35 | 8.00 | 1.30 | 9.30 |
| 1982–4 | 4.95 | 1.35 | 6.30 | 5.40 | 1.30 | 6.70 | 7.00 | 1.35 | 8.35 | 8.05 | 1.30 | 9.35 |
| 1985 | 4.95 | 1.35 | 6.30 | 5.70 | 1.35 | 7.05 | 7.00 | 1.35 | 8.35 | 8.55 | 1.35 | 9.90 |
| 1986–89 | 4.95 | 1.50 | 6.45 | 5.70 | 1.45 | 7.15 | 7.00 | 1.50 | 8.50 | 8.55 | 1.45 | 10.00 |
| 1990–2010 | 4.95 | 1.50 | 6.45 | 6.20 | 1.45 | 7.65 | 7.00 | 1.50 | 8.50 | 9.30 | 1.45 | 10.75 |
| 2011 and after | 5.95 | 1.50 | 7.45 | 6.20 | 1.45 | 7.65 | 7.00 | 1.50 | 8.50 | 9.30 | 1.45 | 10.75 |

**Changes in Contribution and Benefit Bases**

| Years | Old Law[a] | $ Change | % Change Over Previous Year | % Change From 1978 | H.R. 9346 | % Change | % Change Over Previous Year | % Change From 1978 |
|---|---|---|---|---|---|---|---|---|
| 1978 | $17,700 | | | | $17,700 | | | |
| 1979 | 18,900[b] | $1,200 | 6.8% | 6.8% | 22,900 | $5,200 | 29.4% | 29.4% |
| 1980 | 20,400[b] | 1,500 | 7.9 | 15.3 | 25,900 | 3,000 | 13.1 | 46.3 |
| 1981 | 20,900[b] | 1,500 | 7.4 | 23.7 | 29,700 | 3,800 | 14.7 | 67.8 |
| 1982 | 23,400[b] | 1,500 | 6.9 | 32.2 | [c] | | | |

[a]Amounts produced under automatic provisions of the old law.
[b]Estimated by the Social Security Administration, based on the old adjustment mechanism.
[c]Automatically adjusted after 1981, on the basis of average earnings changes.

Source: Social Security Administration, *Legislative Report* No. 17, December 16, 1977, Table 1.

$2,012.40 per year in 1987. This would have been an increase of 108 percent. Under the new law, the estimated tax (assuming that projected changes in average annual earnings will be close to the mark) will be $3,045.90 in 1987, an increase of 215.6 percent over the 1977 tax.[5]

It is quite possible that the wage base, under automatic adjustments, will rise more rapidly than envisioned by the Congress. For example, the automatic adjustment was expected by Congress to put the wage base at $33,900 in 1983.[6] The Congressional Budget Office (CBO), however, projected a wage base of $34,800, a difference of $900.[7] This figure seems to have been accepted by the Social Security Administration.[8] All projections are necessarily speculative, of course. Nonetheless, the projection that inflation will proceed at higher rates than Congress believed seem plausible as of 1978.

The SSA's projections are apparently based on the assumptions underlying the President's budget for Fiscal Year 1979. As seen in Table 6-3, these are somewhat more optimistic than the CBO's, with regard to both inflation and unemployment. If CBO is more nearly correct, then inflation is likely to increase the wage base (see above) and associated tax revenues. It will also increase benefit outlays in the short term—via the indexing of benefits—and in the long term through the rising wage base. The higher unemployment rates imply lower revenues in the short term and lower benefit payments in the long term.

Whatever the case may be, it remains to be seen whether the sharp tax increases in the next decade, for those whose earnings will be at the wage base, will lead to a politically effective tax revolt by this group. If so, the political strategy of confining the financing of Social Security to a payroll tax will finally become operational.

In early years when Social Security taxes were a minuscule percentage of federal tax receipts, little attention had to be paid to the effect of the taxes on the national economy. In 1951 all social insurance taxes (including the small federal unemployment tax) constituted 10.9 percent of all federal receipts and 28.9 percent of personal income tax receipts (see Table 6-4.) At that time, social insurance tax receipts were smaller than receipts from indirect business taxes and corporate income taxes. By 1975 social insurance taxes had risen to almost one-third of all federal tax receipts. This ratio might have in-

**TABLE 6-3** Comparison of Projected Changes in the Consumer Price Index and in Unemployment Rates, Budget for FY 1979 and Congressional Budget Office (Calender Years)

| | 1979 | 1980 | 1981 | 1982 | 1983 |
|---|---|---|---|---|---|
| CPI change, Budget | 6.10% | 5.70% | 5.20% | 4.70% | 4.20% |
| CPI change, CBO | 6.01 | 5.68 | 5.54 | 5.68 | 5.90 |
| Unemployment rate, Budget | 5.90 | 5.40 | 5.00 | 4.50 | 4.10 |
| Unemployment rate, CBO | 6.17 | 5.69 | 5.20 | 4.71 | 4.52 |

Sources: *The Budget of the United States Government, Fiscal Year 1979* (Washington: U.S. Government Printing Office 1978), pp. 30–33, and Congress of the United States, Congressional Budget Office, *Five-Year Budget Projections: Fiscal Years 1979–1983* (Washington: U.S. Government Printing Office, 1978), pp. 132–134.

**TABLE 6-4** Ratio of Social Insurance Tax Receipts[a] to Personal Income Tax Receipts and All Federal Budget Receipts

| Year[b] | Social Insurance Receipts as % of Income Tax Receipts | Social Insurance Receipts as % of All Receipts |
|---|---|---|
| 1951 | 28.9% | 10.9% |
| 1960 | 39.3 | 17.6 |
| 1965 | 47.7 | 20.4 |
| 1970 | 52.6 | 25.2 |
| 1975 | 72.4 | 32.6 |
| 1978 (est.) | 69.4 | 30.9 |
| 1979 (est.) | 74.6 | 32.3 |
| 1980 (est.) | 71.5 | 31.7 |

[a]Includes federal unemployment tax and other contributions.
[b]Fiscal Years ending June 30 until 1976, ending September 30 thereafter.

Sources: For 1951–75, *Economic Report of the President, 1977* (Washington: U.S. Government Printing Office, 1977), p. 271; for 1978–80 estimates, *Budget of the United States Government, Fiscal Year 1979* (Washington: U.S. Government Printing Office, 1978), p. 48.

creased further if inflation had not driven income tax payers into higher brackets, thus increasing income tax receipts even faster.

It is clear from the relative size of the social security tax that significant tax increases present fiscal policy problems. In a sense, this harks back to a somewhat parallel problem in the 1930s when the pioneer Keynesians feared that the tax burden of a fully funded system would retard recovery from the Depression. The decision in 1939 to move to a pay-as-you-go system was partly the result of this fear. At this juncture, full funding is no longer a politically serious consideration,[9] but the 1977 amendments will increase the size of the Trust Fund.

The Social Security tax increases that are needed to build up the Trust Fund create a problem in fiscal policy. In order to build up the fund, the payroll tax collections must exceed increases in total benefit payments. This leads to a decline in aggregate demand in the economy unless offset by an equivalent increase in federal spending or a decrease in other taxes. Whether or not such a brake on demand is desirable depends on the state of the economy and the goals of the fiscal policymakers. However, very few seriously propose to use social security taxes and benefits as discretionary fiscal policy tools. The usual tools are changes in personal and corporate income taxes and changes in expenditures. Accordingly, it may be useful to offset Social Security tax changes and shift the burden of fiscal policy to the more conventional tools. It would, after all, be an unlikely coincidence if the fiscal drag introduced by a Social Security tax change in any one year were precisely the fiscal medicine that was needed in that year.

The Congressional Budget Office estimates that the 1977 amendments will increase Social Security revenues $27 billion by fiscal year 1983 and reduce outlays by $3 billion. This amounts to a fiscal drag of $30 billion. By CBO projections (1978), if the economy is to grow at a rate of 4.8 percent until the unemployment rate declines to 4.5 percent, the $30 billion will have to be offset by an equivalent tax cut or expenditure increase during the period in question.[10]

By now it may occur to the reader that there is something puzzling about a policy to raise payroll taxes and to reduce other taxes. After all, a reduction in personal income and corporate taxes reduces general revenues. Precisely the same thing would occur if, instead of raising Social Security taxes, general revenues were applied toward a reduction in the gap between Social Security benefits and expenditures.

In short, if the Social Security tax increase is offset by a decrease in other taxes or an increase in other expenditures, then the net effect is that general revenues have entered the picture through the back door. They contribute to the financing of the system anyway, because the employer's share is tax deductible, a policy that decreases general revenues and requires that they be made up from other tax sources.

Thus, the question of whether to use general revenues to supplement Social Security tax revenues appears, at first glance, to be an accounting question. The U.S. government is, after all, one government. It has merely chosen to divide certain taxes and expenditures into separate budget accounts, just as a family might wish to separate, say, its savings accounts into a Christmas Club and a regular account. Such a family's asset position is unchanged if it adds $10 to its Christmas Club (earmarked for a certain purpose) and draws out $10 from its regular savings account. The difference between such a family and the government is that, for the latter, this shifting about of funds between accounts may obscure changes in the real economic position of the government. It can deceive both the voters and the policymakers.

So far, we have assumed that the aggregate effect of an increase in Social Security taxes and a corresponding decrease in income and corporate taxes is neutral. On a microeconomic basis, the two types of taxes may well have different impacts. In the previous chapter, it was noted that the Social Security tax may have some effect on decisions of family members to enter the labor market. The evidence on this is weak, but at least in theory there is a distortionary effect, which may become important (on an aggregate basis) in periods of full employment.

Nor are other markets immune from the distortionary effects of a payroll tax. To the extent that employers cannot shift the incidence of their share to employees, the tax discriminates between labor-intensive and capital-intensive sectors of the economy. Labor-intensive industries are led to produce less than they would have in the absence of the tax, thus altering the array of goods available to consumers.[11]

Further problems are generated by the Social Security tax with respect to inflation and unemployment. To the extent that employers cannot shift the tax backward, they may attempt to pass it forward in the prices of their products. Their ability to do so depends not only on the elasticity of demand for their products[12] but also on their market power. Firms with market power, found in the large corporate sector of the economy, tend to set prices by some mark-up over costs and would treat payroll tax increases as cost increases that warrant price increases.[13] To the extent that this leads to a decline in sales, some unemployment results, thus adding a further element to the problem of stagflation.[14]

The foregoing suggests that exclusive reliance on a payroll tax equally divided between employers and employees (or two-thirds of the total for the self-employed) may not be the optimal method of financing Social Security as further pressures on the system develop. In 1977 the Carter Administration proposed that the Trust Fund be allowed to borrow from general revenues to tide it over shortfalls caused by high cyclical rates of unemployment. This proposal was parallel to existing practices whereby states that are overdrawn on their account in the Unemployment Insurance Trust Fund can borrow from the federal government to tide their accounts over high periods of unemployment.

Although this proposal was apparently innocuous, it ran into stormy opposition in Congress. Any use of general revenues, it was said, smacked of welfarism and violated the tradition that beneficiaries have earned their benefits by their payroll tax payments.[15]

Thus, we come full circle to the confusion between insurance and *social* insurance. This confusion appears to be unresolved in the mind of the polity. Social insurance, as in the Social Security program, certainly contains an aspect of welfarism in that benefit scales are skewed to favor low wage earners. Furthermore, the present generation of beneficiaries may have earned beneftis in a moral sense, but they *did not* earn all of them in a fiscal sense; benefits are far higher than would have been earned by equivalent contributions to an annuity fund.

Or perhaps confusion is not the proper word. It may be that Congress or its constituents are bemused by the mythic or symbolic aspects of the system, and that forsaking the myth of an insurance program is too painful to bear. Unfortunately, this prevents serious consideration of the use of general revenues.

It will be recalled that the original Bismarckian conception of social insurance used a trilateral financing system, with the general revenues as the third source. Such arrangements remain common in industrial nations and are worth considering in the United States. Of fifteen leading industrial countries surveyed in Table 6-5, all but one (France) subsidize old age insurance programs with government revenues. There is no *a priori* reason for adopting a symmetrical system—one-third employees, one-third employers, one-third government. No such symmetry is found in other countries. A smaller contribution by government might be a reasonable approach. It could, for example, be limited to making up deficits if unemployment or inflation do not behave as expected, given the present structure of benefits.

There are some advantages to shifting part of the financial cost of the system more overtly to general revenues. One is that general taxes, especially the personal income tax, are less distortionary than payroll taxes. A second is that general taxes (again, specifically the income tax) are more progressive. On the whole, the Social Security tax—at minimum, the employees' share—is regressive. A third is that it puts the focus of fiscal policy where it properly belongs: on general taxes and expenditures.

There are other ways in which general revenues can be introduced.[16] Instead of dealing with revenue losses caused by excessive unemployment or expenditure increases caused by excessive inflation, general revenues can be used to finance some of the benefits based on social adequacy. At present, the benefit structure has three brackets: 90 percent of the first $180 of Average Indexed Monthly Earnings (AIME), 32 percent of the next $905, and 15 percent of the balance up to maximum taxable earnings.[17] In addition, there is a minimum benefit and a special minimum benefit. General revenues could, for example, be used to subsidize the first bracket and/or the minimum benefits. It can be argued that this redistributive portion of the benefit structure should properly be borne by the taxpayers at large rather than by Social Security taxpayers alone.

The redistribution is target inefficient, because some of the high-bracket recipients (low wage earners) are not needy. A number of writers, like Munnell,[18] have suggested that the needy be financed through an expanded means-tested Supplementary Security Income program. This, of course, is merely another way of shifting income support to general revenues, albeit at a lower cost.

**TABLE 6-5** Sources of Funds for Old-Age Programs

| | |
|---|---|
| 1. *Austria* | |
| insured person: | 8.75% of wages (wage earners) or 8.5% of salary (salary earners) |
| employer: | 8.75% of wages paid and 8.5% of salaries paid |
| government: | any deficit |
| 2. *Belgium* | |
| insured person: | 6% of earnings or 5.75% of salary |
| employer: | 8% of payroll (wage and salaried) |
| government: | annual subsidies, according to rising scale |
| 3. *Canada* | |
| insured person: | 1.8% (employees) of earnings or 3.6% (self-employed) |
| employer: | 1.8% of payroll |
| government: | any deficit |
| 4. *Denmark* | |
| insured person: | 3 kroner/week (employment related pension) |
| employer: | 6 kroner/week (employment related pension) |
| government: | universal pension, whole cost |
| 5. *France* | |
| insured person: | 3% of earnings |
| employer: | 7.25% of payroll |
| government: | none |
| 6. *Germany (Federal Republic)* | |
| insured person: | 9% of earnings (none if earnings below 10% of ceiling) |
| employer: | 9% of payroll (18% for employees with earnings below 10% of ceiling—1975—DM 33.600/year) |
| government: | annual subsidy (about 16% of total cost of pension insurance) |

**TABLE 6-5** (*cont.*)

| | |
|---|---|
| 7. *Ireland* | |
| insured person: | £1.27/week (men) or £1.20 (Women) (less in agriculture)<br>earnings related pension—1% of earnings |
| employer: | £1.84/week (male employees) and £1.79/week (female employees)<br>earnings related pension—2% of payroll |
| government: | difference between expenditures and contributions collected (about 20% of cost) |
| 8. *Italy* | |
| insured person: | 6.65% of earnings |
| employer: | 13.45% of payroll |
| government: | lump-sum subsidies |
| 9. *Japan* | |
| insured person: | employees' pension insurance 3.8% (men), 2.9% (women) or 7.6% (voluntarily insured) of earnings |
| employer: | 3.8% or 2.9% of payroll<br>voluntarily insured, 3.8% |
| government: | 20% of benefit costs |
| 10. *Luxembourg* | |
| insured person: | 7% of wage or salary |
| employer: | 7% of wages and salaries paid |
| government: | entire cost of basic pensions, 50% of cost of administration, and any deficit |
| 11. *Norway* | |
| insured person: | employees, 4.5% of pension-producing income plus 4.4% of taxable income (national tax)<br>self-employed, 13.0% of pension-producing income plus 4.4% of taxable income |
| employer: | 16.7% of pension-producing income |

| | |
|---|---|
| government: | national and local governments, each 2.25% of pension-producing income |
| 12. *Spain* | |
| insured person: | 4% of base wage |
| employer: | 9.4% of payroll |
| government: | annual subsidy equivalent to 2.3% of national budget |
| 13. *Sweden* | |
| insured person: | universal pension, no contribution (employees) self-employed—4.2% of assessable income.<br>earnings related pension: no contribution (employees); contribution of self-employed equal to employer contribution |
| employer: | universal pension, 4.2% of wages<br>earnings related pension—10.75% of wages/employee between base amount and 7.5 times base amount |
| government: | universal pension, about 55% of cost<br>no contribution for earnings related pension |
| 14. *Switzerland* | |
| insured person: | 4.2% of earnings (employee)<br>self-employed—7.3% of income; non-working persons with income also contribute |
| employer: | 4.2% of payroll |
| government: | amount equal to about 20% of cost |

Source: U.S. Department of Health, Education, and Welfare, Social Security Administration, Office of Research and Statistics *Social Security Programs Throughout the World*, HEW Pub. No. (SSA) 76-11805 (Washington: U.S. Government Printing Office, 1976).

Still another approach is to reduce the tax rate by transferring Medicare (HI) financing to general revenues. The 1978 level of the HI tax rate is 1 percent to each side, scheduled to rise to 1.45 percent by

1986 (self-employed workers pay only half of the total HI tax, whereas they are scheduled to return to payment of two-thirds of the OASDI tax). In 1977 certain previously scheduled increases in the HI tax were reallocated to OASDI—another example of "solving" problems by changes in accounting procedure. Since Medicare eligibility and need have nothing to do with a worker's earning history, there is no inherent logic in financing Medicare through a percentage payroll tax. A flat tax would do, or, if progressivity is desired, financing could come from general revenues. The latter suggestion was made by the 1975 Advisory Council.[19] and has considerable merit. Should the United States ever adopt a national health insurance system, the issue of how to finance it will have to be faced anyway—it would make little sense to separate health insurance for the aged from health insurance for everyone else.

In 1979, proposals were made in Congress to finance all or part of Social Security by the imposition of a federal Value Added Tax (VAT). Details of the proposals were not available at the time that this book went to press, so that a thorough analysis of them cannot be made here. However, some general comments may be useful.

VAT behaves like a general sales tax. As such, it tends to fall relatively more heavily on lower income households, since they consume a greater proportion of their income than higher income households. Whether or not it is more or less regressive than the existing payroll tax depends on how it is structured. For example, higher rates on luxury goods or lower rates on necessities can reduce the regressive feature of VAT. The extent to which VAT is more or less regressive than the payroll tax is an important issue in any evaluation of the proposal.

The general argument in favor of VAT is that it taxes consumption rather than income from production. It follows that taxes on savings are deferred until the savings are spent on consumption. Hence, at any point in time, VAT encourages saving as compared to a tax on income. Proponents of VAT argue that saving needs to be encouraged in order to form productive capital for future economic growth.

An extensive evaluation of VAT is beyond the scope of this work, although we may note that savings can be encouraged under an income tax system by the creation of tax shelters. Indeed, many such shelters now exist, including occupational pensions that defer taxes on pension fund contributions and earnings.

For our purposes, it is important to realize that there is no *a priori* reason to earmark VAT for Social Security. In Europe, where VAT is prevalent, it usually substitutes in part or in whole for corporate income taxes. It helps to pay for social benefits only to the extent that these are financed from general revenues.

The recent complaints about high Social Security taxes have made Social Security a target of opportunity for those who advocate VAT. This tax can receive support from high-paid employees and from employers who cannot (or believe that they cannot) shift their share of the payroll tax backward to their employees.

However, those who believe that benefits and contributions should be linked will notice that the substitution of VAT for payroll taxes further attenuates this link. I have not heard of any proposal to link benefits to VAT payments. This would defeat the purpose of the exercise by encouraging consumption instead of saving. If benefits continue to be based on the earnings histories of workers, then financing by VAT will introduce the element of "welfarism" that Congress has previously found to be so objectionable.

#### The Regressive Nature of the Tax

A common objection to the Social Security tax is that it is regressive. Even if we leave aside the question of who pays the employer's share, the employees' share takes a greater proportion of income from persons at the low end of the income distribution than from the high end. More strictly speaking, the tax is proportional with respect to labor earnings up to the wage base, and it become regressive past that point. As shown earlier, that point is moving upward along the earnings distribution, so that the point of regressivity will reach the 91st percentile of earners by 1981. However, if the Social Security tax is considered together with the income tax, then the earned income credit helps to offset the Social Security tax for low-earning families with children. Accordingly, the Social Security tax, in such cases, is close to zero for earnings below $4,000, becomes progressive between $4,000 and $8,000 (the phase-out point of the earned income credit), proportional from $8,000 to the wage base, and regressive thereafter.

The concept of regressivity (or progressivity) commonly refers to all income, and not merely to labor earnings. Since the Social Security tax is not levied on income from capital, it becomes regressive before the wage base is reached. This is because, as we move up along the earnings distribution, we encounter more assets that yield income that is not subject to the payroll tax. Since much of wealth holding is concentrated in the upper tail of the income distribution, regressivity becomes more pronounced the farther up we go. Thus, even if all labor earnings were subject to the tax, it would retain its regressive character.

The upward move in the wage base reduces the degree of regressivity as the rate reaches higher incomes. Take the case of someone who, in 1977, earned $29,700 per year. This is the maximum wage base scheduled for 1981, after which automatic adjustments will apply. Assume that the earner will receive annual salary increases of 6 percent per year. As seen in Table 6-6, the percentage of *earnings* taxed (employee's share only) rises from 3.25 percent in 1977 to 5.27 percent in 1981. The percentage of earnings taxed for people at or below the wage base also rises during this period, from 5.85 percent to 6.65 percent, but at a considerably less rapid rate. In a relative sense, therefore, an element of progressivity is introduced. Inasmuch as wage earners above the wage base generally have higher capital incomes and higher untaxed fringe benefits than those below the wage base, the net effect is still regressive, only less so than before the 1977 amendments.

If the Social Security tax is viewed together with benefits over an earner's lifetime, then the progressive nature of the benefit structure helps to offset the regressivity of the tax. The benefit scale enacted in 1977 is sharply progressive at the bottom with respect to AIME (90 percent of the first $180 per month). The next bracket is a broad one (37 percent of the next $905 per month), and will cover a substantial part of the population. At the top bracket, the benefit rate drops to 15 percent of indexed earnings between $1,085 and the wage base. Strictly speaking, the maximum benefit is never attainable at the point of retirement because of lower indexed earnings in the years prior to retirement, the nature of the calculation that confines averaging to the period between ages twenty-one and sixty-two, and the lag in the indexing process that ceases to inflate earnings two years

**TABLE 6-6** Percent of Earnings Taxed (Employee's Share), Earners at or Below Wage Base, and Earner at $29,700 in 1977, with Annual Salary Increases of 6%, 1977–81

| Year | Tax Rate on Wage Base | Tax Rate on $29,700 with Earnings Rising at 6% |
|---|---|---|
| 1977 | 5.85 | 3.25 |
| 1978 | 6.05 | 3.40 |
| 1979 | 6.13 | 4.21 |
| 1980 | 6.13 | 4.49 |
| 1981 | 6.65 | 5.27 |

Source: Computed from Social Security Administration, *Legislative Report*, No. 17, Table 1.

before retirement. Thus, the high earners get a relatively lower rate of return on their Social Security "savings" and, of course, receive no Social Security benefits for incomes that were not subject to the payroll tax.

On net balance, the system remains somewhat redistributive between earners. Whether or not this is vertically equitable is a matter of individual ethical taste. All we note here is that, notwithstanding the regressive nature of the Social Security tax, the total system redistributes income downward. For some observers the degree of redistribution may be insufficient or excessive. There are others who argue that Social Security, taken by itself, should not be redistributive. Among them are writers who, like Munnell, believe that income redistribution should take place in our economy, but through mechanisms other than Social Security.[20] However desirable this may be, it would mark a shift from the goals developed by the founders of the system.

## THE TRUST FUND

The crisis that led to the 1977 amendments focused upon the rapid depletion of the OASI (and DI) Trust Fund. As shown in an earlier chapter, the original fund established by the 1935 act was intended to be actuarily sound, in a manner analogous to an insurance reserve. The shift to pay-as-you-go financing in 1939 removed this function. The fear of "bankruptcy" that was expressed so frequently in the 1976 and 1977 debates over reform indicates that the change in function was not understood by many people. This may be because the change had not been explained.

It may be useful to recapitulate the pay-as-you-go mechanism. The Internal Revenue Service collects a payroll tax and credits the fund. The fund, in turn, makes the necessary disbursements. Any surplus of revenues over disbursements is invested in federal bonds that are purchased directly from the U.S. Treasury. The surplus revenues themselves enter into the stream of general federal revenues, and are used for general purposes. The bonds constitute a claim against future government revenues to be derived from future general taxes—not from the Social Security tax.

So long as revenues exceeded disbursements, the fund could increase. When disbursements began to grow faster than revenues, bonds were redeemed. The interest on the bonds came from general taxes, and the redemptions, taking place when the government generally had budget deficits, were a shift of debt holding from the fund to private lenders. The process of redemption in periods of budget deficit had the effect of increasing the effective liabilities of the government.

If the fund is not an insurance reserve, one can infer other functions for it. The first of these, quite simply, is an accounting device. It separates earmarked taxes and specialized disbursements. This is necessary as long as Social Security, like the construction of interstate highway systems, is perceived as somehow different from other operations of government. The device thus serves to reinforce the mythic or symbolic value of Social Security alluded to above.

A second, and more important, function is to act as a buffer fund. In the ordinary course of operations, inflows of revenue do not necessarily match outflows of expenditures at any moment in time. If the mismatch were a simple seasonal one, it could be bridged either by using a small buffer or by short-term borrowing. However, there are times when the mismatch is considerable because of large swings in unemployment (which reduces revenues) or inflation (which increases expenditures by raising benefits). Again, if the phenomenon is temporary, it can be handled by borrowing, which was proposed by President Carter. If borrowing is politically unacceptable because it introduces general revenues, then the buffer must be great enough to withstand economic shocks of more than seasonal magnitude.

In this respect, the buffer function resembles a bank reserve, not a pension fund. The latter must be actuarily sound against the event that enterprise may close, ending revenues immediately but having a further obligation to pay off pensioners. A bank reserve, beyond the money needed for day-to-day variations in business, must be in relatively liquid form and sufficiently large to provide for unanticipated withdrawals. No such reserve can ever be large enough to protect against the contingency that all depositors want their money at the same time. Analogously, Social Security does not worry about a "run on the bank," because individuals can claim benefits only when they meet the criteria of age, disability, or death of a spouse. However, a contingency reserve or buffer that is too small cannot function well.

In 1977 the size of the OASDI fund at the beginning of the year was 47 percent of outlays made during that year,[21] considerably lower than the comfortable 101 percent of 1968.[22] Although this decline will continue until 1979 and 1980, the 1977 amendments are expected to rebuild the fund to 59 percent in 1987.[23] In the absence of the law, the DI Fund would have been exhausted in 1979, and the OASI Fund would have expired in the early 1980s.

This brings us to the third function. The fund is a barometer. A persistent fall in the fund—or, in the future, a persistent failure to achieve a target size—is a signal that something must be done. The expected exhaustion of the fund compelled a reluctant Congress to legislate changes. Furthermore, the warning signal allows for some time to plan changes. The last decline in the fund began in 1971, when it stood at 98 percent, down from 103 percent in 1968. By 1974 the ratio was down to 73 percent,[24] and it became apparent that the decline was not temporary.

The function—accounting, buffer, barometer—could be performed in other ways. It is the political need to make Social Security self-supporting that makes separate funding such a handy device. A declining fund draws attention to itself, and the system's operational statistics are not simply buried in the mass of data found in federal budget analyses.[25]

The foregoing analysis is broad, and more detail on the operations of the fund may be useful to the reader. I have lumped the OASI and DI Trust Funds together and it should be remembered that, in practice, the two funds are separate, and that Health Insurance (HI) and Supplementary Medical Insurance have their own funds. The discussion below focuses on the OASI Trust Fund.[26]

The receipts of the fund come from four sources. The first and foremost is the contributions collected by the Internal Revenue Service and the deposits arising from state agreements. The latter are reported separately because, legally speaking, coverage of state (and local) public workers is by agreement between sovereign entities. The agreements are revokable by the states. Although nonprofit institutions are also covered voluntarily by revokable agreements, contributions from that source are not broken out in the Trustees' Statement of Operations, presumably because there is no Constitutional question about the federal power to tax such entities. The federal government is barred from taxing states (but it is free to tax employees of states and their subdivisions). In any event, net contributions in Fiscal Year 1976 came to $59.5 billion.

The second source of receipts is interest on the assets of the Trust Fund. The assets consist of Treasury notes and bonds, including special issues available only to the fund, and investments in federally sponsored agency obligations. The special issues constituted 89.4 percent of total assets as of June 30, 1976, and agency obligations were a negligible proportion of the total. The special issues are heavily used because they are exempt from statutory restrictions on the amount of bonds paying more than 4¼ percent that can be held by the public. Special issues purchased in June 1976 yielded 7½ percent. The effective rate of return on all assets in FY 1976 was 6.8 percent. Interest income that year totaled $2.46 billion.

The interest rate on special issues is based on the average market yield on federal obligations that are not due or callable for four years. This has enabled the fund to take advantage of rising interest rates and to acquire a portfolio that produces more advantageous yields than those available to private investors. The latter cannot easily assemble an equivalent portfolio of assets and are, in any event, likely to be concerned with the marketability of their securities. The fund does not worry about marketability or capital gains and losses.[27]

The main purpose of the special issues is to keep the fund out of the open market. Although Section 201(d) of the Social Security Act permits the purchase and sale of assets by the fund, the enormous flows of cash involved could seriously disturb the money markets. Accordingly, the fund no longer enters the market, except on occasions when the Treasury refinances maturing public obligations that the fund might hold. Additionally, the fund never sells any of its public issues. All transactions are handled by the Treasury; the trust's Managing Trustee is the Secretary of the Treasury.

A third but much less significant source of income to the fund consists of certain reimbursements to it from general revenues. These cover the cost of benefits to transitionally insured workers who reached age seventy-two before 1969, of the wage credits granted to persons in military service between 1947 and 1956, and the wage credits given to Americans of Japanese ancestry who were interned during World War II. The last of these, although referred to in the Trustees' Report of 1977, is not carried on its Statement of Operations. The total contribution from general revenues in FY 1976 was $425 million.

As an aside, it may be noted that other instances of "blanketing in" persons who were not previously covered have not involved contributions from general revenues. Has this been done, the fund would have been in a less critical position in the mid-1970s. As it is, Congress apparently does not consider the present general revenue contributions as a serious departure from the principle of self-financing.

The last, and by far the least, source of income to the fund consists of gifts. The fund is empowered to accept gifts and bequests, and actually receives some. In FY 1976, gifts amounted to about $34,000. This was a 143 percent increase over the previous year's $14,000, perhaps reflecting a heightened concern by a few public-spirited citizens about the soundness of the fund.

On the expenditure side, the main outlay of the fund is for benefits. These amounted to $62 million in FY 1976, plus $1.2 million in transfers to the Railroad Retirement Account. A second expense is for the cost of vocational rehabilitation that is chargeable to OASI rather than DI (as, for example, for persons disabled as children who are entitled to benefits on their parents' accounts). This came to $7.5 million in FY 1976. Finally, administrative expenses are charged to the fund. In FY 1976 net administrative expenses came to $935 million, or about 1.5 percent of receipts. This indicates one advantage that social insurance has over public assistance: The cost of administration is relatively low.

### The Future of the Trust Fund

Since the fund serves as a barometer that can predict oncoming problems, it may be useful to look into the future to gauge the extent to which the 1977 amendments have solved the recent crisis. However speculative such crystal ball gazing might be, all of us have some need to predict the future in order to make even current plans, and most of us do. The need is not confined to social policymakers but extends to individuals and business enterprises as well. The need is especially acute when dealing with retirement programs, because these have a built-in tendency to mature. This means that operations in an early point in time will differ from those at a later time.

The OASI Fund in the 1970s faced some short-term and long-term problems. The primary short-term problems resulted from unexpectedly high inflation, which led to automatic increases in benefits, and unexpectedly high unemployment, which reduced tax revenues. The higher tax rates and the increased wage base of the 1977 act should get the fund through the short term. However, there is some possibility of a crunch in the early 1980s, when the Fund will reach its low point (see Figure 6-1). A combination of inflation and high unemployment can reduce the Fund's ratio of assets to disbursements to a danger point.

The two long-term problems were the overindexing of benefits and the demographic "hump" that will occur as the war babies reach retirement age in the next century. The first of these problems, which accounted for half of the projected long-term benefits, was corrected by the 1977 amendment that "decoupled" the tax and benefit structure so that beneficiaries will no longer be compensated twice for inflation. Faced with choices between essentially two decoupling schemes, Congress chose the wage indexing method rather than the price indexing method. The former will cause a smaller reduction in percent of earnings replaced by Social Security, at a correspondingly higher future cost. The second problem was reduced in magnitude but not entirely solved. It was left to the next generation.

To elaborate, the decoupling device reduces future costs by reducing benefits below what they would have been under the 1972 law. Table 6–7 compares the change in replacement rates for three earnings groups between 1979 and 2000, using the actuarial assumptions of the Social Security Administration. The three groups are the SSA's low income group, average earners, and those always at the maximum.

As can be seen, low and average earners face a 10 percent decline in their replacement rates. Those whose earnings histories will entitle them to maximum attainable benefits will face a 26 percent drop in their replacement rates. The primary purpose of this action regarding high earners may have been to preserve the financing of the system, but it also reflects the goal of social adequacy. High earners are presumed to need less, as they should be able to supplement their retirement income from other sources.[28]

The Social Security Administration has projected the future of the fund, taking into consideration the net effect of the changes in the 1977 act. The assumptions underlying their projections are somewhat optimistic regarding future rates of inflation and unemployment.[29] In evaluating these projections, the reader must decide whether the assumptions err on the side of optimism or pessimism. If they are unduly optimistic, the fund's next crisis will occur sooner than expected. If the assumptions are overly conservative, the crisis will occur later. Either way, a crisis will occur unless preventive action is taken.

The SSA actually has three sets of assumptions, although it uses the intermediate set for most of its projections. The first and third set of alternatives are more and less optimistic, respectively, than the intermediate set. The alternative assumptions are a valuable tool for monitoring the progress of the fund and anticipating problems. Under all assumptions in use, the fund is due to expire sometime in the twenty-first century. The question is not whether, but when.

This can be seen by examining the projected ratio between the OASI Fund at the beginning of each year and disbursement during

**TABLE 6-7** Earnings Groups and Replacement Rates, Retirement at 65 (Earnings in Prior Years)

| | Low Earners | Replacement Rate | Average Earners | Replacement Rate | High Earners | Replacement Rate |
|---|---|---|---|---|---|---|
| 1979 | $ 5,271 | 59.6% | $10,572 | 46.7% | $17,700 | 34.8% |
| 2000 | 17,753 | 53.6 | 35,609 | 41.8 | 83,400 | 25.7[a] |
| Decline in replacement rate 1979–2000 | | 10.1% | | 10.5% | | 26.1% |

[a]Will ultimately stabilize at 28%.

Source: A. Haeworth Robertson, "The Financial Status of Social Security After the Social Security Amendments of 1977" (Baltimore: Social Security Administration, processed, January 1978), p. 7.

the year using the intermediate assumptions for future years. This is shown in Figure 6-1. In 1981 the ratio begins its rise from a skimpy 26 percent to a comfortable 99 percent in 1991. At its peak, in 2010, the fund is projected to reach a ratio of 398 percent, or close to four times annual disbursement. The year 2010 is exactly sixty-five years after the end of World War II. Thereafter, the decline sets in, accelerating rapidly after 2010. In 2028, the fund will be exhausted. The Disability Insurance Fund will expire twenty years before that. It should be stressed that these are the SSA's own projections, not mine. Congress presumably has access to the same information.

Another way of looking at this is to express the difference between expenditures and tax revenues as a percentage of taxable payroll. This avoids the difficulties introduced by the depreciation of our currency over time. The Social Security Administration's projections of this actuarial balance for the OASI Fund are shown in Table 6-8. For the period 1977–2051, the fund is projected to show an imbalance of 1.08 percent. This seems like a small amount, but a closer look shows that the principal imbalance is concentrated in the second quarter of the twenty-first century.

Table 6-8 also shows projections for the combined OASDI Funds (that is, including Disability Insurance) and the Health Insurance (HI) Fund. The latter shows a negative balance for all time periods. The combined OASDI Funds show an average imbalance of 1.46 percent, a figure that has been widely used to indicate that the prob-

**FIGURE 6-1** Estimated OASI Trust Fund Ratios (Funds at the Beginning of Year as Percentage of Disbursements During the Year)

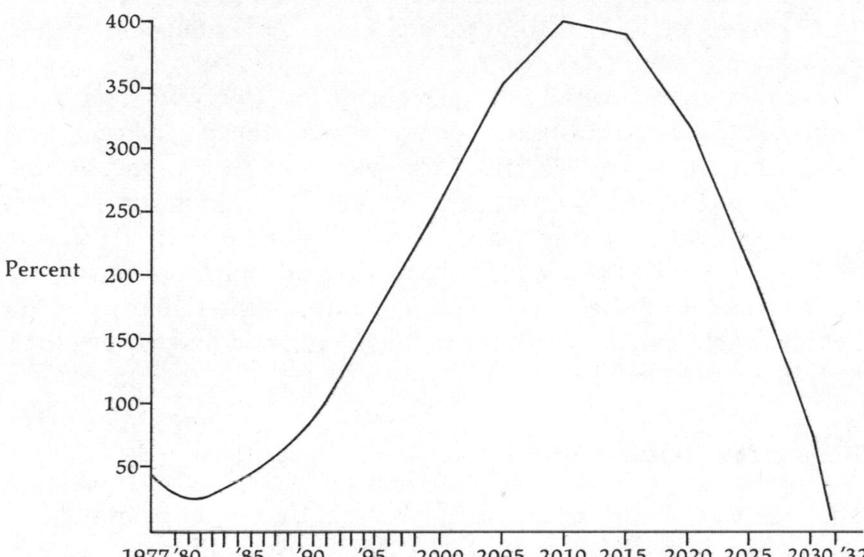


Source: "Table 8—Estimated Trust Fund Ratio for the OASDI System Under the Social Security Act as Amended through Public Law 25-216, Calendar Years 1977-2035," Office of the Actuary, Social Security Administration, February 2, 1978, p. 21.

**TABLE 6-8** Projected Difference Between Income and Expenditures, as Percentage of Taxable Payroll, OASI, OASDI, and HI

| Time Period | OASI | OASDI | HI |
|---|---|---|---|
| 1977–2051 | −1.08% | −1.46% | −3.04% |
| 1977–2001 | 0.89 | 0.97 | −0.90 |
| 2002–2026 | −0.39 | −1.06 | −3.58 |
| 2027–2051 | −3.73 | −4.29 | −4.63 |

Source: Robertson, "Financial Status of Social Security," pp. 18–32.

lem is trivial. However, in the second quarter of the Twenty-first century the imbalance is 4.29 percent. If we add the 4.63 percent imbalance in HI, we find that Social Security taxes would have to rise by close to nine percentage points unless corrective action is taken before that time.

The combined Social Security tax is legislated to be 15.3 percent in 1990, divided equally between employers and employees (10.75

percent for the self-employed). The additional tax needed will be 8.92 percent. When added to the 15.3 percent, we get a payroll tax of 24.22 percent or 12.11 percent for employers and employees. This is not a trivial amount.

Certainly, the overall 1.46 percent deficit in the OASDI Fund represents a considerable improvement over the 8.2 percent projected under the pre-1977 law. More will need to be done. As the former Chief Actuary of the Social Security Administration has pointed out, "It should be noted that a substantial projected deficit of 4.29 percent of taxable payroll in the latter third of the 75-year period remains unresolved. Casual references to the 1.46 percent 'actuarial deficit' may tend to obscure the timing and magnitude of the remaining problem."[30]

## PROBLEMS IN TODAY'S FINANCING

Discussions of financing can easily distract the reader from the real problems that Social Security faces. The Trust Fund, as stated earlier, is an accounting device, a short-term buffer, and a barometer. Projections of the Trust Fund are complex guesses about future price levels, labor force sizes and participation rates, unemployment rates, immigration and future fertility rates. The last two determine future population sizes and age distributions. Other variables, such as possible changes in life expectancy, are also included. In short, projecting the future size of the Trust Fund is basically an attempt to obtain a future barometer reading.

To get at the real problem, let us recapitulate the essence of a pay-as-you-go system. The Social Security tax is a current tax, like any other tax. Those who bear the burden of the tax are thereby foreclosed from buying goods and services, or engaging in private saving, to the extent of the tax. This releases resources that are converted into goods and services used by the current generation of beneficiaries.

If the age distribution of the population were stable, the tax would simply be a transfer of income from each working generation to its elders. Although each worker might look upon the tax as a form of saving invested as an annuity, the total tax contributions by and for workers does not constitute saving in any real sense. The annuity is not secured by assets such as machinery, housing, and raw materials, that is, assets that can produce a future flow of real goods, and therefore, real income. Instead, it is secured by the power of government to levy future taxes. In a mature system, and given a stable distribution of age groups in the population, it is possible to establish tax and benefit levels so that the taxes just pay for the benefits.

In such a case, temporary imbalances can occur. These can be handled by the creation of a buffer fund of modest size—perhaps a half-year's benefit payments. This complicates the explanation, but only slightly. A buffer fund (in fact, the Trust Fund) can hold government securities. If it does, then it may represent some national saving, provided that private investors who would otherwise have bought these bonds now buy private sector securities. The latter, unlike government bonds, are claims against the income of real capital. However, the amount of this national saving is trivial. Accordingly, beneficiaries are not drawing upon accumulated savings, although they may think so.

Just as the Social Security tax is a current tax and not an investment in real assets, the benefits are also current. They represent claims against goods and services that are currently produced in the economy, with the economy's current stock of capital, resources, and labor. This point cannot be stressed too much. Given the stock of resources with which the nation is endowed, our ability to redistribute income (that is, real goods and services) to the aged and other dependents depends on the quality and quantity of our labor and capital, the extent to which they are utilized, and our willingness to make a redistribution. The willingness is constrained by our output.

In a capitalist economy, claims against output by owners of capital are not considered redistributions.[31] Vested rights in employment-related pensions fall into this category, being akin to the ownership of property. Social Security is a redistribution of income, and much of the redistribution is across generations. Confusion arises because this redistribution apparently takes the form of a property right, but it is a redistribution nonetheless.

Over time, the economy's output changes, and with it the amount that can be redistributed across generations. The age distribution of the population also changes, and with it the relative number of retired persons to whom income needs to be redistributed. It may therefore be impossible to devise a Social Security system that can maintain a stable redistribution of income in the face of these changes. Small fluctuations can be smoothed out by the buffer fund, but large ones cannot. The recognition of this problem is recent, conspicuously absent in the discussions by the founders of Social Security.

To clarify this further, it is instructive to ask why the system has been successful in paying such a high rate of return on the "investments" in Social Security made by the previous and present groups of retirees. Three forces were at work to do this.[32] These were the "start-up" phenomenon, the high rate of per capita economic growth, and the low ratio of retirees to workers.

The start-up phenomenon refers to the shorter amounts of time during which workers needed to pay Social Security in order to achieve maximum coverage. At the polar extreme, workers who began paying taxes in 1937 at age sixty-two became eligible for benefits in 1940. Contributions of $68.36 would have been made for a worker of average earnings during 1937–40. At going rates of interest, this would have yielded an annuity of $6.59 per year. Average benefits, however, were $270.60 per year. With only three years of coverage and tax contributions, this average worker obviously got a very good deal. Similar start-up phenomena occurred as coverage was extended to new workers by "blanketing" them in.

By 1978 the maximum period of coverage for persons retiring at sixty-five had risen to forty-one years. Since most workers can be expected to spend about forty-five years in the labor market, the effect of the start-up phenomenon is almost exhausted. Furthermore, there is little scope for further "blanketing" in of uncovered workers, since 90 percent of workers now belong to the system. The largest group without coverage consists of federal employees. Whether or not they would benefit from start-ups, if included in the system, would depend on the terms of the inclusion. It seems unlikely that inclusion, if it ever occurred, would consist of simply adding Social Security benefits to federal pensions.

The second reason for the system's ability to pay beneficiaries more than their tax contributions (plus market rates of interest) was the high growth in real per capita Gross National Product since the system began. Between 1940 and 1970 real per capita GNP grew on average 2.4 percent per year. This led to a growth in real wages that could be taxed in a relatively painless fashion and used to pay more and better benefits. The 1970s have shown a significantly lower rate of growth and concommitantly lower increases in real wages. Indeed, private nonagricultural wages, in 1967 dollars, declined by an average of 0.4 percent during 1970–76, in contrast to an average increase of 1.48 percent during 1960–69.

If this stagnation persists, then payroll taxes to make intergenerational transfers will become increasingly difficult to levy. A return to a better rate of economic growth is needed merely to slow down the rate at which the system will fall behind in its obligations. As indicated elsewhere in this book, growth would need to include more capital accumulation in order to produce the future flows of goods to be consumed by the retired population.

The third reason for the system's success in its premature years was a demographic situation that was slightly more favorable than the present one, and considerably more favorable than the one we shall face when the war babies mature. Table 6-9 shows the average number of workers it took to support one person aged sixty-five or more in selected years. It simplifies matters somewhat by assuming that the working population consisted of all persons aged twenty to sixty-four and that all persons over sixty-five were retired.

As can be seen, this number was declining even before the advent of Social Security, having fallen from 12.5 in 1900 to 8.3 in 1940. This is a long-term trend that merely reflects the gradual aging of the population, due to declining fertility rates and increasing life expectancies at birth. It tells us that over time, the burden of supporting the elderly that is borne by the working population would have increased in any event.

The long-term trend was interrupted by a sharp upward shift in the fertility rate following World War II and a sharp decline thereafter. The upswing has had two effects. The first is to maintain the ratio of about five prime age workers to every person over sixty-five until the beginning of the twenty-first century, regardless of what happens to the fertility rate in the meantime (assuming no change in immigration and no catastrophes). The second is to reduce the number of workers it takes to support each aged person during the time it

**TABLE 6-9** Average Number of Persons Aged 20–64 Needed to Support One Person Aged 65-plus

| Year | Number |
|---|---|
| 1900 | 12.5 |
| 1930 | 10.0 |
| 1940 | 8.3 |
| 1950 | 7.1 |
| 1975 | 5.3 |

Source: 1900–1950, computed from U.S. Bureau of the Census, *Historical Statistics of the United States* (Washington: U.S. Government Printing Office, 1960), p. 10. 1975, computed from 1977 *Annual Report of the Board of Trustees, OASDI*, p. 63.

will take the war babies to pass through the elderly stage of their lives. This second effect would be occurring even if fertility rates had resumed their long-term trend.

The sharp fall in fertility adds a further twist. This is because fewer births now mean relatively fewer future workers to support the aged who will still be alive. Figure 6-2 shows the average number of workers needed to support one aged person under the three assumptions about future fertility rates that are used by the Social Security Actuary. Under the usual assumption that fertility will move toward 2.1 births per woman, the number of workers it takes to support one retiree will begin a significant decline in 2000 from 4.9 to a trough of 2.9 in 2035 and rising back to 3.27 in 2050.

To give meaning to these numbers, consider that only three workers will be available to support each retired person, at the point where the peak of the demographic wave passes through retirement. This is an enormous burden to place on the future population. The Social Security tax and benefit structure established in 1977 will not suffice, since the Trust Fund will have been exhausted by then. Should births persist at a lower rate, then the burden on each worker will be considerably greater.[33]

The prospects for the long term are subject to factors that can worsen or mitigate the expected problems. The demographic projections alone do not tell the whole story.[34] The probable outcomes are sensitive to such things as future LFPRs of older workers, young people, and women, as well as the extent of such participation—whether full time or part time. Expected rates of unemployment, in-

**FIGURE 6-2** Projected Average Number of Persons Aged 20-64 Needed to Support One Person Aged 65+, Under Three Assumptions About Fertility Rates, 1980-2055

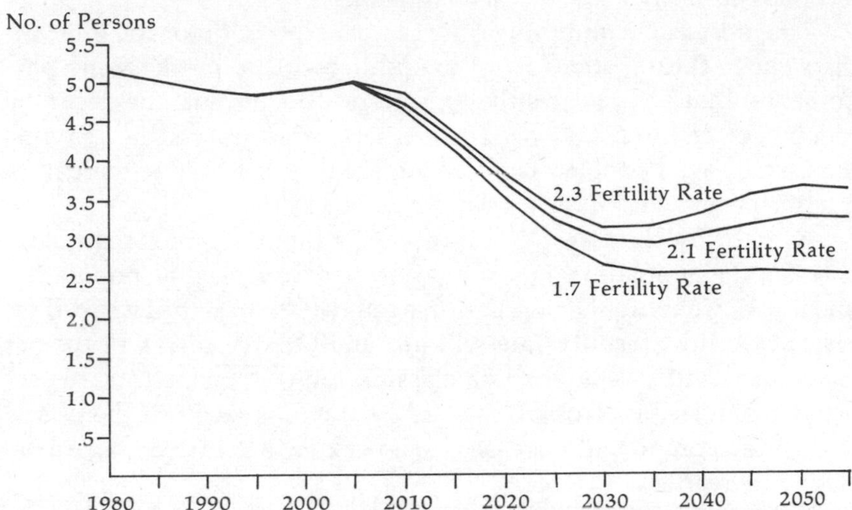


Source: "1977 Annual Report of the Board of Trustees of the Federal Old-Age and Survivors Insurance and Disability Insurance Trust Funds," Social Security Administration, Washington, D.C. (U.S. Government Printing Office: 1977), Appendix Table B, Projections of the U.S. Population by Broad Age Groups, p. 63.

flation, and real economic growth also matter. Most of these variables appear as assumptions in projections of the future of the Trust Fund.

For example, the current trend toward early retirement can, if it accelerates, speed up the advent of the next crisis by increasing the size of the actual dependent population. The same would be true if younger people delay their entry into the labor market at greater rates than at present. This trend can also increase the size of the dependent population. It is possible, of course, that the trend toward early retirement may reverse itself. The raising of the mandatory retirement age from sixty-five to seventy may delay retirements. By the end of the century, the relative shortage of older and experienced workers may raise their wages, thus holding some in the labor market for a longer period of time.

Similarly, the future role of women in the labor market is anyone's guess. The Bureau of Labor Statistics estimates that the percent of women in the labor force will rise from 46.3 percent in 1975 to

51.4 percent in 1990.[35] A previous projection, made in 1973, underestimated the female labor force participation rate, and current projections can easily make the same mistake.

The most important mitigating factor, especially for the intermediate range future, stems from the falling birthrate—the same phenomenon that complicates the long term. Simply put, the declining number of children that need to be supported offsets the growing number of aged people. This can be seen by looking at the demographic projections of the total dependency ratio.

As used by the OASDI Trustees, this figure expresses the ratio between the population aged sixty-five and over plus the population under age twenty to the population aged twenty to sixty-four.[36] If we assume that the fertility rate will gradually move to 2.1 births per woman by 2005 (the intermediate assumption), then the total dependency ratio declines from .829 in 1975 to .662 in 2010. It then rises, as the aged component increases, to a peak of .828 in 2035, again declining thereafter.

If the 2.1 fertility assumption proves to be correct, then the burden on the age twenty to sixty-four group of supporting both the young and the old will return to 1975 levels only once. To put it another way, the average number of people in the twenty to sixty-four age group who share the burden of supporting all dependents will rise from 1.2 in 1975 to 1.5 in 2010, returning to 1.2 in the peak year of 2035, and rising to 1.3 in 2050. It can be argued that if the nation was capable of supporting its dependents in 1975, it should be capable of doing so again at some future point if the burden on the working population is no greater.

In real terms, this means that resources that are not needed for the young can be reallocated for use by the aged. The usual way of getting a reallocation is through the market mechanism. There, consumers use their income to bid for the goods and services they want, and sellers respond by shifting the quantity and array of goods that they offer. In this case, however, the market mechanism cannot make the reallocation. This is because much of the income of the aged depends on Social Security, which relies on the willingness of the population to be taxed. Thus, even though the resources may be available, their transfer from the young to the old becomes a political rather than an economic issue.

The political factor is likely to be quite powerful. There may be many reasons why families choose to have fewer children, but such reasons probably include the desire for a higher standard of living for themselves and their children. If real incomes rise over the long run, then there is reason to believe that expenditures per child will increase.[37] If this is the case, then parents will be unenthusiastic about taxes that deprive them of their family's ability to consume more in order that resources can be transferred to the elderly.

### The Problem of the Future

By now it should be evident that even a Congress consisting of Solons and Solomons cannot create a Social Security system on a once-and-for-all basis. It is a common human experience that promises made now cannot always be kept in the future—ask any holder of Penn Central bonds. But there is a difference between private and social commitments. The worker whose pension fund holds Penn Central bonds did not purchase them individually, nor did he voluntarily undertake the risk. Not surprisingly, the pension reform act (ERISA) affords him some protection. The Social Security taxpayer has even less choice. The tax is compulsory, and benefits in a pay-as-you-go system must come from future taxes, levied on future generations in an unpredictable political climate. The founders of Social Security hoped to remove this uncertainty. They failed.

It will be recalled that current benefits are always spent on goods that are, for the most part, currently produced. Some durables, like housing, can be stocked for the future. Most goods cannot be saved up. Attempts to mitigate the uncertainty of future benefits must look toward the size of future output of goods and services, their allocation among different uses, and their distribution among different generations.

Although distribution is a political issue, there is some economic scope available for redistribution to the elderly. This comes from the favorable total dependency ratio that will ensue if the fertility rate gradually moves from 1.7 births per woman to 2.1 births. Should the rate move higher, this scope is diminished for the next seventy-five years but enhanced thereafter (to take a long view) as the additional children enter the labor market. The reverse is true should the fertility rate persist at levels close to the present. Indeed, the long-range implications of such a low rate are unthinkable. It literally implies a population that will die out in time unless replenished by immigration and strenuous domestic pronatalist policies.

This brings us to questions of future output. One question deals with future allocation of output between those goods that are directly usable by consumers and those that are not. The latter include government goods, such as defense production, and capital goods. Only consumer goods can be redistributed, except that services like public health care and education may be substitutes for what people would ordinarily buy on the open market. Capital goods, however, have the property of being able to produce more consumer goods, so that increasing the stock of capital can increase the future output of consumer goods.[38]

Given any allocation between public and private sector goods, what is needed is a policy that generates enough economic growth to provide satisfactory levels of income for both the working population (and their children) and the retired population. This is what proposals for full or higher funding of the Trust Fund are all about. The essence of the proposals is to increase national saving in the expectation that this will increase the capital stock and future output.

Unfortunately, the present state of economic science is not very helpful in the design of such a policy. There is some consensus that relatively lower government deficits would increase national savings, investment, and output. However, this rests on the proposition of full employment without continued deficits.[39] It may well be that economists of the stagnant 1970s are, like their 1930s counterparts, unduly pessimistic. The leading candidate for a policy that might yield price stability, high employment, and economic growth is incomes policy—wage and price restraint. This proposal is not only controversial among economists; it is heartily opposed by business and labor as well.

Thus the search for a policy to secure the long-range future of Social Security coincides with the search for a policy to promote and sustain higher levels of economic growth. The bigger the economic pie, the bigger the slices. There is nothing like a growing pie to make people happier and more altruistic about a redistribution of income.

## FINANCING SOCIAL SECURITY FOR CAPITAL ACCUMULATION

In an earlier section of the book, it was noted that exclusive reliance on equally divided payroll taxes might not be the best way to finance Social Security. The discussion assumed that Social Security, whatever other vices it might have, did not diminish the supply of capital to the United States and thereby reduce our standard of living. If it does, changes are needed, because a system that make more people worse off than better off leaves something to be desired.

The major proposal for reform comes from Feldstein, who argued that his studies showed a serious loss of savings and capital investment, and therefore lower income, as a result of the pay-as-you-go method of financing. Although the evidence on the subject is still inconclusive, it will be useful here to review his proposal for full funding on the chance that he may, after all, be right.[40] Variants on the proposal will also be discussed below.

The essence of Feldstein's proposal is the creation of a fully funded system in place of the present pay-as-you-go system. This requires a Trust Fund that is far more than a contingency reserve, one so large that its earnings will pay current benefits. Once the fund is in place, there would no longer be a need to levy payroll taxes until the cohort of post–World War II births reaches retirement. At that point or earlier (in anticipation of the event), payroll taxes would be needed to rebuild the fund and enable it to survive the demographic "hump." Thereafter, payroll taxes could again be abolished and could remain abolished if the age distribution of future populations remains stable. The creation of such a fund would add to national savings and partially offset the loss of saving that is attributed to the system.

This method of financing may be called the investment method, and Feldstein reasons that it is preferable to the pay-as-you-go method. He arrives at his conclusions through a theoretical analysis of both methods, assuming that benefits will grow over time but that the rate by which earnings are replaced by benefits (the replacement rate) will remain stable.[41]

To build up a fund of the needed size ($600 billion as of 1974) would require very high payroll taxes for a short period of time. A combined payroll tax of 20–25 percent without an increase in the wage base (instead of the approximately 10 percent in effect in 1974) would create the needed fund in five to six years. Although these high taxes would cause considerable decline in people's well being in the short run, the long-period gains would be considerably greater than the short-term losses. The principal gainers would be younger workers whose tax distribution over their remaining working lives would be reduced. Feldstein estimates that workers with more than twenty-seven years before retirement would benefit. Given the relatively large proportion of younger workers in the labor market, the proposal would pass on the basis of democratic choice.[42]

A fundamental reason for the optimality of the investment method lies in the difference between the before-tax rate of return on capital (the social rate of return) and the after-tax rate of interest available to workers who save.[43] The social rate of return measures the effective return to the economy from its stock of capital before the intervention of corporate and personal income taxes. It is always higher than the private rate. The fund, in the proposal, would be credited with earnings at this rate and would pass the benefit through to workers in the form of reduced or abolished payroll taxes.[44] This, in turn, would reduce the distortions in labor and capital markets that currently act to reduce saving, capital accumulation, and economic growth and that redistribute income from plentiful labor to the relatively scarcer capital.

This leads to three questions: (1) How would such a fund be invested? (2) How would it earn a social rate of return, something that is not available to private investors? (3) What condition is necessary for the success of the plan?

Feldstein rejects investment in equities, because this would involve the government in the management of private enterprise. His policy might make the fund the sole owner of the national debt, and possibly of all federally guaranteed obligations. This would then force private investors into other investment channels, primarily stocks and bonds. Thus, their savings would be available for capital formation. If the stock of federal obligations is insufficient, resort can be had to state and local bonds (municipals) and, if need be, to private sector bonds or mortgages.

None of these obligations yield the social rate of return. However, as private investors are "crowded out" of the public sector into private sector securities, their savings would stimulate investment in real capital (plant and equipment). This would increase national income and thereby increase corporate and personal income tax revenues. The increment in tax revenues would then be credited to the fund; it could be earmarked for this purpose, but that is theoretically not necessary. The combination of the fund's own earnings, plus the contribution from tax revenues, would produce a yield equal to the social rate of return. Note that this is a variant on proposals to finance Trust Fund benefits out of general revenues. In Feldstein's plan, however, this diversion of general revenues does not compel government to decrease its expenditures on other services or to increase its tax rate, since the operation of the plan would generate the necessary additional revenues through the existing tax structure.

As for the third question, the necessary condition for the plan is that the federal government operate so as not to increase future deficits in its budget. This is because budget deficits are financed by selling federal bonds and other obligations to the public. That, in turn, would allow private investors to forsake the private sector money market and enable them to invest in government bonds, which, unlike private investments, do not add to the nation's stock of real capital.

Higher levels of funding than ours are not unknown. The two countries that are usually cited in this regard are Canada, whose public pension plan is invested in provincial obligations, and Sweden, whose pension fund plays a prominent role in that country's long-term capital market. From the viewpoint of economic theory, a fully funded Social Security system may well be superior to a pay-as-you-go system. As Munnell points out, this will be the case when the real rate of return on capital is greater than the implicit rate of return on Social Security contributions. The latter consists of the growth rate of the population plus the growth rate of real earnings. For the period 1956–1976, the real pre-tax return to capital ranged from 9 percent to 16 percent, and the implicit rate of return on Social Security was 3.2 percent. By this criterion, a fully funded system would be preferable if we could start from scratch, since lower Social Security taxes would be needed to sustain any given level of benefits.[45]

We are, to some extent, the prisoners of our history. The original 1935 act provided for full funding,[46] but the 1939 amendments opted for current financing. The shift was, in effect, a gift from the younger population to its predecessors, who were spared the pain of the forced saving needed to build up the fund. To undo this decision requires another gift, this time from the population of mature workers to their successors.[47] Whether a return to full funding today is desirable, or even necessary, is open to question.

The critiques of the Feldstein proposal center on four groups of issues: (1) the regressive nature of the tax and the inequity of the short-term sacrifice; (2) the impact, at least in the short term, of the budget surpluses that would be generated; (3) whether the shift to full funding would accomplish its objectives; and (4) whether an increased Social Security tax is the best way to increase saving and the stock of capital.

The Social Security tax, taken by itself, is regressive, bearing more heavily on lower- and median-income households than on higher-income groups. If it is assumed that saving is too low, why use a payroll tax as the corrective mechanism? Doubling the payroll tax on lower and median earners forces more saving by families whose current needs are great and who would not engage in saving in the absence of Social Security. To ask members of the current generation to make such a sacrifice not only for themselves but, in the case of the mature ones, for a future generation violates commonly held notions of equity and distributive justice.[48]

The budget surpluses coming from a doubling of the Social Security tax may have a negative impact on national income and savings. This Keynesian idea is dismissed by Feldstein, who argues that firms would tailor their investments in real capital to the available stock of savings. When the last is increased, capital becomes cheaper. In turn, firms would be induced to acquire cheap capital and shift to more capital-intensive methods of production. However, the Keynesian analysis is more easily dismissed when unemployment is low, as it was in the 1950s and 1960s. Unemployment rates in the 1970s have been persistently higher than the average of 4.8 percent in the first twenty-five years after World War II and are unlikely to fall below 5 percent in the forseeable future.[49]

Under the circumstances, the Keynesian fear of a budget surplus may not be unreal. Although the negative aspect could be offset by an easy money policy, the Federal Reserve's monetary policy has traditionally been constrained by a fear of inflation. It is unlikely, as Munnell points out, to become expansive enough to offset the deflationary effect of higher government saving.[50] Worse yet, even if cheaper capital increased employment in industries that produce the new capital, and in some industries that use it, a sudden shift toward capital-intensive production would disemploy people in the labor-intensive sector of the economy. Such workers tend to be low paid and relatively unskilled, and it would be difficult to reabsorb them into the labor market. The high unemployment among blacks in our central cities is eloquent testimony to what happened when agriculture shifted from labor-intensive to capital-intensive production in the decade or two after World War II.

Next, it may be asked whether full funding would achieve the objective of increasing our capital stock. This has been examined by two economists, von Furstenberg and Malkiel. Their view is that the negative impact of Social Security on saving does not imply that U.S. capital stock would necessarily have been much higher with full funding. This is because the size of our capital stock also depends on the ability of greater government surpluses (or reduced deficits) to increase Gross National Product in the long run, something that they, like Munnell, do not take for granted if the long run includes long periods of high unemployment. At minimum, periods of high unemployment are poor times for increasing the full employment budget surplus (that is, the hypothetical surplus that would exist if we had full employment) by increasing payroll taxes.

Moreover, there are two other factors that would have affected the stock of capital. One is the response of savers to the decline in interest rates[51] that full funding would induce. The extent of the fall in savings as a result of lower interest rates is hard to gauge. Conceivably, the percent decline in savings could be greater than the percent decline in interest, thus leading to a lower stock of savings than anticipated. Some slippage would certainly occur.[52] The second is the likelihood that some of the added savings would flow out of the United States and build up the capital stock of foreign countries. The extent to which this might happen depends on conditions in international capital markets.[53] In short, the evidence that a fully funded system would have increased the capital stock in the U.S. is inconclusive.

A fourth critique hinges on the question of whether a high Social Security tax is the best way to engage in forced saving, even if such saving is necessary. Munnell's objections, on grounds that the tax is too regressive, were noted above. Michael R. Darby has shown that essentially full funding is nothing more than a proposal to run a large government budget surplus. If this is the case, then there is no *a priori* reason to tie the surplus to Social Security. Social Security may affect the size of the nation's capital stock, but it is not necessary to use the system itself to alter this stock to a more optimal level. This may not even require a large surplus. Other policy tools, such as changes in income tax laws, can be used to encourage saving and investment.[54]

In addition to the four points made above, full funding would create problems in economic stabilization policy. Because it is, in itself, a fiscal policy to run budget surpluses (or at least to restrain deficits), it makes discretionary fiscal policy impossible. If it works, then it will promote economic growth, but nothing in the plan guarantees that growth will be stable. Should business fluctuations persist—and they will—an important tool for stabilization will have been lost. The main emphasis of stabilization policy will shift to the monetary authorities. These will find that their chief tool, open market operations, will no longer exist. At the moment, the Federal Reserve System's open market operations consist of purchasing U.S. government securities to reduce interest rates and increase the money supply, and selling them for the opposite purpose. If the fund were to be the sole owner of U.S. government securities, then open market operations would have to be conducted in other securities, or else new policy tools would have to be devised.

Of course, full funding is, in itself, a monetary policy to reduce interest rates. Although this may be desirable over the long haul, it is not necessarily optimal at any particular point in time. Accordingly, proposals for full funding need to be accompanied by proposals for new stabilization policies.

In a subsequent work,[55] Feldstein modified his proposal for rapid full funding. Instead, he offered three new proposals using level tax rates. One was to get the fund through the demographic crisis coming in the twenty-first century, when the bulge in the retirement age population will appear. This is for a Terminal Fund for Transactions Only, which is designed to return the system to pay-as-you-go after the passing of the bulge and which may require higher taxes thereafter. The second proposal is for a Terminal Capital Fund that is large enough at the end of the bulge period to make some permanent contribution to capital formation. At the end of the bulge period, the fund's assets would equal one year's Gross National Product. The third proposal uses a tax rate high enough not only to get through the bulge but to endow all future benefits. This last proposal is a gradual substitute for the rapid full funding idea.

All of the above proposals rest on Feldstein's notions that (1) Social Security depresses savings and (2) surpluses of payroll taxes over benefits are used to purchase outstanding government debt so as to force private investors into the private capital market. The latter implies that government may not increase its deficits. Otherwise, the additional availability of government bonds would divert private investment back into the market for government obligations.

A further underlying proposition is that Feldstein's savings-investment mechanism would work—that the additional national saving caused by the restriction of government deficits would be invested in real capital and thus produce greater output for the economy. For the purpose of simulating the results of the proposals, Feldstein assumed a fertility rate of 2.1 births per woman and an annual growth in real wages of 2 percent. While the former is still used as the intermediate assumption by the OASI Trustees, the latter is no longer used. The current intermediate assumption about real wages is that their growth will decline to 1.75 percent by 1983. Feldstein also assumes a social rate of return on private investment of 12 percent, although he admits that the effect of his proposals might be to reduce this rate to 10.6 percent.[56] The 12 percent estimate may be on the high side. Critics have pointed out that the 12 percent figure is derived from the historical return on corporate investment, which accounts for less than half of all private capital. The return on all private capital, even excluding recessions, has averaged substantially less than 12 percent per year.[57]

For all three proposals, Feldstein presents level tax rates (combined for both employers and employees) under three possible rates of return to the Trust Fund, 3 percent, 6 percent, and 12 percent. The first is the real rate of return on government bonds, after adjusting for inflation, and assumes that the fund would not capture any of the additional income and corporate tax revenues that would come from the additional income generated by his system. The 12 percent represents the social rate of return and assumes that all additional income is taxed and given to the fund. This is unlikely, for forcing private investors into private securities adds to their risks. Thus, the 6 percent rate is a compromise, and we shall focus on it.

For two of the three proposals, Feldstein also presents level tax rates for two ways of indexing the benefit formula: (1) by changes in average annual earnings, which was the formula actually adopted in 1977, and (2) by changes in the Consumer Price Index. The third proposal, for an eventually fully funded endowment, is given only for the price indexing method, presumably because the necessary payroll tax rate under wage indexing would be too high.

The proposals are summarized in Table 6-10, using only the intermediate 6 percent rate of return. As can be seen, the tax rates look low when compared to the payroll taxes that will be needed to get the system through the demographic bulge. The 1978 OASDI tax on both employers and workers is 10.1 percent of covered earnings and is scheduled to rise to 12.4 percent by 1980. These rates are insufficient to maintain the system, and very substantially higher rates will be needed if reliance on payroll taxes is continued.

On their face, the revised Feldstein proposals look appealing. A payroll tax of 10.45 percent, one close to the present 10.1 percent, buys a pay-as-you-go system that survives the demographic bulge beginning in 2010. To be sure, there is a price to pay in changing from wage indexing to price indexing, since replacement rates will be lower. To stay on wage indexing requires a 12.7 percent tax rate now, close to the 12.4 percent to become effective 1990. However, this would mean an immediate 22 percent jump in the payroll tax. A gradual phase-in is possible but raises the ultimate tax rate that would be needed to accomplish the goal. In any event, all of Feld-

**TABLE 6-10** Level Tax Rates for Three Types of Funds Proposed by Feldstein (Rate of Return to Fund = 6%; Difference Between Real Yield on Assets and 6% as Transfers from General Revenues)

| | Wage Indexing | Price Indexing |
|---|---|---|
| Terminal Fund for transactions only | 12.70% | 10.45% |
| Terminal Capital Fund | 13.15% | 10.90% |
| Endowment Fund | — | 14.30% |

Source: Martin Feldstein, "The Social Security Fund and Capital Accumulation," *Funding Pensions: Issues and Implications for Capital Markets* (Boston: Federal Reserve Bank of Boston, 1976), pp. 54–55, 58–59, 60.

stein's estimated tax rates are lower than those likely to be needed, as a practical matter, after the turn of the century.

Most of the critiques of the original full funding proposals are applicable to the new proposals. These can be recapitulated briefly.

One is that the proposals rest on the controversial proposition that savings are substantially reduced by Social Security and that national saving needs to be increased. Although there may be a depressing effect on savings, it may not be anywhere near the magnitude estimated by Feldstein. The second critique is that an increase in saving may not lead to a corresponding increase in investment and output. Even if it does, there is no *a priori* reason to use regressive payroll taxes, inasmuch as general tax increases or expenditure reductions will yield similar results. For example, a 1.1-percentage-point increase in income tax rates raises as much revenue as a one-percentage-point increase in the payroll tax.[58]

Strictly speaking, none of the Feldstein proposals requires the use of payroll taxes. The underlying strategy is the reduction or (ultimate) elimination of government securities from the financial capital market in order to crowd private investors into the private capital market. This can be done by a long-term fiscal policy aimed at reducing the national debt and using general taxes to buy back outstanding government obligations.

James Tobin has pointed out that the history of Social Security contains periods of unemployment that were caused by insufficient aggregate demand in the economy. In those periods, benefits increased output and did not displace investment.

Because Social Security should not be funded when the economy is slack, Tobin suggests another procedure. Congress should make appropriations for funding as part of the regular budget. It should then decide, each year, how much of the appropriation should be paid out of payroll taxes and how much of a deficit to run.[59]

Tobin's idea introduces an element of flexibility but sacrifices the long-term planning that may be needed to see the system through the first part of the twenty-first century. An alternative approach would be a more or less consistent policy of lower deficits and greater emphasis on fiscal policy for economic stabilization. Such a policy should produce periodic surpluses in the federal budget. These could be used to buy back federal (or state) bonds. Such bonds could then be given to the Trust Fund to build up an endowment. Corresponding monetary policy would be needed to avoid stimulating the economy at an inflationary stage in the business cycle.

The crux of the matter is whether the additional national savings would indeed be invested and yield a high enough social rate of return. This and the other foregoing critical points suggest that Feldstein's proposals for full or partial funding are not yet ready for acceptance. Certainly, the sacrifice entailed by full funding is comparable to the economic sacrifice of a good-sized war. Our present state of economic knowledge is not great enough to determine whether so large a sacrifice, or lesser ones envisioned by the partial funding proposals, is worthwhile.

What *is* important is that we must now begin to take steps to increase the economy's future ability to produce more so that adequate benefits can be available to the aged. In this regard, we can no longer ignore the issues of savings and capital formation when looking at Social Security and the optimal ways of financing it. The system simply cannot be examined apart from the rest of the economy.

# CHAPTER SEVEN

# Analysis: The Needs for Change

## THE GOALS OF THE SYSTEM REVISITED

As the preceding chapters have shown, the problems surrounding Social Security are extremely complex. The system touches upon all aspects of the economy and has developed a large variety of clienteles with special interests that need to be accommodated through the political process. These include the aged, those nearing retirement, workers in mid-career, and those just entering the labor market. Their interests conflict among themselves and may conflict with the future interests of the young and the as yet unborn.

Other groups with their own interests are also involved. Employers and employees, unions and managers, males and females, the poor and the affluent, pension planners and those who administer the system. Since these interests are so diverse, it is possible for one individual to find himself a member of conflicting groups. Viewed in this light, the confusion surrounding the politics of Social Security is not astonishing. It could hardly be otherwise.

In order to see how well the system functions, given such diverse interests, it may be useful to review the underlying principles of social insurance that were adduced from the pioneering German experiment, as well as the intentions of the founders of the American system. These ideas can then be incorporated into the issues and problems that have emerged since 1935 and can give some ideas about the directions for change that are indicated today.

The first principle (see Chapter 1) was an income security system that helped to promote social and political stability in a capitalist economy. All social welfare policies have this objective, of course, and no one policy can ensure against all possible stresses. Still, a policy under which people anticipate poverty at the end of their lives is likely to create considerable dissatisfaction. In an industrial setting, a population with a growing proportion of older people would exacerbate such unrest. It is likely that Social Security, together with other social insurance programs and the rise of private pensions, has helped to keep American politics in their relatively centrist position.

The second principle is that social insurance is more effective than public assistance in allaying unrest in industrial societies. Public assistance, like charity, is simply too demeaning, and an industrial society, whether socialist or capitalist, cannot rely on means-tested programs to cover more than a peripheral portion of its population. Whatever might be the economic advantages of laissez-faire, the politics of ending social insurance are impossible. Workers in all industrial societies have come to rely on social insurance systems. It is noteworthy that the occasional advent of conservative regimes in democratic industrial nations has never led to the dismantling of their welfare states.

From the third principle, we learn that national income security programs are better than local ones (especially the local public assistance systems that preceded them) because of the uneven distribution of the population at risk. A national system can spread the risk over a larger pool of the taxpaying population.

It has been widely noted that the uneven distribution of the poverty population in the United States creates heavy tax burdens for welfare programs in the states and cities where the poor are concentrated. Similarly, while Unemployment Insurance is statewide, not nationwide, the federal government in effect reinsures the states by making loans available to their UI programs. In 1977 it became necessary for the federal government to raise the wage base of the tax in order to restore an element of fiscal soundness to the UI system. Any one state would have found it difficult to raise its UI tax substantially for fear of losing more employment.

The fourth principle is that there is no *a priori* reason for making social insurance redistributive from owners of capital to workers. The system's redistribution of income within a generation is a matter of political choice. In the United States, as in some other countries, the goal of socially adequate benefits leads to a redistribution of income on the benefit side, from affluent workers to poor workers, but not from capitalists, as such, to workers as a class.[1]

Furthermore, there is no *a priori* reason for Social Security taxes to be evenly divided between employers and workers or for the total exclusion of general revenues. Whether general revenues introduce an element of income redistribution depends on how progressive the total tax structure is.

However, the fifth principle of social insurance is that benefits are a matter of right. This suggests that *some* contribution by employees is necessary if beneficiaries are to treat their benefits more like a property right than a handout. Even if all of the tax is ultimately shifted to workers, they may not perceive this. The argument cannot, however, be carried too far, in view of the fact that our Unemployment Insurance taxes are generally levied only on employers, and benefits are not considered demeaning, or at least not as demeaning as welfare.

Linking benefits to contributions is the sixth of the Bismarckian principles. The link in the United States is not direct because of the redistributive aspects of benefits. The original strategy was to limit popular demands for higher benefits by making the cost obvious. The Trust Fund is a useful vehicle for this purpose.

As pointed out earlier, this strategy, when applied to the United States, did not work well so long as revenues to the system exceeded expenditures. The response to the system's consequent "unsoundness" led to the 1977 amendments. Even if general revenues are introduced (they were always in the German system), some linkage remains to remind taxpayers of the cost of the benefits.

Turning to the seventh principle, social insurance can affect savings behavior and, thereby, capital markets and economic growth. The extent to which this happens is a matter of dispute and has been reviewed in a preceding chapter. In addition, there are labor market impacts, some of which are the result of the design of the system, especially the retirement test.

The final principle to emerge from the German pioneers is that social insurance does not fully replace public assistance. The two systems can grow together and complement each other. This has been the experience in the United States and elsewhere. To be sure, social insurance does substitute for public assistance, in the sense that in the absense of the former the latter would bear a substantially greater burden. Nonetheless, the two systems not only coincide but interact, a matter that affects those who are caught in the overlap. It is probably impossible to separate the two systems fully, but more coherent integration is certainly possible. It can also be argued that greater separation is possible by placing the burden of income redistribution on public assistance.

As the body of this work suggests, the American model of Social Security has remained close to the basic Bismarckian principles, at least with respect to its old age provisions. The most significant deviation is in the fourth principle. The progressive scaling of benefits was deliberately intended to make Social Security a vehicle for income redistribution, although this redistribution occurs entirely within the class of those who work in covered employment. When taxes and benefits are considered together, the regressive nature of the tax tends to offset the progressivity of the benefits except to the extent that the Earned Income Credit for poor families with children is an effort to restore progressivity.

Another deviation from the fourth principle is the avoidance of the use of general revenues as part of the financing process (at least as of early 1978). So far, the principle of equal contributions has remained sacrosanct, except that the self-employed rate is (or will soon be) three-quarters of the full rate. Even here the balance is not made up from general revenues. Instead, the employed subsidize the self-employed.

Close to a hundred years have passed since the introduction of the Bismarckian reforms. The United States, like other industrial nations, has become much more of a welfare state than was even envisioned by Count Otto von Bismarck. Still, the fundamental principles of public old age security have remained remarkably stable. Changing circumstances will require some change, and that will be the focus of this concluding chapter.

### Back to the American Founders of Social Security

The principal goals of the founders were detailed in Chapter 1 of this book, as adduced from the Report of the Committee on Economic

Security. The goals and underlying principles of the American founders are worth re-examination here for two reasons. One is that their vision was not that of a Bismarckian German society, even though they borrowed heavily from countries whose systems evolved from that of the German pioneers. The second reason is that times have changed since the enactment of the law, and some of the goals, principles, and means are now subject to debate. In particular, the founders were very conscious of the Great Depression, both in economic terms and in terms of the ideological shift that occurred at the time. A proper evaluation must take into consideration today's economic and ideological climate—and perhaps even tomorrow's.

Under the heading of goals, the first two, which overlap, were the prevention of dependency and retardation of the growth of public assistance. For the aged, Social Security has certainly reduced the degree to which they are dependent on their relatives and on public assistance. Figure 7-1 shows the decline in the proportion of the population aged sixty-five and over receiving public assistance cash payments.[2] Between 1940 and 1970, the proportion declined from almost a quarter of the aged (22.9 percent) to 10.4 percent.

Some of the replacement of public assistance by Social Security would have occurred even if Social Security benefits were strictly wage-related or merely somewhat progressive. This is because, as Milton Friedman put it, the law compels workers to "buy an annuity"; absent Social Security, some persons might have used other, including riskier, ways of accumulating assets. In the nature of risk, there would have been those who would have lost their bets. Others might not have made any provision at all for old age. The debate that is developing is over the role of the minimum benefits, or of any progressivity, in displacing public assistance.

The problem of public assistance was very much in the minds of the founders when they posited the goal of encouraging thrift. Persons who expected to rely on public assistance in their old age were discouraged from saving, since the ownership of assets would disqualify them. Because Social Security is not means-tested, it was expected to offset such antisaving tendencies. The founders expected workers to complement expected benefits by savings, inasmuch as these savings would not disqualify recipients from benefits under Social Security.

**FIGURE 7-1** Decline in the Proportion of the Aged Population Receiving Public Assistance, 1940-1977

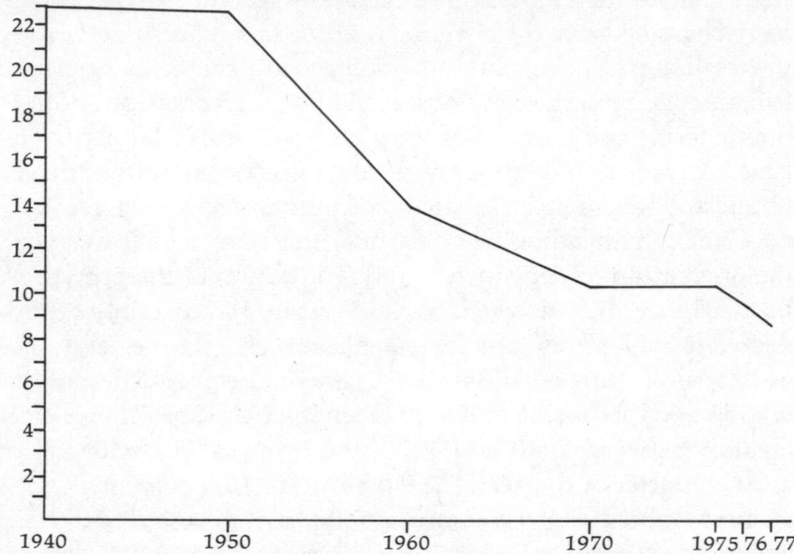


Sources: *Statistical Abstracts of the United States;* 1975 *Annual Statistical Supplement to the Social Security Bulletin* (1976); HEW *Monthly Benefit Statistics,* December 1976; *Social Security Bulletin,* April 1978.

Some of the Keynesian economists of the early 1940s (including Keynes himself) foresaw the possibility that personal saving would nonetheless be discouraged by Social Security. To them, saving might be a personal virtue, but it was a public vice that depressed the economy. It was only recently that Feldstein and others raised the possibility that the possible antisaving property of Social Security could be a public vice, retarding the long-run growth of the economy. This is leading to a reexamination of the financing of Social Security so as to reduce the antisaving property that it may have or to devise a mechanism that overcomes this effect by, in effect, compelling an increase in national saving.

Given the massive unemployment of the 1930s, it was to be expected that a goal of the founders would be to reduce the labor supply of older workers. This was to be achieved not only by the provision of retirement income but also by the retirement test that, in its early version, was quite punitive. Its immediate purpose was not only to make room in the labor market for younger workers but also to maintain wage standards for them. Because a reduction in labor supply would tend to raise wages for all workers, some older ones might wish to remain in the labor market. Either this was not perceived by the founders or else they believed (correctly) that on net balance older workers would leave.

Although unemployment has returned to haunt us in the stagnant 1970s, it is no longer self-evident that a social policy that drives older workers out of the labor market is desirable, especially for the long run. The reasons for a re-examination of the policy include both sociopolitical and economic factors.

To begin with, there is an obvious conflict between our policies on age discrimination and Social Security. Under legislation passed in 1977, virtually all workers have some protection against mandatory retirement below age seventy. In effect, the law encourages them to stay in the labor market. Social Security benefits (and pensions), coupled with the retirementtest, discourage labor force participation. In the 1930s, discrimination was taken for granted.

In the second place, workers perceive their Social Security benefits as earned annuities. The retirement test is thus a continuing political irritation. Its relative liberalization over the years reflects the political pressure generated by older persons.

Any income-tested tax or benefit program encourages evasion, and Social Security is no exception. The retirement test encourages "chiseling" on the part of retired workers, for it enables them to evade both the benefit loss and the income and payroll taxes associated with working. The dimensions of the subterranean labor market are unknown, and the importance of this problem is hard to gauge. It it is a problem, it will grow through time as the population ages. In any event, a policy that encourages ordinary people to cheat seems undesirable.

The retirement test creates a peculiar inequity between those who invested in human capital—education, training, and experience—and those who chose to invest in physical or financial capital. The payoff to human capital is in the form of wages, which are subject to the retirement test.

The foregoing discussion leads to a reconsideration of the economic consequences of a policy that diminishes the supply of educated, trained, and experienced labor. Such labor is a scarce resource, and its waste reduces the economy's ability to generate income, including income for those who choose to retire. As the cohort of war babies matures in the next few decades and is followed by a relatively smaller cohort of younger workers, skills and experience will be more badly needed. Presumably, the labor market will respond with higher wages, but it will be struggling to overcome a policy that creates an artificial shortage.

Thus, the goal of removing older workers to make way for the young, whatever its short-term usefulness might have been, can be deleterious in the long run. To disguise unemployment as retirement is, in any case, treating the symptom rather than the cause of an economic malaise.

The next goal of the founders was to promote economic stability by stimulating consumer expenditures among the aged. Here again, we encounter the ghost of the Great Depression, as well as the less sophisticated economics of the 1930s. In the first place, Social Security benefits are largely offset by Social Security taxes. In periods when the Trust Fund is being built up (as in the next few decades), the taxes exceed expenditures and the stimulus is lost. The reverse is true when the fund is being run down. In a "steady state," if we ever achieve it, the only stimulus comes from the probability that pensioners are likely to spend a greater proportion of their income than, say, mid-career workers.

What is noteworthy is that the founders treated stabilization and stimulus as synonymous. Economic stabilization today consists of policies that smooth out the peaks and valleys of business fluctuations. This has been accomplished, with some moderate success, since World War II.[3] In formulating their stabilization goal, the founders made a serious confusion between long-term and short-term policy. By its nature, Social Security is not a useful vehicle for short-term policy, and the stabilization goal belongs elsewhere.

A principal goal of the founders was to provide for the basic needs of the aged. Although the word "basic" was never clearly defined, it meant less than the full needs of the aged. Presumably, the benefits were to be building blocks, to be supplemented by savings and help from adult children. It is doubtful that private pensions played a role in their thinking, given the small size of the pension sector and its debacle in the 1930s. It will be recalled that the founders expected to stimulate saving, and it is likely that private transfer payments from family members were more prevalent then than now. In addition, public assistance was provided for those whose benefits, if any, were too low and who were poor enough to satisfy the means test.

Generally speaking, the goal was achieved. The aged are especially prone to poverty. In Chapter 4, I estimated that the poverty rate among the aged, as defined by the HEW poverty line, falls into a range of 6 percent to 14 percent. If the poverty line defines basic needs, then zero percent remains an elusive goal. Still, much of the reduction in poverty among the aged can be attributed to Social Security and Medicare, as well as to public assistance. Of the 2.3 million aged SSI recipients, 70 percent also received Social Security benefits in 1975. This indicates that Social Security benefits for them were inadequate by the standards of the SSI means test. If basic refers to the low standard estimated by the Bureau of Labor Statistics, then 20 percent of aged families still fall below this measure.

Alternatively, basic may refer to previous earnings. For the very low wage earners retiring at age sixty-five, replacement rates of 60 percent (single individuals) and 90 percent (couples) seem to satisfy this criterion. Among higher wage earners, the lower replacement rates caused by the progressive benefit structure make benefits indeed "basic." Sole reliance on Social Security for such persons would occasion drastic declines in their living standards. Thus, for most workers, the benefits are a building block to which other sources of income must be added. In this regard, the goal remains intact, as of now.

The long-term goal of the founders was an average replacement rate for an individual of 50 percent. It appears that this goal is not quite attainable under existing legislation. At present, the average replacement rate at age sixty-five is 46.7 percent, and this will decline to 41.8 percent in the year 2000. There was, in the last few years, considerable debate over future replacement rates, but the subject was disguised under the rubric of decoupling, that is, correcting for the overindexing of earnings histories so as not to overcompensate beneficiaries for inflation.

In choosing the method of decoupling through wage changes, Congress opted for a device that generates higher replacement rates than the alternative method of indexing wage histories through price changes. The cost, of course, is in terms of higher payroll taxes. The debate was not well reported, and it is unlikely that the public was aware of it. It is possible that the issue of the "proper" replacement rate will resurface if the existing decoupling method does not work well or if the payroll tax becomes politically too onerous.

Underlying the goals discussed above were a number of principles that are also subject to debate and modification in the future.

One was the use of age sixty-five as the retirement age. This was modified downward later by the early retirement option at age sixty-two, but sixty-five remains the "normal" retirement age for Social Security purposes. As noted earlier, this conflicts with the new civil rights law's designation of age seventy as normal. More than that, the financial problems of the system, together with longer life expectancies and better health among older workers, raises the question of whether a higher Social Security retirement age might be desirable. Suggestions have been heard that, for future generations, the eligibility age be raised to sixty-eight, with age sixty-five as the eligibility point for actuarily reduced benefits.

Any attempt to change the Social Security retirement age now would run into serious political opposition, because it would deprive older and mid-career workers of "rights" that they have accumulated. Such workers prefer a further relaxation of the retirement test. However, gradual phase-in of the higher age over a forty-year period would not affect the bulk of the present working population, although it would further reduce the value of the retirement benefits of future workers. It would, however, have the advantage of providing some fiscal relief at the time when it will be greatly needed, in the third decade of the twenty-first century. It would also maintain the nation's stock of human capital.

Obviously, a phased-in higher benefit age is simply a different way of getting younger generations to pay for the benefits of the elderly. It is a partial substitute for the higher taxes that will have to be paid in the future if the existing mechanism is retained. It is in the nature of Social Security that, for better or worse, Congress must legislate for the distant future. Future generations, however, are not represented in Congress. The proposal for a phased-in higher benefit age will not be forgotten, but it must be dealt with soon if it is to be helpful when the retirement bulge occurs. In any event, sixty-five is losing its magic qualities. It is only one of a number of possible ages for retirement and benefits.

A second underlying principle of the founders was that benefits should be based both on covered earning histories (i.e., tax contributions) and on some measure of minimum need. From the very beginnings, the system encompassed the conflicting notions of individual equity and social adequacy. Thus, the original 1935 law established a progressive benefit structure anchored to a relatively high minimum benefit. Social Security was seen as a vehicle for income redistribution, at least within a given generation.[4]

Presumably, Congress could have rejected the redistributive features of Old Age Insurance and could have made a clear distinction between equity and social adequacy. After all, the same law established a means-tested Old Age Assistance program to succor the indigent aged. However, the 1935 Congress chose to mix equity with social adequacy. In the years that followed, Congress continued in this vein, further shifting the mix of equity and social adequacy in the direction of the latter.

One of the pronounced shifts occurred in 1939, when the influence of the founders was still very great. In that year survivors' and dependents' benefits were added without a change in the tax rate in order to accommodate, at least minimally, the needs of family units rather than workers as such. In other words, the taxing unit remained the individual (and his or her employer), but the basic benefit unit became the family. Furthermore, intergenerational transfers were introduced by the change from full funding to pay-as-you-go. Succeeding Congresses extended eligibility for benefits to new groups without requiring equivalent contributions. Like their predecessors, they accepted the idea that Social Security should, in part, be redistributive.

The question of equity versus social adequacy will be reviewed in more detail in another part of this chapter. Suffice it to say here that the principle of social adequacy remains very much a cornerstone of Social Security. There are those who want to separate equity and adequacy by relying on public assistance for the latter, and their voices will continue to be heard. Others grope for some "proper" balance of the two. There is no objective way to determine a "proper" balance. It was, and is, a matter of political taste and compassion.[5]

A leading principle enunciated by the founders was that the system be self-financing through a payroll tax levied equally on employers and employees. The equal division seemed "fair" at the time, and not much attention was paid to the possibility that the employer's share might be shifted. The later inclusion of the self-employed at a lower total tax rate was not considered a breach of the principle, although it certainly is one.

In the context of the time (1935), the equal division of taxes made some sense. The original payroll tax was low. Most workers did not pay income taxes at all, and income taxes levied on employers were lower than today. Over time, taxes would rise gradually, but no one foresaw the present payroll tax levels.[6] The system was seen as a mechanism by which workers and their employers paid for a national pension scheme.

Self-sufficiency was a vital aspect of this. One reason for this, now long forgotten, was the basically conservative fiscal outlook of men like President Roosevelt and Treasury Secretary Mortgenthau. The New Deal's federal budget deficits were always seen as temporary, and a balanced budget was a goal to be achieved as soon as times became normal again. Accordingly, the founders were directed to create a system that would not generate perpetual demands on general revenues. Indeed, Social Security was for decades treated as separate from the federal budget.

A second reason, one already noted above, was that self-sufficiency would curb future political demands for higher benefits by making the cost immediately obvious to workers and employers. The polity at large was not to be trusted, especially when most of its members paid no income tax.

The third reason is still very much with us. Because benefits are "earned" by the payment of "contributions," any use of general revenues would constitute welfare handouts, with all their attendant pejorative implications. This reason lost some of its cogency in 1939, when pay-as-you-go replaced full funding. This is because one generation now paid for the benefits of its predecessors, making sizable transfers in the first several decades of the system's operation. Today's benefits exceed the joint contributions of the beneficiaries. One could reasonably argue that the excess is a welfare handout that has not impaired anyone's dignity, and that the principle of social adequacy also introduces a welfare feature. However, ideology is not generally susceptible to logical analysis.

The final basic principle of the founders was compulsory participation. Total coverage was not achieved in 1935, although subsequent extensions now cover 90 percent of the labor force. The founders believed that many workers could not, and some would not, provide for their old age. These would then become a burden on the public assistance system or on their children. (Pay-as-you-go makes the older generation a burden on the younger one, but it converts the burden from an individual to a social one.)

The founders also knew that compulsion provided the system with a broad pool of risks. Risk pooling is necessary in any insurance or annuity system. Some annuitants lose by dying earlier than expected, and others gain by living longer. In the private sector, sellers of annuities can reject poor risks. Hence voluntary participation in Social Security was not deemed feasible, because the system would be compelled to accept the poor risks, leaving the good ones to the private sector.

The presence of a welfare component in Social Security extends the reason for compulsion. The welfare component should, on the grounds of equity, be financed by a broad base of the population. If the principle of self-sufficiency bars the use of general revenues to finance the welfare component, then at least the 10 percent of workers outside Social Security should be brought in. Most of these are federal and other civil servants with their own pension systems. Their inclusion is not needed to compel them to save or even for risk pooling. It is needed to help finance the welfare component, especially as some 40 percent of federal civil servants benefit from its existence. The omission of these groups is a small but serious breach in the principle of compulsion.

It is possible to summarize goals and principles of the founders and to see how the system, after close to forty-five years, has behaved with respect to them.

1. Social Security, the nation's largest income transfer, has gone a long way toward preventing dependency in old age.

2. By the same token, it has retarded the growth of public assistance for the aged. Nonetheless, total expenditures for the aged component of SSI have grown, fueled by the growth of the aged population, longer life expectancies at age sixty-five, and relatively higher benefits. The growth would have been greater were it not for the Social Security benefit structure, expecially the relatively high minimum benefits.

3. Current evidence on the goal of encouraging thrift is mixed. At best, it has not discouraged personal saving significantly. At worst, it has done so with very deleterious results for the economy. However, if Social Security helped to stimulate the development of employment-related pensions, it encouraged thrift in a different form.

4. The system has undoubtedly stimulated the removal of older workers from the labor market, an effect reinforced by the growth of pensions. This has made room for younger workers. Given the current high rates of unemployment, a number of Western countries are encouraging policies to stimulate early retirement.[7] Whether the removal of older workers is a desirable goal is questionable.

5. It is doubtful whether the system promotes economic stability. The advent of the payroll tax in 1937 worked to impede recovery from the Depression. The first benefits were payable in 1940, just when the nation began to enter a phase of wartime prosperity and (suppressed) inflation. Indexing benefits can be destabilizing during periods of inflation caused by excess demand.

The possibility that Social Security can be destabilizing is not an argument against it. Economic stabilization is simply not a proper goal for the system. The task belongs to those who make economic policy for the nation.

What were called the underlying principles are no longer taken for granted.

1. There may be a question as to whether trends to *earlier* retirement will persist, or whether *later* retirement is desirable, but sixty-five is no longer taken for granted.

2. There seems to be political consensus that the system should engage in some income redistribution. Historically, the balance between individual equity and social adequacy has changed. It may change in another direction as the system is subjected to closer scrutiny or if political attitudes become altered.

3. Self-sufficiency, once sacrosanct, is now open to question. There are economists, in both the liberal and conservative wings of the profession, who advocate partial or total reliance on general revenues. As the payroll tax burden rises, policymakers may re-examine their aversion to the use of general revenues, or (what amounts to the same thing) consider financing some of the system's functions, such as Medicare, with general revenue funds. The proposal to finance benefits from a Value Added Tax may also gain support as a way of reducing the burden of a high payroll tax.

4. Compulsory participation remains a firm principle, although objections continue to be heard from libertarians. Federal employees, as well as Congressmen, have managed to stay out of the system on terms favorable to themselves. The same is true of a minority of other public servants. The fear that many state and local governments might withdraw has not materialized as yet. Sould this happen on a large scale, the system could be seriously damaged, because the initial loss of revenue would exceed ther initial reduction in benefit payments.

## DYSFUNCTIONAL BEHAVIORS AND FUTURE PROBLEMS

### Interaction with Private Pensions

The rise of Social Security taxes and real benefits in the last decade is likely to retard the growth of private pensions. Although the Pension Reform Act (ERISA) will make private pensions more secure and increase the number of covered workers who will benefit, it will also contribute to slowing the growth of pensions. The costs of vesting and compliance will cause employers to recalculate the benefits they receive from providing pensions and may alter their bargaining stance in the unionized sector. In this section I shall focus on the interaction of pensions with Social Security apart from ERISA.

Some erosion of pensions plans can be expected at the lower wage end of the labor market, where coverage is spotty in any case.

The relatively high replacement rates of Social Security lessen both the need and the demand by workers for pensions. Higher wages may be preferable to both sides. Employers who nonetheless find some pension coverage for workers desirable may prefer the simpler Individual Retirement Account (IRA). No great growth of IRAs carried by individuals is likely, however, because IRAs, like any tax shelter, favor those who have higher incomes.

Where the tradition of pensions is well entrenched in low-wage firms and industries, one can expect a relative reduction rather than a cessation of contributions. This will be especially so where collective bargaining occurs, because unions have a strong motive of their own to engage in pension bargaining.

The rising Social Security taxes and benefits may lead to a renewed interest in pensions plans that are integrated with Social Security. Integrated plans were popular in the 1950s, when the pension movement was just getting started. Two methods of integration developed. One was the "excess" method, which provided benefits (or higher benefits) above certain compensation levels (step-rate plans). The usual step was the Social Security wage base. Frequent changes in the base and uncertainty about future changes made private pension planning difficult.[8]

"Offset" plans defined a combined benefit and deducted from it increases in Social Security benefits. Inasmuch as every increase in Social Security benefits led to a visible and explicit decrease in private benefits, such plans were understandably unpopular with workers and unions. These perceived a loss in compensation previously agreed to, a loss caused by decisions over which they had no control.[9] It should be noted that while ERISA prohibits benefit reductions past the point of retirement, it permits integration before that point is arrived at.

Integrated plans lend themselves to the achievement of some desired replacement rate of previous earnings. If they are understood in this light, they may become more acceptable to workers, who are thereby enabled to make retirement plans in advance. Because only the Social Security portion is likely to be indexed to consumer prices, the real replacement rate will decline with unintegrated plans. On the other hand, further rises in benefits caused by wage inflation will reduce the unindexed proportion of the total retirement package, thus reducing the erosion of combined real benefits because of inflation.

Widespread adoption of integration would lead to a stabilization of replacement rates and concurrent reduction in contributions to pension plans. Taken by itself, this implies a decrease in national saving for investment in the private sector.

There may be some possible offsets to this. If workers anticipate relatively lower retirement incomes, they may respond by increasing personal savings. They cannot do so on a one-to-one basis unless further tax shelters are extended to retirement savings by workers covered by pension plans.

The second offset comes from the use of corporate funds that would otherwise be contributed to pension plans. If the funds are paid out as higher wages, some additional personal saving may result, depending on workers' propensities to save and the possible increase in such propensities if lower retirement benefits are anticipated. If the funds are used to increase corporate profits, some will undoubtedly be retained for reinvestment, and a portion of those paid as higher dividends will find their way into capital markets. Again, the tax advantage will be lost unless corporate and personal income tax rates are reduced in response to higher corporate or personal earnings.

The principal factor that may serve to maintain relative growth in pensions—or to slow the decline—is the tax advantage to workers of employer contributions to pensions funds.[10] This provides higher rates of return than can be obtained on savings that are not tax-deferred. The tax advantage, it will be recalled, stems from the fact that the employer's contribution and the earning of the fund are sheltered until the point of retirement. At that point, retired workers are in a lower tax bracket because of the tax-free nature of Social Security benefits, the double exemption at age sixty-five, and the Retirement Income Credit (where applicable).

The advantage varies directly with the age of workers, with incomes, and with inflation. The labor force continues to age, albeit at a slower rate for the time being, real incomes can be expected to rise—again, more slowly than before—and some inflation seems inevitable in the future. As workers perceive the tax advantage, unions are likely to continue to demand pensions. In the open labor market employers may continue to find that pensions are an attractive device for recruiting and holding workers. More time is needed to determine the net effect on pension growth of the interaction with Social Security.

If the tax advantage sustains pensions or retards their relative decline, this will be accomplished at a cost. It is, in effect, a subsidy by all taxpayers to pension recipients. The tax subsidy reduced personal income tax collections in fiscal year 1977 by an estimated $6.5 billion.[11] The subsidy is paid in part by those who will benefit from it, and in part by those not covered by pension plans.

There is an inequity here that has not excited the imagination of that part of the labor force not covered by pension plans. From another point of view, the subsidy may be worthwhile if, indeed, pension funds make net additions to the nation's capital stock.

Several other interactions between Social Security and pensions are worth exploring. One is the possibility of some shift from ordinary pension plans to profit-sharing plans. The second may be a greater reluctance to incur unfunded liabilities by crediting workers with past service.

Pension plans based on profit-sharing have the same tax advantage as regular defined contribution plans. From the employer's point of view, they have some additional advantages. They convert a quasi-fixed cost into one that is variable and shift some of the enterprise's risks to employees. The advantage is most pronounced for large enterprises that are generally profitable, insofar as the expectation of pensions, albeit with a little more uncertainty, reduces labor turnover and induces self-discipline in employees who are led to avoid discharge in order to preserve their pension rights. For firms with frequent low-profit years, profit-sharing may be a useful form of variable compensation but carries few of the personnel management advantages of regular pensions.

There are some further problems with profit-sharing. Should this option spread, accounting questions about profits will be raised by the agencies that enforce ERISA and by unions that bargain with profit-sharing employers. Employers may hesitate to subject themselves to further regulation by external forces. In general, unions are likely to resist profit-sharing, preferring to deliver more concrete benefits to their constituents.

Where new pension plans are introduced, there may, however, be a tendency to avoid crediting past service. There is always less need to do so in new firms where the work force is likely to be young. Unions, faced with a choice between higher wages and more pensions, may acquiesce more readily to a start-up that involves full funding.

As can be inferred, the interaction of rising Social Security taxes (and benefits) with pensions will alter the pattern of collective bargaining. In low-wage industries, where Social Security replacement rates are relatively higher, there may be less pressure by unions for more than minimal pensions, and less resistance to integration. On all bargaining fronts employers are likely to resist pension demands.

The union response can take several forms. One might be to opt for relatively lower wages or for other benefits. This would be rational policy for unions with older or high-paid members who understand the tax advantage of fringe benefits. Unions with a mix of high and low-wage workers, or of older and younger workers, would face internal political problems in shaping their bargaining demands.

### Interaction with Public Pensions

Since most public sector workers have pensions plans, there is little scope left for expansion of coverage. At the state and local level, the rise in Social Security taxes will affect those public employers (the majority) whose employees are also covered by Social Security. At first glance the temptation to withdraw from the system may grow in an effort to contain the costs of compensation, and employers outside the system might be even warier of joining it.

Attempts may also be made to reduce the liberality of public pensions. However, this is likely to occur only at the margin, that is, for new employees, because pension plans for existing employees are difficult to alter. In some states, a constitutional amendment would be required for this, and public employees are well organized to protect their pension rights. The trend toward more liberal pensions is probably slowing of its own accord, as the policymakers begin to realize how costly some plans are. This realization may be particularly acute in cases where plans are poorly funded.

If inflation can be expected to continue, the indexation of Social Security benefits will make the system more attractive to nonfederal public workers. Although some state and local pensions make adjustments to beneficiaries for rising prices, this is commonly *ad hoc*, and employees cannot count on it. By remaining in the system employees can count on retaining, in real terms, at least part of their retirement benefits. By the same token public employers will be under less pressure to make sizable postretirement adjustments. Those outside the system may find that inflation reduces the benefits of exclusion. In short, the much touted threat of mass withdrawal by states and localities may be chimerical. It will also be resisted by public employee unions.

For public employees not covered by Social Security—primarily federal employees—the progressive Social Security benefit structure interacts with public pensions. It creates the incentive to pick up enough coverage in the covered sector to reach at least the lower rungs of the benefit structure. Over time, this will be constrained as we move toward the point where ten years' coverage, at $1,000 earnings per year in 1978 prices, will be required for beneficiaries and as the earnings averaging period for benefit calculations nears thirty-five years, but it will not cease.

There is nothing inherently wrong about having federal employees moonlight or take postretirement jobs. The issue, as mentioned in an earlier chapter, is one of equity. The progressive nature of Social Security benefits is intended to redistribute income to the needier members of our society. Career federal employees whose benefits are both adequate and indexed are hardly the proper objects of such a policy. Attempts to overcome this by integrating the federal retirement system with Social Security were easily defeated in Congress in 1977. Instead, the law calls for a study of how universal coverage could be achieved. Nothing on the immediate horizon suggests that the policies on this matter will change. Congress is also outside the Social Security system, so that the interests of its members coincide with those of federal employees.

**Interaction with Public Assistance**

Although Social Security is redistributive, the primary job of aiding the needy poor has been assigned to such public assistance programs as Supplemental Security Income, Medicaid, and Food Stamps. Nonetheless, about half of SSI recipients also receive Social Security. The systems differ and interact on the benefit side.

All but the first $240 per year of Social Security benefits are deductible from SSI. Social Security benefits are indexed beyond price increases of 3 percent a year. SSI benefits are partially indexed. The federal component moves with the Consumer Price Index, but the state component need not do so. Accordingly, double recipients are vulnerable to some decline in their real benefits as prices rise, unless their state is willing to raise its supplement. At the margin, an increase in Social Security benefits can take some double recipients past the eligibility point for SSI, Medicaid, or Food Stamps, thus reducing their benefits. Furthermore, the different retirement tests imposed by Social Security and SSI (the latter, strictly speaking, has a means test) impose extremely high marginal tax rates on any work effort.

Interactions of this type are common to multiple-program–multiple-benefit systems. Coordination of income maintenance programs has proved to be an elusive goal, partly because of the different politics of each program. Nonetheless, coordination is necessary if we are to avoid impoverishing people whom we are trying to help.

**Problems of Equity and Social Adequacy**

The Social Security system is a tangle of inequities. This is not surprising, because many of the provisions reflect ideas of social adequacy as well as equity, and the two concepts are antithetical. So long as both goals remain inherent in the system, any attempt to rectify an inequity will affect social adequacy and possibly generate new inequities.

From a political point of view, the principal problem for the future stems from the differential treatment of men and women. This is not merely because the present law contains no less than ten gender-based distinctions, some of which exist to protect women and others of which damage their interests.[12] Whatever the intent of the founders may have been, family behavior is now substantially different from the original model of the intact one-earner family. About half of all married women are in the labor force, and high divorce rates have shattered theimage of the intact family. Over the years, incremental changes in the law have attempted to cope with some of the new problems. An example is the provision for divorced dependent spouses who, beginning in 1979, need only ten years of marriage to be eligible for dependents' benefits. But, at 50 percent of the primary benefit, such a dependent's benefit is clearly inadequate for divorced women with low earnings records and not helpful for those whose own earned benefits are greater.

The search for a change that will reduce the differential between one-earner and two-earner families (equity), while providing some protection for divorced women (social adequacy), is likely to lead to some mechanism that attaches benefit rights to individuals rather than families. If we wish to discard our present notions of vertical equity, all that needs to be done is to phase out all spouses' benefits, thus letting each person collect benefits based on his or her earnings. Progressivity in benefits can be retained under this option or eliminated. The latter would make benefits strictly earnings-related and shift much of the cost of supporting widowed and divorced homemakers to the public assistance budget.

The mechanism that shows greatest promise of reducing horizontal inequity between one- and two-earner families, while providing protection to divorced women (whose benefits now tend to be low because they have, and will continue to have, lower earnings) is combining the earnings records of family members, and basing benefits for each spouse on half of such combined earnings.[13] This approach presents some administrative problems, because it would require information on the marital status of individuals. It would also require considerable ingenuity in the design of the specifics, as undesirable side effects could easily creep in. However, it need not increase the total direct burden of the system if the transfer is principally from divorced men (with higher present benefits) to divorced women (with lower present benefits).

In a report released early in 1979, the Social Security Administration suggested two alternative possibilities to reduce inequities (and for other purposes). One was the combined earnings approach. The second, a variant on this, would provide a basic benefit for all aged and disabled persons (Tier I) and an earnings-related benefit (Tier II) for persons who had employment covered by Social Security. Tier II benefits would be based on combined earnings. Unfortunately, the report was issued too late for detailed analysis here. All that can be said is that both proposals, in effect, attach benefits to individuals rather than to families, as suggested in Chapter. 4.[14]

## SOCIAL SECURITY AND THE NATIONAL ECONOMY

### Labor Markets

As pointed out in Chapter 5, the functioning of the Social Security system may have adverse effects on the national economy. The main effects that have recently been discussed are on the supply of human resources and on the supply of capital. Because both labor and capital are needed to produce goods and services, a reduction in the supply of either may reduce the real income available for both the working population, including their dependents, and the retired and disabled population.

Whether or not the payroll tax reduces the supply of labor is, as yet, indeterminate. It may interfere with the efficient functioning of all markets, which would be an argument in favor of alternative means of financing, such as a value-added tax. However, this is speculative. There is little doubt that benefits, accompanied by a retirement test, reduce the supply of older workers. Pensions have a similar effect, although the law that prohibits age discrimination below age seventy may ameliorate the force by which they induce workers to retire.

There are many reasons why older workers retire, not the least being problems of health. Nonetheless, the retirement test that penalizes earnings above a given limit plays an important role in the retirement decision. At the individual level it affects the choice between retirement and work (to the extent that free choice is possible) by making work costly relative to retirement. Where after-tax earnings are high, some workers may be willing to postpone retirement. The lower the earning abilities of the individual, the more work is discouraged, thus keeping poor people poor. To the economy, the work disincentive entails a loss of potential human resources.

The impact of the retirement test has been mitigated by recent legislative developments. One is the new age discrimination law that protects workers, except highly pensioned managers, to age seventy.[15] The second is the 1977 amendment to the Social Security Act.

This raises the exempt amount of earnings in stages from $3,000 a year in 1977 to $6,000 in 1982, after which the exemption will be indexed to changes in average annual earnings. This will be helpful if wages rise, on average, by less than 20 percent a year between 1977 and 1982. The 1977 law also lowered the age at which the test no longer applies from seventy-two to seventy in 1982. In addition, it increased benefits payable past delayed retirement from 1 percent to 3 percent per year (¼ of 1 percent per month).

There are various ways to reduce the work disincentive of the system. One is to raise the age at which benefits become available. This would have to be phased in over several decades. It would, in the long run, reduce the lifetime benefits to those who retire.

The second direction increases rather than decreases costs. There are three options, which can be used in combination. One is to increase the benefits from delayed retirement. However, raising them to their full value (about 7 percent) would cost as much as dropping the retirement test. The second is to increase the amount of wages that are exempted before benefit loss takes place. The third is to reduce the rate of benefit loss past the exemption from 50 percent to some lower figure. The rate of benefit loss behaves like a marginal tax rate on earned income. Reducing it toward the marginal income tax rate paid on earnings would overcome some of the work disincentive.[6] The last option is probably the least costly one.[17]

Alternatively, we can go outside of the system. For example, it might be possible to adjust the federal income tax in order to overcome the work disincentive effect. This can be done by reducing the income tax liability on earned income to the extent of the benefit loss incurred by working. The double exemption for persons aged sixty-five or over does some of this already, but its value varies with the taxable income of the household. A precise offset might make for a more complicated tax return than most persons are accustomed to and might create administrative problems for the Internal Revenue Service and the Social Security Administration.

The reverse approach is another possibility. The rate of benefit loss from working can be reduced, as suggested above, and the additional cost can be financed from general revenues. Either way, the cost is shifted from Social Security taxpayers to taxpayers at large. Because the benefits from the retention of human resources (which should exceed the outlay) accrue to the entire economy, this may be an equitable way of financing such an option.

The availability of human resources does not guarantee that they will be used. In periods of high unemployment a policy that retains older workers in their jobs will make it harder for younger workers to obtain jobs. It is difficult, however, to design a national retirement system that adapts to short-run changes in unemployment. This problem must be solved in the context of a broader economic policy. In the next few decades the relative number of younger workers will decline, reflecting today's low birthrates. At some reasonable rate of economic growth, workers in both age groups will be needed. And the need for experienced workers will become acute as people born during the baby boom reach retirement age, unless drastic changes are made in our immigration policy.

In light of the above, the cost-reducing option of gradually extending the age at which full benefits are available may be the best choice. It is consonant with the nation's policy against age discrimination below age seventy. It will ease the financial strains of the system that are bound to become acute after the year 2010. A similar adjustment in the employment-related pension sector is desirable for the same reason. In terms of real resources, the consumption of the aged always comes from current output. Given the future demographic structure of the population, the burden on the working-age population may, at some point, become politically unbearable. In that event, promises made now, including those made by private pensions, will not be kept.[18]

### Savings and Capital Markets

Chapter 5 reviewed the controversy over the question: Does Social Security reduce saving, and does this reduce the stock of capital and the economy's output? The answer was generally inconclusive. The weight of the evidence, as of 1978, is that they system may, on net balance, deter private saving. Even so, it is not clear whether the deterrent effect significantly impedes the accumulation of capital. Given this imperfect state of knowledge, it may be premature to consider reforms that may correct this problem. Such reforms, should they be necessary, can take place outside the Social Security system and do not, *a priori*, require the excruciatingly high payroll taxes needed to move the system toward a fully funded basis, as proposed by Feldstein. Any long-term and persistent reduction in government budget deficits (or creation of surpluses) will increase national saving.

It is nonetheless instructive to consider the impact of recent retirement legislation on savings, assuming (for the sake of argument) that Social Security and occupational pensions *do* affect saving. This is done below without any attempt to quantify anything, so that no judgment is possible about net effects.

First, the 1977 amendments. The higher earnings limit before benefits are diminished reduces the inducement to retire and thus the need to save. The effect is likely to be negligible, because the work incentive is strongest at the lower wage level, where personal savings are least likely to occur. Considerable improvements in the retirement test, or its elimination altogether, might have a significant effect on saving.

If working people expect continuing increases in real benefits at retirement, then the stabilization of the average replacement rate should induce more private saving to make up for the shortfall between benefits expected on pre-1977 and post-1977 calculations (this does not affect the cohort in the transition period ending after 1984). However, knowledge about replacement rates is not widespread among the population, and the realization of reduced replacement rates may take time.

The 1977 law reduced replacement rates most sharply in the higher earnings brackets, where personal saving is feasible. If this becomes apparent to high-wage workers, then personal saving would be increased by this provision.

On the Feldstein–Munnell argument, the Pension Reform Act (ERISA) might also affect saving, although the net effect is equally unclear. Just touching the highlights: (1) Greater certainty of benefits could reduce personal saving; however, (2) the stricter need to fund unfunded liabilities can increase pension saving; (3) the shake-out of weak plans and the deterrent to further growth of pensions can reduce pension saving. According to the Feldstein–Munnell theory, this should be offset, at least in part, by more personal saving, possibly through Individual Retirement Accounts (IRAs). Weak plans are most common in industries characterized by small employers and low wages, where workers are not likely to do much saving; (4) apart from this, IRAs and the liberalized Keogh Plan should increase saving via these tax shelters.

It should be noted that all tax-subsidized savings—pension plans, IRAs, Keogh Plans, and tax-favored home ownership—can have a negative effect on national saving by making smaller federal budget deficits harder to achieve.

If the 1977 Age Discrimination Act induces longer stays in the labor market, then the Feldstein–Munnell effect will act to reduce saving, because less time will be spent in retirement. The immediate impact of the law is not likely to be significant, but it may make itself felt in the long run when experienced workers are in short supply. For the savings effect to operate, this long-range labor market outlook must be anticipated *now* by the war babies. This strikes me as unlikely.

The proposal gradually to increase the age at which full Social Security benefits become available should tend to reduce life-cycle savings (again, less time expected in retirement). For a different reason, the proposal to use general revenues to help finance Social Security would also retard saving—national saving is the issue here—by keeping federal budget deficits higher than they might otherwise be.

The foregoing illustrates how complex the savings issue is in terms of the operation of Social Security and pensions. Hasty legislation is inadvisable, but the issue cannot be ignored. Capital accumulation takes a long time. Accordingly, further research must be done, and done now. If our retirement system is found to retard capital formation, then some macroeconomic policy tools must be found to generate tomorrow's capital stock *and* to put it to use.

## FINANCING SOCIAL SECURITY: ALTERNATIVES

It is noteworthy that the recent crisis in Social Security was not generated by such issues as equity or the adequacy of benefits. Rather, it developed from the rapid and highly visible depletion of the Trust Fund. The question was not whether something worthy should be done. Circumstances *compelled* Congress to do something. Questions of financing touch upon all other issues of the system, for other issues involve costs.

The summary to follow is confined to the prominent issues and the possible directions for change. I shall assume the problem of decoupling—preventing overcompensation for inflation—has been settled by the 1977 amendments. However, the reader is warned that the issue is not entirely dead. Given two options, Congress chose the more expensive one, which maintains higher replacement rates. It is conceivable that this may be reconsidered if the tax burden proves to be too high or if undesirable quirks develop that cause the system to behave poorly. However, immediate change strikes me as unlikely.

### Insurance or Welfare

Some of the confusion found in debates about Social Security stems from the term social insurance. It was stressed earlier that *social* insurance is not fully analogous to *private* insurance. It is, in fact, whatever the polity wants it to be. In our case, as in most countries, social insurance programs have some elements of income redistribution. Accordingly, contributions (taxes) and benefits are not linked on a one-to-one basis.

One aspect of this is that while payroll taxes are levied at the same rate (up to the maximum) for all covered workers, benefits are skewed to give low earners a better rate of return on contributions than high earners. In addition, features such as dependents' benefits, the minimum benefit and the special minimum benefit also exist. The purpose of such provisions is to put money where the need is presumed to be the greatest. Because there is no means test, this produces some anomalies, which were earlier discussed under the heading of equity.

A second aspect, as we move through time, is the fact that earlier beneficiaries, including those who were "blanketed in" when coverage was extended, have fared relatively better than later beneficiaries. Had the system operated closer to an annuity basis, as envisioned in 1935, benefits in the first few decades would have been pitifully inadequate. In effect, a gift was made by the working population to the retiring population.

This gift must be repaid over time, because the population is growing older, with relatively fewer active workers to make transfer payments to retired workers. The repayment of the gift—perhaps it is better called in intergenerational loan—takes the form of a declining ratio of benefits to contributions. With the present schedule of taxes and benefits, another gift will be needed as the postwar generation moves through retirement.

Underlying both aspects is the concept of social adequacy. A civilized society supports its dependent population in some form and at some level of living. In choosing the Social Security mechanism as the principal income transfer to the aged, Congress provided an element of dignity along with the cash. This is not necessarily a bad idea.

### The Payroll Tax and General Revenues

Over the years, the payroll tax has been a continuing source of controversy. An important reason for this is that the tax, viewed by itself, is regressive, especially if it is assumed that the employers' share is shifted to workers. One can argue about the justice of progressive taxes, but regressive taxes have few defenders.

The degree of regressivity has diminished with the rise of the maximum level of taxable earnings (the wage base), and it will diminish further as a result of the 1977 amendments. If benefits are considered together with taxes, the system is by no means regressive, because the benefits are progressive. The earned income credit on the federal income tax, available to low wage earners with children, reduces regressivity. This was not a matter of philosophical principle. It was legislated to relieve the heavy burden of the tax on poor workers with children. Considerations of both equity and need suggest that this tax credit be extended to all low-wage workers,regardless of whether they have children. Such a policy is preferable to such options as levying the payroll tax in progressive brackets, or providng an exemption at the bottom. People accept progressivity in income taxes, and are used to a flat rate Social Security tax—but this is a political judgment, and not an economic one.[19]

If desired, the system can be made more progressive by taxing benefits. This suggestion has been made by a number of observers, including the former Commissioner of Social Security, Robert M. Ball.[20] Under this proposal, half the benefit would be taxable, on the argument that the employers' contribution was not taxed. (Employees' contributions are made with after-tax dollars.)

There is something appealing about this, for it would treat Social Security benefits like pension benefits. In the latter, benefits that amount to the return of employee's contributions (in contributory plans) are not taxed, since they were made with after-tax dollars. The taxable portion of benefits consists of the part attributed to the employer's tax-deductible contribution, plus all interest. The general principle, in short, is: tax-free in, taxable out; taxable in, tax-free out.

Applying the principle to Social Security benefits creates some problems. If the general benefit structure, in real terms, is at some acceptable level now, it would have to be increased to compensate for the tax. Persons with occupational pensions who are now paying low or no income taxes would be taxed. In turn, employers and unions might find themselves under pressure to revise pension plans—at least for future pensioners—to make up the difference. As Social Security benefits are adjusted to inflation, the progressive income tax would drive beneficiaries, including those who also receive pensions, into higher tax brackets. This would erode the value of the inflation adjustment.

It is questionable whether all this is worth the effort in order to catch the relatively few retirees with high incomes from capital. The present income tax system is a maze of cross-subsidies and inequities already. The agenda for tax reform is a large one, and there is no special reason for beginning with a tax on the aged, a group that is notoriously poverty-prone.

Finally, it should be remembered that there is, in effect, a progressive tax on Social Security benefits. This is in the benefit formula that pays a lower percentage of Average Monthly Indexed Earnings to the higher earners. A progressive tax on progressive benefits does not make much sense.

A more interesting question is whether the payroll tax should continue to be equally divided between employers and employees. The proposal by the Carter Administration to tax all of the employers' payrolls instead of stopping at the wage base was emphatically rejected by Congress.

In 1977 Social Security revenues were divided as follows: 48 percent from employers, 47 percent from employees, and 5 percent from the self-employed. Enactment of the proposal would have altered this proportion to 51 percent from employers, 45 percent from workers, and 4 percent from the self-employed.[21] Although there is nothing sacrosanct about the approximately 50–50 split that now obtains (leaving aside the self-employed), a change can create peculiar distortions.

These distortions arise because employers' ability to shift the burden of the tax backward to employees or forward to consumers is probably not uniform. The enterprises (and their employees) most directly affected would be those with high-skill and high-technology components. Technology plays an important role in our economic growth, and it may not be a good idea to penalize it by raising its price or lowering its relative wages.[22]

If the employers' share is shifted backward, in the form of relatively lower wages for high-wage employees, then an inequity may occur. Most employees with salaries above the wage base are likely to have made heavy investments in education and training. In addition to being less favored by the benefit structure, they are heavily penalized by the retirement test. Those whose investments are financial are not so penalized. Reducing the relative income of the former group compounds the inequity.

Contributions from general revenues were lawful between 1947 and 1950, although none were made. Since then, Congress has resisted this option, although there are signs that the resistance is weakening.

As indicated in Chapter 6, there are good reasons for moving in this direction. One is that payroll taxes distort the operation of the economy more than general taxes. This is a matter of growing importance as payroll taxes keep rising. Those who object to the regressive nature of the payroll tax (without reference to benefits) might also prefer use of the more progressive income tax. When the demographic "squeeze" occurs in the early part of the next century, general revenues might be a handier device for transferrring resources from the diminishing number of children to the growing number of aged persons. It would be helpful to have the mechanism in place before this crisis occurs.

The political objections to use of general revenues have some merit, and need to be considered. Principally, these are (1) that it would lead to excessive benefit increases; (2) that the system would be politicized if it were subject to annual budget reviews by the President and Congress; and (3) that the system would lose political acceptability and deteriorate into a welfare program—something that voters appear to dislike.[23]

It is possible to cope with these objections and retain much of the contributory nature of the system. This can be done by limiting the scope of general revenue contributions to one or more specific purposes on which a consensus can be obtained. Among these are:

1. The welfare components of the benefit structure, either as a whole of by specifying particular components, such as dependents' benefits, minimum benefits, and the lowest benefit bracket.

2. Medicare benefits. In the event that the United States adopts a broad national health insurance system, Medicare should be combined with it. Should national health insurance be financed through payroll taxes, some provision for people who are not working would have to be made in any event, and general revenues are a good candidate for financing such benefits.[24]

3. "Windfall" benefits, i.e., benefits that exceed contributions plus market rates of interest during the employees' working life. All present retirees and future ones (at diminishing rates) receive such windfalls. Because the windfall is a form of income redistribution (it is, in effect, part of the welfare component), it is reasonable to finance it from general revenues instead of payroll taxes.[25]

There are two problems with financing the windfall component from general revenues. One is that the computation of the windfall is sophisticated and might not be easily understood. This could create political difficulties. The second problem is that the windfall diminishes over time. If the sole purpose of general revenues is to finance the windfall, then the general revenue mechanism will not be effective when it is most needed in the years when the demographic crunch sets in.

4. Periods of excessive unemployment or inflation. High unemployment causes a shortfall in revenues. High inflation increases expenditures, although the latter finances itself, in part, through the automatic increase in taxable wages. If trigger points are established at which general revenues come in, then the Trust Fund need not be built up as much as presently contemplated, and the payroll tax rate could be lowered.

This option does not solve the long-term problem except by leaving scope for future higher payroll taxes. If used, it would be best to use it as a supplement to the use of general revenues for the welfare component or Medicare.

**Ending the Welfare Component**

An alternative way of financing the welfare component is to take it out of Social Security altogether and to shift the income redistribution to an expanded Supplemental Security Income program. There, it would be financed from federal and state general revenues. In turn, Social Security benefits would become strictly earnings-related.

The principal arguments in favor of the proposal are that it is more equitable to finance income redistribution out of general revenues and that it is more efficient in concentrating welfare benefits where they are needed. As noted earlier, the problem of equity can be solved within Social Security by financing its welfare component from general revenues. There is, however, little doubt that the welfare component lacks target efficiency—it reaches people who are not in need.

Target efficiency has its costs, however. Administrative costs are high in any income maintenance system that has a means test. SSI, as now structured, is only partly indexed; state supplements do not automatically respond to changes in the Consumer Price Index. Moreover, state supplements come from taxes that are less progressive than the federal income tax; indeed, some states do not even have income taxes. Finally, SSI carries with it the usual stigma of an overt welfare program and the concommitant unpopularity of welfare programs with legislators and voters.

The 1977 amendments have gone some way toward reducing the welfare component. The minimum benefit for future beneficiaries will no longer rise as average annual earnings rise, although it will be indexed to the CPI. In addition, Social Security benefits for spouses will be reduced by the amount of any governmental retirement benefit payable to the spouse that is based on his or her own earnings in employment not covered by Social Security. This provision begins in 1983 and serves to eliminate windfalls primarily to men with federal pensions whose wives are eligible for Social Security benefits on their own earnings.

### The Trust Fund

The crisis of the 1970s focused on the rapid depletion of the Trust Fund. It was asked whether the Social Security System was bankrupt, and both present and future beneficiaries began to worry. It is useful, therefore, to review the nature and function of the Trust Fund.

It is *not* an insurance reserve, because benefits are largely paid out of payroll taxes. As noted earlier, it is an accounting device that earmarks payroll taxes for benefits. It serves as a buffer or contingency fund for periods when expenditures and revenues do not match. It is a barometer that warns of future problems and signals the need for possible action.

The 1977 amendments were intended to rebuild the size of the Fund from 47 percent of annual outlays to a peak of 398 percent in 2010 under the intermediate set of actuarial assumptions. Although this peak appears to be high, the impact of the demographic "hump" is dramatic. Under the same set of assumptions, only eighteen years are needed thereafter to exhaust the fund. Indeed, there is no reasonable set of assumptions under which the fund can survive, given the present structure of benefits and method of financing.

It is not really the fund that is at issue. The fund, after all, is something of an artifact. The underlying issue is the willingness and ability of the working-age population in the early twenty-first century to support its dependents. The total dependency rate (ratio of working-age population to children plus over-sixty-fives) will not change, because the decline in children offsets the rise in the aged. Adequate support for the aged will therefore be possible, provided that the working-age population is willing to see a transfer of resources from children to the aged.

Such a reallocation may be politically difficult, especially if it is to be effected through the mechanism of the payroll tax. The broader base of general revenues may be needed to spread the pain somewhat more thinly. The warning signals on the barometer are apparent now. It would be useful to plan ahead by making contributions from general revenues an acceptable device for funding, along the lines followed by most European systems. Whether or not value added taxes are a proper vehicle for this depends on the reader's preferences between regressive or progressive taxation.

## ECONOMIC GROWTH

Only a growing economy can provide higher living standards for people in all phases of their life cycle. It has been noted that, over the long haul, Social Security may retard growth by reducing the supply of older workers and possibly by retarding the accumulation of capital. With regard to the former, some change to encourage a longer work life is desirable. Some options for change add to the money costs of the system. These include reduction or elimination of the retirement test, reducing the benefit loss from work, and increasing benefits for delayed retirement from 3 percent per year toward their actuarial value. It is possible that the benefits may exceed the costs, but this has not been established as yet. The less popular but less costly option is to raise the Social Security retirement age gradually (say, over a forty-year span) by three years. If enacted now, the full effect of this measure would come into play just when the demographic squeeze is at its worst. It would then serve to relieve the financial and real strains on the system.

The system's impact on capital formation is less certain. Further study is needed before a decision is made to accept or reject Feldstein's proposals for full funding or at least substantially greater funding. Even if Feldstein is correct in saying that Social Security retards capital formation and economic growth, his goals can be achieved by a fiscal policy that persistently reduces government deficits or creates surpluses. Should forced national saving be desirable, fiscal policy might be a better tool for this than the less flexible format of Social Security.

Recommendations for a policy to stimulate and sustain future economic growth are beyond the scope of this book. There is, of course, no one policy that can assure growth. The search must be for a combination of policies that are theoretically valid and politically practicable. The first requirement has not been met, as evidenced by the continuing disagreements among economists on the subject. The second requirement is equally important, for growth generally entails losses to some and gains to others.

It cannot be stressed too much that the success of a program that redistributes income depends on the economy's ability to generate income—real goods and services. Social Security is no exception to this rule. SSI is bound by it, as are public and private pensions, even if soundly funded. Long-term economic growth is needed if our aspirations for retirement—and for living standards prior to retirement—are to be satisfied.

Moreover, the growth must proceed under conditions of low unemployment, so that workers can accumulate benefit rights while adequately financing the benefits of their retired colleagues. Low unemployment is also necessary if occupational pensions are to make adequate payoffs. Stable prices or a lower rate of inflation is also needed. More stable prices reduce the strains on Social Security. At the same time, they protect the value of savings and pensions benefits.

From the viewpoint of the late 1970s, policies that promote economic growth, low unemployment, and relatively stable prices seem unattainable. If they cannot be found, then more than a workable retirement system is at stake. At the risk of sounding dramatic, what is at stake is our way of life.

# Appendix: Additional Tables to Chapter 4

**TABLE 4–10** Annual Earnings History with Projections (1951–1986)

| Year | Low Earnings Model | Retail Trade Annual Earnings | Services Annual Earnings | Manufacturing Annual Earnings | Construction Annual Earnings |
|---|---|---|---|---|---|
| 1951 | $1,708.70 | $ 2,226.64 | $ 2,321.00 | $ 3,293.68 | $ 4,001.92 |
| 1952 | 1,777.05 | 2,255.76 | 2,489.00 | 3,492.32 | 4,308.72 |
| 1953 | 1,848.14 | 2,358.72 | 2,623.00 | 3,664.44 | 4,493.32 |
| 1954 | 1,922.07 | 2,446.08 | 2,736.00 | 3,665.48 | 4,623.32 |
| 1955 | 1,998.95 | 2,535.00 | 2,831.00 | 3,936.40 | 4,726.80 |
| 1956 | 2,078.91 | 2,609.36 | 2,963.00 | 4,096.56 | 5,011.76 |
| 1957 | 2,162.07 | 2,714.40 | 3,110.00 | 4,242.68 | 5,214.04 |
| 1958 | 2,248.55 | 2,813.20 | 3,220.00 | 4,300.98 | 5,396.56 |
| 1959 | 2,338.49 | 2,919.80 | 3,364.00 | 4,589.52 | 5,637.32 |
| 1960 | 2,432.03 | 3,003.52 | 3,513.00 | 4,665.44 | 5,878.08 |
| 1961 | 2,529.31 | 3,050.32 | 3,642.00 | 4,801.68 | 6,140.16 |
| 1962 | 2,630.48 | 3,196.92 | 3,783.00 | 5,021.12 | 6,368.44 |
| 1963 | 2,735.70 | 3,258.32 | 3,924.00 | 5,180.76 | 6,613.88 |
| 1964 | 2,845.13 | 3,367.00 | 4,129.00 | 5,354.44 | 6,867.12 |
| 1965 | 2,958.93 | 3,463.72 | 4,292.00 | 5,591.56 | 7, 195.76 |
| 1966 | 3,077.29 | 3,565.64 | 4,514.00 | 5,841.68 | 7,605.52 |
| 1967 | 3,200.38 | 3,698.40 | 4,770.00 | 5,974.80 | 8,057.40 |
| 1968 | 3,328.40 | 3,897.40 | 5,088.00 | 6,370.52 | 8,576.36 |
| 1969 | 3,461.54 | 4,090.32 | 5,505.00 | 6,734.52 | 9,420.32 |
| 1970 | 3,600.00 | 4,288.44 | 5,946.00 | 6,953.96 | 10,151.96 |
| 1971 | 3,744.00 | 4,503.72 | 6,648.00 | 7,406.88 | 11,006.84 |
| 1972 | 3,893.76 | 4,731.48 | 7,015.00 | 8,043.88 | 11, 570.52 |

| | | | | | |
|---|---|---|---|---|---|
| 1973 | 4,049.51 | 4,969.64 | 7,486.00 | 8,635.12 | 12,255.88 |
| 1974 | 4,211.49 | 5,254.08 | 8,141.00 | 9,172.80 | 12,952.16 |
| 1975 | 4,379.94 | 5,627.44 | 8,600.00 | 9,854.52 | 13,798.20 |
| 1976 | 4,555.13 | 5,990.00[a] | 9,100.00[a] | 10,795.20[b] | 14,816.36[b] |
| 1977 | 4,782.89[c] | 6,453.63[d] | 9,804.34[d] | 11,630.75[d] | 15,963.15[d] |
| 1978 | 5,069.86[e] | 6,920.87 | 10,514.17 | 12,472.82 | 17,118.88 |
| 1979 | 5,424.75[f] | 7,464.85 | 11,340.58 | 13,453.18 | 18,464.42 |
| 1980 | 5,804.48 | 8,105.33 | 12,313.60 | 14,607.46 | 20,048.67 |
| 1981 | 6,210.79 | 8,790.23 | 13,354.10 | 15,841.79 | 21,742.78 |
| 1982 | 6,645.55 | 9,460.05 | 14,371.68 | 17,048.93 | 23,399.58 |
| 1983 | 7,110.74 | 10,121.31 | 15,376.26 | 18,240.65 | 25,035.21 |
| 1984 | 7,608.49 | 10,828.79 | 16,451.06 | 19,515.67 | 26,785.17 |
| 1985 | 8,141.08 | 11,585.72 | 17,600.99 | 20,879.82 | 28,657.45 |
| 1986 | 8,710.96 | 12,395.56 | 18,831.30 | 22,339.32 | 30,660.61 |

[a]Estimated.

[b]Annual earnings 1976 based on average weekly earnings from U.S. Department of Labor, Bureau of Labor Statistics, *Employment and Earnings, September 1977* (Washington: U.S. Government Printing Office, 1977), p. 73.

[c]1977 increased by 5 percent.

[d]1977–86 estimated; 1977–83 increased by same percentage as Average Wages in Social Security Administration, "Projected Workers with Taxable Earnings 1973–83"; 1984–86 increased by 6.99 percent.

[e]1978 increased by 6 percent.

[f]1979–86 increased by 7 percent.

Sources: This table updates Table 7 in Peter Henle, "Recent Trends in Retirement Benefits Related to Earnings," *Monthly Labor Review*, 95, No. 6 (June 1972): 14. Annual earnings for retail trade, manufacturing, construction 1971–1975 based on average weekly earnings from U.S. Department of Labor, *Handbook of Labor Statistics 1976* (Washington: U.S. Government Printing Office, 1976), p. 191, multiplied by 52 weeks. Services data 1971–75 from U.S. Department of Commerce, *The National Income and Product Accounts of the United States, 1929–1974 Statistical Tables*, (Washington: U.S. Government Printing Office, 1975), pp. 210–213. Projected figures from Social Security Administration, "Projected Workers with Taxable Earnings 1973–83," processed, 1978.

**TABLE 4–11** Pension Plan Benefits

| Industry | Pension Plan | Assumed Career Average Annual Earnings (25 Years' Service) | Monthly Benefit (Worker Retired) at Age 65) |
|---|---|---|---|
| Service | Bronx Realty Advisory Board, Inc. | $ 4800 | $ 135 |
| Manufacturing | Pfizer, Inc. | 10000 (20 years' service) | 233 |
| Retail | Distributive Workers of America, District 65 | 4800 | 182 |
| Construction | Boilermakers (National Plan) | 7800 (contributory plan) | 379 |

Sources: U.S. Department of Labor, *Digest of Selected Pension Plans*, 1973 ed. Supp. III (August 1975), pp. 37, 175, 307; for construction, Supp. II (October 1974), p. 55.

**TABLE 4–12** Indexed Earnings for Worker Retiring 1987 (Age 65)

| | INDEXED EARNINGS | | | | |
|---|---|---|---|---|---|
| Year | Low-Earnings Model | Retail Trade | Services | Manufacturing | Construction |
| 1951 | $9,083.94 | $11,837.45 | $12,339.11 | $15,948.87[a] | $15,948.87[a] |
| 1952 | 8,949.11 | 11,359.87 | 12,534.45 | 15,107.81 | 15,107.81 |
| 1953 | 8,740.36 | 11,155.03 | 12,404.88 | 14,187.82 | 14,187.82 |
| 1954 | 8,935.93 | 11,372.11 | 12,719.99 | 13,947.35 | 13,947.35 |
| 1955 | 8,944.97 | 11,343.71 | 12,668.26 | 17,614.74 | 18,794.31 |
| 1956 | 8,752.88 | 10,986.24 | 12,475.18 | 17,247.83 | 17,683.34 |
| 1957 | 8,779.03 | 11,021.75 | 12,628.07 | 17,053.98 | 17,053.98 |
| 1958 | 8,924.97 | 11,166.19 | 12,780.86 | 16,670.69 | 16,670.69 |
| 1959 | 8,838.41 | 11,035.49 | 12,714.36 | 15,874.05 | 15,874.05 |
| 1960 | 8,899.72 | 10,991.02 | 12,855.41 | 17,072.62 | 17,550.08 |

| | | | | | |
|---|---|---|---|---|---|
| 1961 | 9,126.19 | 11,006.08 | 13,140.96 | 17,319.23 | 17,319.23 |
| 1962 | 9,065.00 | 10,923.98 | 13,036.74 | 16,541.46 | 16,541.46 |
| 1963 | 9,163.07 | 10,913.55 | 13,143.21 | 16,077.32 | 16,077.32 |
| 1964 | 9,108.37 | 10,779.08 | 13,218.54 | 15,366.67 | 15,366.67 |
| 1965 | 9,240.92 | 10,817.41 | 13,404.18 | 17,400.33 | 14,990.70 |
| 1966 | 9,092.92 | 10,535.92 | 13,338.18 | 17,261.27 | 19,501.99 |
| 1967 | 8,963.57 | 10,333.21 | 13,359.73 | 16,734.11 | 18,485.16 |
| 1968 | 8,764.24 | 10,262.52 | 13,397.57 | 16,774.66 | 20,538.73 |
| 1969 | 8,539.26 | 10,090.39 | 13,580.26 | 16,613.36 | 19,241.79 |
| 1970 | 8,463.02 | 10,081.43 | 13,978.09 | 16,347.64 | 18,336.54 |
| 1971 | 8,388.54 | 10,090.71 | 14,895.03 | 16,595.32 | 17,476.12 |
| 1972 | 8,129.29 | 9,878.26 | 14,645.73 | 16,793.80 | 18,789.96 |
| 1973 | 7,901.66 | 9,697.08 | 14,607.16 | 16,849.40 | 21,073.65 |
| 1974 | 7,685.00 | 9,587.49 | 14,855.45 | 16,738.25 | 23,634.71 |
| 1975 | 7,475.99 | 9,605.32 | 14,679.09 | 16,820.40 | 23,551.75 |
| 1976 | 7,194.01 | 9,460.13 | 14,371.82 | 17,049.09 | 23,399.79 |
| 1977 | 7,010.92 | 9,459.94 | 14,371.52 | 17,048.73 | 23,399.31 |
| 1978 | 6,929.67 | 9,459.70 | 14,371.15 | 17,048.30 | 23,398.06 |
| 1979 | 6,874.66 | 9,460.03 | 14,371.65 | 17,048.89 | 23,399.52 |
| 1980 | 6,774.52 | 9,459.88 | 14,371.44 | 17,048.65 | 23,399.19 |
| 1981 | 6,684.16 | 9,460.19 | 14,371.91 | 17,049.20 | 23,399.94 |
| 1982 | 6,645.55 | 9,460.05 | 14,371.68 | 17,048.93 | 23,399.58 |
| 1983 | 6,646.25 | 9,412.82 | 14,299.92 | 16,963.80 | 23,282.75 |
| 1984 | 7,608.49 | 10,828.79 | 16,451.06 | 19,515.67 | 26,785.17 |
| 1985 | 8,141.08 | 11,585.72 | 17,600.99 | 20,879.82 | 28,657.45 |
| 1986 | 8,710.96 | 12,395.56 | 18,831.30 | 22,339.32 | 30,660.61 |

[a]Manufacturing over taxable earnings, 1951–1954, 1957–1959, 1961–1964, and construction over taxable earnings, 1951–1973, indexed by maximum taxable earnings. Indexed: base year 1982—$12,892. Assumes 6.99 percent increase in annual average earnings 1984–1986.

Sources: Table 4-10 and Social Security Administration "Projected Workers with Taxable Earnings 1976–83."

**TABLE 4–13** Estimated Pension Plan Benefits, 1987

| Industry | Pension Plan | Assumed Career Average Annual Earnings (25 Years' Service) Updated by Changes in Average Earnings per Worker 1977–87[a] | Monthly Benefits (Worker Retired at Age 65) Updated by Changes in Average Earnings per Worker, 1977–87[a] |
|---|---|---|---|
| Retail | Distributive Workers of America, Dist. 65 | $ 9,900.00 | $350.00 |
| Service | Bronx Realty Advisory Board, Inc. | 9,900.00 | 278.00 |
| Manufacturing | Pfizer, Inc. | 19,207.00 | 479.00 |
| Construction | Boilermakers (National Plan) | 16,029.00 | 779.00 |

[a]From Social Security Administration; assumed earnings increased by 6.99 percent for 1984–87.

Sources: Table 4–11 and Social Security Administration, "Projected Workers with Taxable Earnings, 1973–83."

# Notes

## CHAPTER 1: AN OVERVIEW OF THE PROBLEM ISSUES (pp. 1–26).

1. *New York Times*, May 6, 1975.
2. William E. Simon, "How to Rescue the Social Security System," *Wall Street Journal*, November, 3, 1976, p. 20.
3. *Annual Report of the Board of Trustees of the Federal Old Age and Survivors Insurance and Disability Insurance Trust Funds*, 1974 House Document 93-313 (Washington: U.S. Government Printing Office, 1974), pp. 22–27. The 1974 Advisory Council on Social Security had also warned of the impending crisis.
4. See the comments by Representative James A. Burke (D-Mass.) in U.S. Congress, *Decoupling the Social Security Benefit Structure*, Hearings Before the Subcommittee on Social Security, House Ways and Means Committee 94th Cong., 2d sess., on H.R. 14430, June 18, 1976 (Washington: U.S. Government Printing Office, 1976), p. 65.
5. Memo from Robert J. Meyers citing his own estimate (1970) and the estimates made in the *Annual Report of the Trustees*, 1975, cited in Subcommittee on Social Security, *Decoupling*, pp. 134–35.
6. See Chapter 2 below.
7. Social Security Administration, *Research and Statistics Note*, No. 14, August 3, 1977. Similar conclusions were reached by Lawrence H. Thompson and Paul N. Van de Water, "The Short Run Behavior of the Social Security Trust Funds," Technical Analysis Paper No. 8, Department of Health, Education, and Welfare, Office of the Assistant Secretary for Planning and Evaluation, July 1976.
8. For an excellent discussion of the problem, see Alician H. Munnell, *The Future of Social Security* (Washington: Brookings Institution, 1977), pp. 30–61, 134. See also *Reports of the Quadrennial Advisory Council on Social Security*, House Document No. 94-75 (Washington: U.S.

Government Printing Office, 1977), pp. 13–16. The subject is covered in great detail in Subcommittee on Social Security, *Decoupling.* This document includes a full text of the *Report of the Consultant Panel on Social Security to the Congressional Research Service*, commonly known as the *Hsiao Report* for its chairman, William Hsiao. It is also well explained in Robert S. Kaplan, *Indexing Social Security: An Analysis of the Issues* (Washington: American Enterprise Institute, 1977).

9. *Annual Report of the Board of Trustees of the Federal Old Age and Survivors Insurance and Disability Insurance Trust Funds*, 1977 (Washington: U.S. Government Printing Office, 1977), p. 113.
10. Ibid., p. 113.
11. See Yung-ping Chen and Kwang-wen Chu, "Total Dependency Burden and Social Security," in Industrial Relations Research Association, (IRRA), *Proceedings of the 29th Annual Winter Meeting, 1976* (Madison, Wisc.: Industrial Relations Research Association, 1977), pp. 43–51. Dependency ratios used in this article differ slightly from the ones I used, but the conclusions are essentially similar. I came across the paper after writing the early drafts of the above paragraphs on demographic change and am pleased to see my analysis confirmed by the more rigorous work of Dr. Chen and Dr. Chu.
12. There are exceptions to this in the sense that a nation may deliberately conserve its natural resources for future use. Existing stocks of real capital are also national savings to the extent that they are not depreciated.
13. An example of a public trust fund that created real capital is the Highway Trust Fund, built up from gasoline tax revenues and used to help finance the Interstate Highway System.
14. Military hardware may be thought of as capital in that it produces a service: defense or warfare. But it is not strictly comparable to the usual kind of capital that produces goods and services that are useful to consumers in the ordinary course of their lives.
15. Note that this is also true in a socialist economy, where capital is publicly owned. The methods of producing the savings needed for such investment would, however, be different from ours.
16. The leading proponent of the argument that Social Security diminishes savings is Professor Martin C. Feldstein. For a concise summary of his findings, see his "Social Security" in Michael J. Boskin, ed., *The Crisis in Social Security* (San Francisco: Institute for Contemporary Studies, 1977), pp. 21–24. A more extended bibliography will be given in Chapters 5 and 6.
17. It is a common belief among economists that the full burden of the tax is borne by the worker. See George F. Break, "Social Security as a Tax," in Boskin, *Crisis in Social Security*, pp. 114–115 and Richard A. Musgrave and Peggy B. Musgrave, *Public Finance in Theory and Practice* (New York: McGraw-Hill, 1973), pp. 390–395 and John A. Brittain,

*The Payroll Tax for Social Security* (Washington: Brookings Institution, 1972), pp. 60–81. The empirical evidence on the subject is not as clear as one might hope. See, for example, the controversy between Feldstein and Brittain in the *American Economic Review*, 62, No. 4 (September 1972): 735–742, based on Brittain's "The Incidence of Social Security Payroll Taxes," *American Economic Review*, 61, No. 1 (March 1971): 110–125.

18. This is unlikely in the long run on the common theoretical proposition that, in the long run, all costs must be covered. Furthermore, there is no empirical evidence that the tax has led to a reduction in profit rates.
19. Feldstein, "Social Security," pp. 21–24. The argument about the displacement effect on savings follows Feldstein very closely.
20. Robert J. Lampman, "The Future of Social Security," in IRRA, *29th Annual Proceedings*, pp. 40–41.
21. For another doubtful view, see Joseph A. Pechman, "The Social Security System: An Overview," in Boskin, *Crisis in Social Security*, pp. 37–38.
22. All income maintenance systems, including welfare, can have this effect.
23. *Employment and Training Report of the President, 1978* (Washington: U.S. Government Printing Office, 1978), pp. 235–236.
24. Unpublished projections by the Office of the Chief Actuary, Social Security Administration. See *New York Times*, July 10, 1977.
25. U.S. Department of Health, Education and Welfare, Social Security Administration *Preliminary Findings from the Survey of New Beneficiaries* (Washington: U.S. Department of Health, Education, and Welfare, June 1973), pp. 14–15.
26. U.S. Congress, Joint Economic Committee, Studies in Public Welfare, Paper No. 20, *Handbook of Public Income Transfer Programs, 1975* (Washington: U.S. Government Printing Office, 1974), pp. v–vi.
27. In New York, the state supplement adds $60.85 for an individual and $75.94 for an aged couple who are not living with someone else.
28. Robert Tilove, *Public Employee Pension Funds* (New York: Columbia University Press, 1976), pp. 128–129.
29. U.S. Department of Health, Education, and Welfare, Social Security Administration, *Research and Statistics Note #18*, September 30, 1976.
30. Edwin E. Witte, *The Development of the Social Security Act* (Madison: University of Wisconsin Press, 1962), p. 111.
31. Frances E. Perkins, *The Roosevelt I Knew* (New York: Viking Press, 1946), p. 284.
32. See the testimony of Murray W. Latimer in U.S. Congress, House Ways and Means Committee, *Hearings on H.R. 4120, Economic Security Act* (Washington: Senate Library, Vol. 699, 1935), pp. 220–224.
33. Ibid., p. 203.

34. U.S. Committee on Economic Security, *Social Security in America* (Washington: U.S. Government Printing Office, 1937).
35. Perkins, *The Roosevelt I Knew*, p. 283.
36. For further discussions of the goals of the Social Security Act, see J. Douglas Brown, *An American Philosophy of Social Security* (Princeton, N.J.: Princeton University Press, 1972), and Wilbur J. Cohen, *Retirement Policies Under Social Security* (Berkeley: University of California Press, 1957), especially pp. 5–6. Both men were prominent in the development of the act.
37. Cohen, *Retirement Policies*, p. 5.
38. Brown, *American Philosophy*, p. 18–19.
39. See Cohen, *Retirement Policies*, pp. 17–25.
40. In certain cases, benefits are available at lower ages.
41. Milton Friedman, *Capitalism and Freedom* (Chicago: University of Chicago Press, Phoenix, 1962), pp. 182–189. Friedman does not, of course, hold that benefits are annuities in the usual sense of the word. They are merely payments financed by a tax.
42. My own value judgments do not lead me to believe that compulsory social insurance is objectionable, even though I have a strong attachment to personal liberty. One may as well argue that drivers should not be compelled to obey traffic signals.
43. Doctors complained that Medicare would rob them of *their* freedom of choice and patients' freedom to choose their doctors, but the law was drafted so as initially to overcome these objections.
44. Aaron Wildavsky, "Doing Better and Feeling Worse: The Political Pathology of Health Policy," in John H. Knowles, ed., *Doing Better and Feeling Worse* (New York: Norton, 1977, p. 109. The entire essay, pp. 105–123, is one of the most perceptive pieces in the literature of health economics, even though (or because) its author is not an economist but a political scientist.
45. See *Annual Report of the Board of Trustees of the Federal Hospital Insurance Trust Fund*, 1977 (Washington, mimeo, May 9, 1977), especially p. 39–40; *Annual Report of the Board of Trustees of the Federal Supplementary Medical Insurance Trust Fund*, 1977 (Washington, mimeo May 9, 1977), p. 30; and A. Haeworth Robertson, "The Financial Status of Social Security After the Social Security Amendments of 1977" (Baltimore: Social Security Administration, processed, January 1978), pp. 21–26.
46. See Milton Friedman, "Payroll Taxes, No: General Revenues, Yes," in Boskin, ed., *Crisis in Social Security*, (note 16 supra), pp. 25–30.
47. In more technical language, there is a dynamic interaction. Industrialization breaks up extended families and leads to demands for state income maintenance mechanisms, which, in turn, further break up families and help to further industrial process by enabling the working population to be more mobile in labor markets. Once the interaction is in

full swing, it ceases to matter what the original cause is, especially when the process is irreversible.

**CHAPTER 2: PUBLIC INCOME MAINTENANCE SYSTEMS IN AMERICA (pp. 27–64).**

1. M. M. Postan, E. E. Rich, and Edward Miller, eds.,*The Cambridge Economic History of Europe, Vol. III: Economic Organization and Policies in the Middle Ages* (Cambridge, England: Cambridge University Press, 1965).
2. For a discussion of Vives and his impact on England, see W. J. Ashley, *An Introduction to English Economic History and Theory* (New York: Sentry Press, 1966), pp. 343–346.
3. The classic history of the Poor Law is Sidney Webb and Beatrice Webb, *English Local Government: English Poor Law History Part I: The Old Poor Law* (Hamden, Conn.: Archon Books, 1927), esp. pp. 315–316. A dramatic view of the changing attitude is found in R. H. Tawney, *Religion and the Rise of Capitalism* (London: Hazell, Watson & Vinly, 1926), pp. 262–266.
4. Scotland and Ireland had variations on the system as it developed, but Wales fell under English law. I shall concentrate on the English system. For a brief description of the early Scottish Poor Law, see J. F. Sleeman, *The Welfare State: Its Aims, Benefits and Costs* (London: George Allen & Unwin, 1973), p. 10.
5. Webb and Webb, *English Local Government,* pp. 315–316.
6. For an interesting discussion of this issue, see Paul Mantoux, *The Industrial Revolution in the Eighteenth Century* (New York: Harper & Row, 1962).
7. Adam Smith, *The Wealth of Nations* (London: Oxford University Press, 1904), vol. 1, pp. 153–160; vol. 2, pp. 49–51.
8. During part of my childhood, my family received aid from a private charitable organization, because the terms of our immigration status then precluded us from public assistance. I remember being coached by my mother to tell the nice social worker that I went through a quart of milk every day. In point of fact, I loathed the stuff and rarely drank it. Because the aid was in the form of cash, and cash is fungible, this enabled my mother to reallocate the milk money to purposes for which family needs were greater than the aid budget provided.
9. For example, the Prussian Common Law promulgated in 1794 embodied the principles of the early English Poor Law. See William Harbutt Dawson, *Social Insurance in Germany 1883–1911: Its History, Operation, Results, and a Comparison with the National Insurance Act, 1911* (London: T. Fischer Unwin, 1912), p. 2.
10. J. Walker, *British Economic and Social History, 1700–1967* (London: MacDonald & Evans, 1968), pp. 353–354.

11. *Knappschaftskassen* in Germany and *Bruderladen* in Austria, which were made compulsory in Prussia on a joint contributory basis. See Dawson, *Social Insurance*, pp. 4–5.
12. Ibid., pp. 6–10.
13. Walter Vogel, *Bismarck's Arbeiterversicherung: Ihre Enstehung im Kraftespiel der Zeit* (Braunscwheig: Georg Westerman Verlag, 1951), pp. 13–15.
14. Walter Sulzbach, *German Experience with Social Insurance*, Studies in Individual and Collective Security, No. 2 (New York: National Industrial Conference Board, 1947), pp. 3–5. The quotation is from Bismarck.
15. Dawson, *Social Insurance*, p. 14.
16. Arthur J. Altmeyer, *The Formative Years of Social Security* (Madison: University of Wisconsin Press, 1966), p. 11.
17. Dawson, *Social Insurance*, pp. 102–127.
18. Ibid., pp. 38, 135.
19. In the Marxian, as well as in the mid-nineteenth century classical economic systems, wages tended toward subsistence levels. This implies that the employer's contribution would be shifted to the workers through a diminution of cash wages offset by the insurance contribution.
20. See Norbert Pinkus, "Workmen's Insurance in Germany, III," *Yale Review*, November 1904, pp. 296–323.
21. Ibid., pp. 420—421.
22. For a good survey of ten social welfare systems now in operation, see P. R. Kaim-Caudle, *Comparative Social Policy and Social Security: A Ten Country Study* (New York: Dunellen, 1973).
23. U. S. Committee on Economic Security, *Social Security in America* (Washington: U. S. Government Printing Office, 1937), p. iii.
24. A third category, consisting of contributory laws of very limited coverage in a few countries, also existed but is of no interest to this work. See ibid., p. 184.
25. Ibid., pp. 181–188. The Polish law was passed in 1933. The Yugoslav law of 1922 was not enforced.
26. Ibid., p. 184.
27. The Netherlands and Spain divided contributions between the employer and the government. In the Soviet Union, the entire cost was assessed on the employer, who by 1933 was largely the government. Ibid., p. 185.
28. Ibid., pp. 204—207. Historically, Congressional preference has been to exclude government subsidies in social insurance. President Roosevelt, although he supported the committee recommendations that would introduce subsidies in 1965, directed the committee to develop a self-sustaining plan (excluding subsidies) as soon as possible. See Altmeyer, *Formative Years* (note 16 supra), p. 29.
29. Committee on Economic Security, pp. 191—197.

30. Ibid., p. 203.
31. See Eveline M. Burns, *Toward Social Security: An Explanation of the Social Security Act and a Survey of the Larger Issues* (New York: McGraw-Hill, 1936), p. 34. Also see Eveline M. Burns, *Social Security and Public Policy* (New York: McGraw-Hill, 1956), p. 31. Dr. Burns was an adviser to the Committee on Economic Security.
32. I have relied upon the act itself, rather than on secondary sources. A complete text is found in Appendix XVI of Committee on Economic Security, *Social Security in America*, pp. 531–538.
33. Altmeyer, *Formative Years*, p. 89.
34. Burns, *Toward Social Security*, p. 27.
35. I have dealt with this subject elsewhere. See Bruno Stein, *On Relief: The Economics of Poverty and Public Welfare* (New York: Basic Books, 1971).
36. The categorical indigent are those who qualify for public assistance. The medically indigent are those whose incomes are low enough to enable them to qualify for Medicaid. Not all states provide for the latter.
37. Arizona refused participation until 1975.
38. Provisions of some of our income maintenance laws are extremely complex, and Medicaid and its interactions with other programs may well head the list of complexity. For a good description of Medicaid, see U. S. Congress, Joint Economic Committee, Studies in Public Welfare, Paper No. 20, *Handbook of Public Income Transfer Programs, 1975* (Washington: U.S. Government Printing Office, 1974), pp. 220–239. Hereafter JEC *Handbook*.
39. U.S. Department of Health, Education, and Welfare, cited in Sar A. Levitan, *Programs in Aid of the Poor*, 3d ed. (Baltimore: Johns Hopkins Press, 1976), p. 64.
40. Persons ineligible for Social Security cash benefits who reached the age of sixty-five before 1968 were covered. Those reaching sixty-five after 1965 were covered by a transitional requirement of some Social Security wage credits, rising from three quarters of coverage in 1968 to twenty-one quarters in 1974. Those reaching sixty-five after 1974 need the same number of wage credits as are needed for cash benefits from Social Security. See U.S. Department of Health, Education and Welfare, Social Security Administration, DHEW Publication No. (SSA) 73-11915, *Social Security Programs in the United States* (Washington: U.S. Government Printing Office, 1973), p. 45.
41. For a provocative critique of the impact of Medicaid on the nursing home industry, see Mary A. Mendelson, *Tender Loving Greed* (New York: Vintage Books, 1975), pp. 34–52.
42. Except in Puerto Rico, Guam, and the Virgin Islands, which, as of 1977, continue under the old adult categorical welfare programs.
43. JEC *Handbook*, p. 113. Unless otherwise noted, the description of SSI relies heavily on this source. See pp. 113–139.
44. The income and asset exclusions are quite complicated, and the income

exclusion is somewhat more favorable to the blind and disabled. See ibid., pp. 115–118.

45. In 1975, 69.8 percent of aged SSI recipients also received Social Security benefits. See *Social Security Bulletin*, 38, No. 12 (December 1975): 75.
46. For some households, this is in excess of their needs or wants. In such cases, recipients may upgrade rather than increase their food intake, hence the popular anecdotal complaint that recipients are buying expensive meat or selling their surplus stamps on a black market.
47. U.S. Congress, Joint Economic Committee, Studies in Public Welfare No. 17, *National Survey of Food Stamp and Food Distribution Recipients* (Washington: U.S. Government Printing Office, 1974), p. 15.
48. JEC *Handbook*, p. 172.
49. Burns, *Toward Social Security*, p. 21.
50. Joseph A. Pechman, Henry J. Aaron, and Michael K. Taussig, *Social Security: Perspectives for Reform* (Washington: Brookings Institution, 1968), p. 33. For a discussion of the politics of the 1939 reforms, see Altmeyer, *Formative Years* (note 16 supra), pp. 74–117.
51. As projected by the Committee on Economic Security, *Social Security in America*, p. 212, Table 45, based on its recommended tax of 5 percent (joint) by 1957. The act, as adopted in 1935, projected a tax rate of 6 percent by 1949, but this would only have delayed the onset of a need for subsidies. See also Altmeyer, *Formative Years*, p. 20. Actually, the initial tax of 2 percent was not raised until 1950.
52. Subject, of course, to applicable state laws, many of which provided a "widow's mite," a percentage of the estate that must be payable to a widow.
53. Alicia H. Munnel, *The Future of Social Security* (Washington: Brookings Institution, 1977), p. 177. This and other parts of my historical analysis have benefited from the concise history developed by Munnell in the appendix to her book. Munnell also prepared the historical appendix for Pechman, Aaron, and Taussig, *Future of Social Security*, Appendix B, pp. 251–272.
54. Stein, *On Relief* (note 35 supra), p. 71.
55. However, the 1977 amendments to the Age Discrimination in Employment Act protect persons to the age of seventy.
56. California, Hawaii, New Jersey, New York, and Rhode Island. See John G. Turnbull, C. Arthur Williams, Jr., and Earl F. Cheit, *Economic and Social Security*, 4th ed. (New York: Ronald Press, 1973), pp. 363–375.
57. Recent Supreme Court decisions may eliminate the distinctions between the rights of males and those of females.
58. A good description of HI and SMI is found in George E. Rejda, *Social Insurance and Economic Security* (Englewood Cliffs, N.J.: Prentice-Hall, 1976), pp. 233–246.
59. In economic theory, the utility derived from one dollar of public assistance may be less than the utility from one dollar of Social Security.

**CHAPTER 3: EMPLOYER-RELATED PENSIONS (pp. 65–115).**

1. The 46.2 percent figure (as of 1975) was estimated by Martha Remy Yohalem, "Employee-Benefit Plans, 1975," *Social Security Bulletin*, 40, No. 11 (November 1977): 22. *Pension Facts 1976* (New York: American Council of Life Insurance, 1976), p. 17, estimates private sector coverage at "nearly one half of workers in the private sector, and 75% of public sector workers." Tilove estimates public sector coverage as virtually all state and local employees (virtually all federal full-time workers are also covered); see Robert Tilove, *Public Employee Pension Funds*, (New York: Columbia University Press, 1976), p. 49. Alicia H. Munnell, *The Future of Social Security* (Washington: Brookings Institution, 1977), p. 15, cites the 1972 Census for governemnt's figure of approximately 75 percent of state and local employees. Addition of federal employees would raise the figure, but not to 100 percent.
2. Parts of the description here are drawn from Peter F. Drucker, *The Unseen Revolution: How Pension Fund Socialism Came to America* (New York: Harper & Row, 1976), pp. 11–20. Although Drucker is not a qualified pension expert, the clarity of his prose has been helpful to me. For more technical explanations, see Everett T. Allen, Jr., Joseph J. Melone, and Jerry S. Rosenblum, *Pension Planning*, 3d ed. (Homewood, Ill.: Richard D. Irwin, 1976).
3. Median income for households in 1976 was $12,690. Median income of households in owner-occupied homes was $15,350, compared to $8,800 for households in rental buildings. U.S. Department of Commerce, *Current Population Reports*, Series P-60, No. 109 (January 1978), pp. 1,3.
4. Murray W. Latimer, *Industrial Pension Systems in the U.S. and Canada*, Vol. 1 (New York: Industrial Relations Counselors, 1933), pp. 21–22.
5. *Pension Facts 1976*, p. 7.
6. Latimer, *Industrial Pension Systems*, pp. 24–25.
7. *Pension Facts 1976*, p. 7. When railway pension plans faced bankruptcy in 1934, they were federalized.
8. In economic terms, the demand for railway services was relatively inelastic, so that general increases in their rates led to a less than proportional decline in the quantity of the service demanded. Price regulation assured them of a fair return on the fair value of their property, a formula that virtually compelled the Interstate Commerce Commission to pass cost increases forward.
9. *Pension Facts 1976*, pp. 7–8. See also Latimer, *Industrial Pension Systems*, pp. 18–48, and William C. Greenough and Francis P. King, *Pension Plans and Public Policy* (New York: Columbia University Press, 1976), pp. 27–40.
10. For details, see Latimer, *Industrial Pension Systems*, pp. 44–48.

11. See Greenough and King, *Pension Plans*, pp. 40–42, for a discussion of union pension plans.
12. P.L. 101, 80th Congress, Sec. 302(c).
13. 21 LRRM 1310, April 12, 1948; 22 LRRM 2506, September 23, 1948; 24 LRRM 2019, April 25, 1949.
14. Yohalem, "Employee-Benefit Plans," (note 1 supra), p. 26.
15. Drucker, *Unseen Revolution* (note 2 supra).
16. Ibid., pp. 1–2.
17. except in the minor case of Employee Stock Ownership Plans.
18. According to a study by the U.S. Department of Labor, employer representatives on joint boards tend to entrust pension management decisions to the union representatives. See U.S. Department of Labor, Bureau of Labor Statistics, *Administration of Negotiatied Pension, Health, and Insurance Plans*, Bulletin 1425-12 (Washington: U.S. Government Printing Office, 1970), p. 1. This situation probably has not changed since the study was published.
19. This is not entirely a coincidence, but the ERISA standards are probably reasonable in many respects.
20. Yohalem, "Employee-Benefit Plans," pp. 20, 24, 26.
21. Alfred M. Skolnik, "Private Pension Plans 1950–74," *Social Security Bulletin*, 39, No. 6 (June 1976): 4.
22. For details of the law, see Samuel H. Murray, *Analysis of the Pension Reform Act of 1974* (New York: Matthew Bender, 1974); *Handbook on Pension Reform Law* (Englewood Cliffs, N.J.: Prentice-Hall, 1974); and Edward A. Stoeber, *Pension Reform Act Explained* (Cincinnati: National Underwriters, 1974). See also the relevant sections in Greenough and King, *Pension Plans* (note 9 supra).
23. U.S. Department of Health, Education, and Welfare, *Coverage and Vesting of Full Time Employees Under Private Retirement Plans: Findings from the April 1972 Survey*, DHEW Publication No. (SSA) 74-11908, BLS Report No. 423 (Washington, D.C., mimeo, 1974), p. 2.
24. *1975 Study of Corporate Pension Plans* (New York: Bankers Trust, 1975), pp. 8–10.
25. Ibid., p. 22.
26. Robert Tilove, "ERISA—Its Effect on Collective Bargaining," in Richard Adelman, ed., *Proceedings of the New York University 29th Annual Conference on Labor* (New York: Matthew Bender, 1976), p. 189.
27. See Daniel Halperin, "Sex Discrimination and Pensions: Are We Moving Toward Unisex Tables?" in Richard Adelman, ed., *Proceedings of the New York University 30th Annual National Conference on Labor* (New York: Matthew Bender, 1977), pp. 236–38. The Supreme Court has so far made only one significant ruling on the pension status of men and women. A contributory plan that required greater contributions from female employees for equal monthly benefits was held to violate Title VII of the Civil Rights Act. This was qualified in two ways: (1) It is

lawful for the employer to set aside equal retirement contributions and let each retiree purchase the largest benefit that the accumulated contribution commands on the open market; (2) the decision does not call into question the insurance industry practice of considering the composition of an employer's work force in determining the probable cost of a retirement or death benefit plan. *City of Los Angeles* v. *Manhart*, reported in Bureau of National Affairs, *Daily Labor Report*, April 25, 1978.

28. Tilove, "ERISA," pp. 195–96. For a discussion of enforcement issues, see Earl Palay, "Arbitration and Pension Benefits," pp. 223–233, and Steven Sacher, "Current Issues in Compliance," pp. 257–273, in Adelman, *Proceedings, 30th Annual Conference*.
29. *1975 Study of Corporate Pension Plans*, p. 26.
30. Employers and unions can establish IRAs in which funds are pooled, provided that separate accounts are kept for each participant. By their nature, IRAs are fully vested, and participants can add individual contributions up to the maximum of 15 percent of pay or $7,500.
31. Yohalem, "Employee-Benefit Plans" (note 1 supra), p. 25.
32. Inasmuch as only 595 plans out of 730 answered the questionnaire, there is the problem that the findings may be biased, but the direction of the bias, if any, is unknown.
33. Again, this is subject to considerable error. Of the 730 plans sampled, only 524 replied to this quesiton. In this instance, the direction of the bias, if any, is unknown.
33. Again, this is subject to considerable error. Of the 730 plans sampled, only 524 replied to this question. In this instance, the direction of the bias seems clear. My guess is that most nonrespondents did not provide alternative coverage, hence the 41 percent figure is an overstatement.
34. U.S. Comptroller General, *Effect of the Employee Retirement Income Security Act on the Termination of Single Employer Defined Benefit Plans* (Washington: U.S. General Accounting Office, April 27, 1978), pp. 5–6, 26–28.
35. Ibid., pp. 19–28.
36. A. F. Ehrbar, "Those Pension Plans Are Even Weaker Than You Think," *Fortune*, November 1977, pp. 104–14.
37. Kenneth K. Keene and Sandra M. Kazinetz, Comparing Unfunded Liabilities: Net Worth Provides Good News (New York: Johnson and Higgins, 1978).
38. I am assuming that the incidence of the combination falls upon workers, even though it may be paid by employers. I am not sure, however, that this assumption is any sounder than the assumption that the employer's share of the Social Security tax is borne by workers.
39. Munnell, *Future of Social Security* (note 1 supra), pp. 113–24.
40. Philip Cagan, *The Effect of Pension Plans on Aggregate Saving: Evidence from a Sample Survey*, NBER Occasional Paper No. 95 (New York: Columbia University Press, 1965), and George Katona, *The*

*Mass Consumption Society* (New York: McGraw-Hill, 1964), Chap. 19.

41. Alicia H. Munnell, "Private Pensions and Saving: New evidence," *Journal of Political Economy*, 84, No. 5 (October 1976): 1031–1032 (see especially p. 1031).
42. *1975 Study of Corporate Pension Plans* (note 24 supra), pp. 10–15.
43. The Consumer Price Index rose by 13.5 points from 1974 to 1975. During that period, personal savings rose from $8.1 billion to $8.2 billion. *Economic Report of the President, 1976* (Washington: U.S. Government Printing Office, 1976), pp. 193, 187.
44. Alicia H. Munnell, "The Interaction of Social Security and Private Pensions," unpublished paper (mimeo, 1977), p. 1.
45. Ibid., p. 16
46. Robert J. Myers, "The Future of Social Security: Is It in Conflict with Private Pension Plans?" *Pension and Welfare News*, January 1970, pp. 38–48.
47. James H. Schultz and Guy Carrin, "The Role of Savings and Pension Systems in Maintaining Living Standards in Retirement," *Journal of Human Resources*, 7, No. 3 (Summer 1972): 343–365.
48. Robert D. Paul, "Statement Before the Subcommittee on Retirement Income and Employment, April 6, 1978," (Martin E. Segal, mimeo). For a similar view, see Robert Tilove, "Comment on Schulz," in G. S. Tolley and Richard V. Burkhauser, eds., *Income Support Policies for the Aged* (Cambridge, Mass.: Ballinger, 1977), pp. 37–44.
49. These are countries that place heavy reliance on their private pension systems. See James Schultz et al., *Providing Adequate Retirement Income: Pension Reform in the United States* (Hanover, N.H.: University Press of New England, 1974), p. 266.
50. James H. Schultz, "Public Policy and the Future Roles of Public and Private Pensions," in Tolley and Burkhauser, *Income Support Policies*, pp. 30–32. See also *Pensions: Britain's Great Step Forward* (London: HMSO, n.d. [1977]). The plan replaces a previous all-public earnings-related plan that was terminated in 1975.
51. John K. Dyer, Jr., "Coordination of Private and Public Pension Plans," in Dan M. McGill, ed., *Social Security and Private Pension Plans: Competitive or Complementary* (Homewood, Ill.: Richard D. Irwin, 1977), pp. 39–40.
52. Where firms are induced to substitute capital for labor, the disemployment effect would be greater in the long run.
53. The decline would be smaller than the additional pension contribution because of the operation of the income tax system. There might also be some reduction in the supply of marginal workers.
54. ERISA permits the exclusion of workers employed within five years of retirement age.
55. Robert J. Myers, "The New Social Security Amendments: How They Affect Private Pension Plans," *Pension World*, March 1978, p. 14.

56. Strictly speaking, it is a transfer cost. It transfers income from the working population to the retired population.
57. The discussion to follow relies in part on the Johnson and Higgins *Benefit Bulletin*, March 17, 1978.
58. Strictly speaking, changes in the Primary Insurance Amount (PIA), the benefit without reference to additional dependents' benefits. The latter are linked to the PIA.
59. Computed from data in the 1977 *Employment and Training Report of the President*, p. 165.
60. The best work on the subject is Tilove, *Public Employee Pension Plans* (note 1 supra), and I have placed heavy reliance on this source for materials on the public sector. See also John P. Mackin, *Protecting Purchasing Power in Retirement* (New York: Fleet Academic Editions, 1971).
61. See Greenough and King, *Pension Plans* (note 9 surpa), pp. 49–52 and Tilove, *Public Employee Pension Plans*, pp. 5–8.
62. Greenough and King, *Pension Plans*, pp. 58–59, and Board of Actuaries of the Civil Service Retirement System, *Fifty-second Annual Report*, House Document 94-203 (Washington: U.S. Government Printing Office, 1975), pp. 11–13.
63. Computed from *Annual Report of Financial and Statistical Data for Year Ended June 30, 1975* (Washington: U.S. Civil Service Commission, 1975), p. 8.
64. Board of Actuaries, *Fifty-second Annual Report*, p. 5.
65. Board of Actuaries of the Civil Service Retirement System, *Fifty-fifth Annual Report* (Washington, processed November 4, 1977), pp. 5, 9.
66. Board of Actuaries, *Fifty-second Annual Report*, p. 11.
67. U.S. Department of Health, Education, and Welfare, Social Security Administration, *Research and Statistics Note*, No. 8, July 11, 1978.
68. For a further discussion of military pensions, see Martin Binkin, *The Military Pay Muddle* (Washington: Brookings Institution, 1975), pp. 11–13, 55–57.
69. U.S. Department of Commerce, Bureau of the Census, *Finances of Employee-Retirement Systems of State and Local Governments, 1975–76*, GF 76, No. 2, 1978, pp. 1–3.
70. Taken from James A. Maxwell, "Characteristics of State and Local Trust Funds," in David J. Ott et al., eds., *State-Local Finances in the Last Half of the 1970s* (Washington: American Enterprise Institute, 1975), pp. 51–58.
71. The ratio of payments to assets are correspondingly higher in these state and local systems, running about three times the national average.
72. However, Massachusetts is an example of a pay-as-you-go system.
73. *Pensions and Investments*, July 18, 1977.
74. Tilove, *Public Employee Pension Funds*, pp. 261–289.
75. Bruce W. Marcus, "Will Public Plans Sink the Cities?" *Pension World*, 13, No. 4 (April 1977): 11–14.

76. Section 3031, cited in *Handbook on Pension Reform Law*, p. 729. The studies themselves are in U.S. Congress, House Committee on Education and Labor, *Interim Report of the Activities of the Pension Task Force of the Subcommittee on Labor Standards* (Washington: U.S. Government Printing Office, 1976).
77. Bernard Jump, Jr., *State and Local Employee Pension Plans: Watching for Problems* (Columbus, Ohio: Academy for Contemporary Problems, October 1976), p. 8.
78. Marcus, "Public Plans," p. 11.
79. Computed from data in U.S. President, *Eighth Annual Report on the National Housing Goal* (Washington: U.S. Government Printing Office, 1976), p. 107. I have assumed that "cash and other assets" are largely demand deposits, and therefore in the private sector. The data for private plans are for noninsured ones only. Insured plans' assets are also heavily in the private sector, where insurance companies hold most of their assets.
80. Tilove, *Public Employee Pension Funds*, pp. 37–38.
81. Thomas P. Bleakney, *Retirement Systems for Public Employees* (Homewood, Ill.: Richard D. Irwin, 1972), pp. 70–71.
82. Tilove, *Public Employee Pension Plans* (note 1 supra), pp. 339–340.
83. *1975 Study of Corporate Pension Plans* (note 24 supra), pp. 26–28. It should be recalled that ERISA protects beneficiaries from reductions in pensions due to Social Security benefit increases; the offsets, where encountered, pertain to contributions into the plan or reduced future plan benefits.
84. Jerome M. Rosow, "Public Sector Pay and Benefits," *Public Administration Review*, 36, No. 5 (September–October 1976): 38.
85. Bleakney, *Retirement Systems*, pp. 53–54.
86. *1975 Study of Corporate Pension Plans*, p. 34.
87. Rosow, "Public Sector Pay," p. 541.
88. *Employee Benefits, 1975* (Washington: Chamber of Commerce of the United States, 1976), p. 11.
89. Alicia H. Munnell and Ann M. Connolly, "Funding Government Pensions: State–Local, Civil Service and Military," in *Funding Pensions: Issues and Implications for Financial Markets* (Boston: Federal Reserve Bank of Boston, n.d. [1976]), p. 125.

**CHAPTER 4: SOCIAL SECURITY IN A TIME OF CHANGE (pp. 116–152).**

1. Kathleen Bond, "Retirement History's First Four Years: Work, Health and Living Arrangements," *Social Security Bulletin*, 39, No. 12 (December 1976): 13–14.
2. For an alternative measure of intrafamily transfers, see Marilyn Moon, *The Measurement of Economic Welfare: Its Application to the Aged Poor* (New York: Academic Press, 1977), p. 74. Moon's intermediate

estimate is that 12.16 percent of aged families make transfers (of less than $5,000), 15.59 percent receive transfers, and 72.24 percent neither give nor receive. The net mean dollar value of positive and negative transfers is close to zero.

3. There is also a scattering of benefits available in various localities that may be mentioned here but are not important in the aggregate. They range from reduced property taxes to such services as public housing, private and public social work, senior citizens' programs, and meals-on-wheels. No complete list of such services has ever been compiled.
4. *Annual Report of the Board of Trustees of the Federal Old Age and Survivors Insurance and Disability Insurance Trust Funds*. 1977, House Document 95-150 (Washington: U.S. Government Printing Office, 1977), p. 63.
5. Moon, *Measurement of Economic Welfare.*
6. This is not intended to disparage Dr. Moon's work, which is valuable for its theoretical contribution and its demonstration that, were good data available, a better measure of economic welfare would exist and could be used by policymakers.
7. For a discussion of the conceptual problems, see Bruno Stein, *On Relief: The Economics of Poverty and Public Welfare* (New York: Basic Books, 1971), pp. 5–14.
8. Congressional Budget Office, *Poverty Status of Families Under Alternative Definitions of Income* (Washington: U.S. Government Printing Office, June 1977), pp. 11–12. The analysis is based on 1975 data from the current population survey, adjusted to FY 1976 levels.
9. However, see Harold Watts and Felicity Skidmore, "An Update of the Poverty Picture Plus a New Look at Relative Tax Burdens," *Focus*, 2, No. 1 (Fall 1977): 5. The authors estimate that 4.6 percent of persons sixty-five and over and 5.6 percent of families with an aged head were poor after all public transfers in 1976.
10. James N. Morgan et al., *Five Thousand Americans: Patterns of Economic Progress*, Vol. 1 (Ann Arbor: Institute for Social Research, University of Michigan, 1974), pp. 22, 29.
11. U.S. Department of Labor, *Three Budgets for a Retired Couple* (Washington: Bureau of Labor Statistics, August 4, 1977, USDL 77-690, and August 19, 1976 USDL 76-1133).
12. Computed from U.S. Bureau of the Census, Current Population Reports, Series P-60, No. 105, *Money Income in 1975 of Families and Persons in the United States* (Washington: U.S. Government Printing Office, June 1977), Table 23, p. 102.
13. This point is often overlooked by economists who treat leisure as simply a normal good. There are some people who prefer employment not only for its income but also for its own sake, the status it confers, the sociability of the work place, or simply because an excess of leisure is boring to them.

14. Peter Henle, "Recent Trends in Retirement Benefits Related to Earnings," *Monthly Labor Review*, 95, No. 6 (June 1972): 12. The analysis that follows relies heavily on Henle. See also Walter W. Kolodrubetz and Alfred M. Skolnick, *Pension Benefit Levels: A Methodological Analysis*, Social Security Administration Publication No. 72-11851 (Washington: U.S. Government Printing Office, 1972).
15. This was done by updating Henle's earnings histories, which end in 1971. See his table, Henle, "Recent Trends," p. 14.
16. Strictly speaking, male workers. In 1977 there was a slight difference for females, which was being phased out.
17. To avoid confusion, integrated pension plans were omitted from consideration. Thus, the annual benefits in Tables 4-2 and Appendix Table 4-11 are fully additive.
18. No attempt has been made to project after-tax replacement rates and real replacement rates for workers retiring in 1987. Future tax legislation is too uncertain. Price level projections are hypothetical enough when made as far as 1987.
19. U.S. Department of Health, Education, and Welfare, *Monthly Vital Statistics Report, Final Divorce Statistics, 1975*, Health Resources Administration, 26, No. 2, Supp. 2 (May 19, 1977): 1, 3.
20. Paul C. Glick and Arthur J. Norton, "Frequency, Duration and Probability of Marriage and Divorce," *Journal of Marriage and the Family*, 33 No. 2 (May 1971): 310. Data are for 1966.
21. For an excellent discussion of the issues surrounding the spouse's benefits, see Alicia H. Munnell, "Social Security," in Joseph Pechman, ed., *The 1978 Budget: Setting National Priorities* (Washington: Brookings Institution, 1977), pp. 238–243.
22. The problem remains for individuals subsisting on Supplemental Security Income who wish to get married, because benefits are lower and the benefit reduction is consequently more painful.
23. The Supreme Court has ruled that a female employee cannot be compelled to make a greater contribution than a man in a contributory plan. See *City of Los Angeles* v. *Manhart*. Presumably, pension plans can average the life expectancies of men and women if they seek to achieve equal contributions and equal benefits.
24. However, Social Security may have discouraged private savings. For an extended discussion of this, see Chapters 5 and 6.
25. This is especially so if the tax is not a one-shot matter but continues to increase, so that long-run equilibrium lies beyond the horizon.
26. Munnell, "Social Security," pp. 237–238.
27. The Social Security retirement test of $4,000 per year (1978) will rise in stages to $6,000 by 1982 and will be indexed to changes in average annual earnings in subsequent years.
28. For a discussion of horizontal and vertical equity in taxes, see the classic work by Richard A. Musgrave, *The Theory of Public Finance* (New

York: McGraw-Hill, 1959), pp. 160–183. The topic as applied to benefits is also covered in Alicia H. Munnell, *The Future of Social Security* (Washington: Brookings Institution, 1977), and Rita R. Campbell, "The Problems of Fairness," in Michael J. Boskin, ed., *The Crisis in Social Security* (San Francisco: Institute for Contemporary Studies, 1977), pp. 125–145.

29. See Munnell, *Future of Social Security*, pp. 56–57. Munnell Suggests that PIAs be adjusted to length of service.
30. This is a self-liquidating problem, over the long run.
31. J. Douglas Brown, *Essays on Social Security* (Princeton: Industrial Relations Section, Princeton University, 1977). p. 5. Brown was among the founders of Social Security.
32. Computed from *Employment and Training Report of the President, 1978* (Washington: U.S. Government Printing Office, 1978), pp. 233–234.
33. Karl E. Taueber, "Demographic Trends Affecting the Future Labor Force," University of Wisconsin, Institute for Research on Poverty, Special Report Series, SR 14, 1977, p. 33.
34. It will, of course, have "bought" Survivors and Disability coverage during their working years.
35. A full discussion of sex discrimination is found in U.S. Department of Health, Education, and Welfare, *Report of the HEW Task Force on the Treatment of Women under Social Security* (Washington, processed, February 1978).
36. However, Munnell estimates the cost of supporting an additional household member at 30 percent. If she is correct, then the spouse's benefit exceeds the bounds of adequacy. See Munnell, *Future of Social Security*, p. 38, n. 15.
37. The emerging theory of optimal taxation may provide a firmer basis for questions of equity. At this juncture, the state of knowledge is not sufficiently advanced to be helpful to this work, although the possibility of treating benefits as negative taxes suggests that future possibilities for application to Social Security are inherent in this line of analysis. For an interesting empirical effort to treat horizontal equity in optimal taxation, see Harvey S. Rosen, "An Approach to the Study of Income, Utility and Horizontal Equity," Princeton University, Econometric Research Program, Research Memorandum No. 212, February 1977.
38. See Musgrave, *Theory of Public Finance*, pp. 20, 91, 160–183.
39. I am here inverting the concept of equal marginal sacrifice in taxation in order to apply it to benefits.
40. Munnell, *Future of Social Security*, pp. 38–52.
41. Brown, *Essays*, pp. 4–5. Emphasis added.
42. Ibid., p. 23.
43. See J. S. Fleming, "Optimal Payroll Taxes and Social Security Funding," *Journal of Public Economics*, 7, No. 3 (June 1977): 330.

44. E. S. Phelps, *Golden Rules of Economic Growth* (New York: Norton, 1966), p. 5.

## CHAPTER 5: LABOR MARKETS AND CAPITAL FORMATION (pp. 153–170).

1. See Edgar K. Browning, "Labor Supply Distortions of Social Security," *Southern Economic Journal*, 42, No. 2 (October 1975): 243–252.
2. The data are not strictly comparable: The first number excludes men over sixty-nine and is taken from Census data, whereas the second number includes all men sixty-five and over and comes from the Current Population Survey. Comparable data from the latter source show a decline from 46.8 percent in 1948 to 20.3 percent in 1976. *Employment and Training Report of the President, 1978* (Washington: U.S. Government Printing Office, 1978), p. 142.
3. That is, the first derivative
4. See the data in Barry R. Chiswick and June O'Neill, *Human Resources and Income Distribution* (New York: Norton, 1977), p. 131. Their data are from the *Economic Report of the President, 1976* (Washington: U.S. Government Printing Office, 1976).
5. See, for example, U.S. Department of Health, Education, and Welfare, Social Security Administration, *Reaching Retirement Age: Findings from a Survey of Newly Entitled Workers 1968–70*, Office of Research and Statistics, Research Report No. 147 (Washington: U.S. Government Printing Office, 1976), p. 3.
6. The study was limited to white married men, and it may not be possible to generalize the results to others.
7. Joseph F. Quinn, "Microeconomic Determinants of Retirement: A Cross Sectional View of White Married Men," *Journal of Human Resources*, 12, No. 3 (Summer 1977): 329–346.
8. That is, the group's labor supply was elastic in respect to net earnings.
9. Michael J. Boskin, "Social Security and Retirement Decisions," *Economic Inquiry*, 15, No. 1 (January 1977): 1–25. Boskin is careful to note that his findings are tentative, but they strike me as plausible. See also Martin J. Feldstein, "Social Security, Induced Retirement and Aggregate Capital Accumulation," *Journal of Political Economy*, 82, No. 5 (September–October 1974): 905–926. See especially his observation that although the system's intent was income maintenance for the aged, this goal is partly vitiated by the earnings test, which reduces levels of income and consumption for many of the retired population (pp. 924–925). For an excellent summary of the literature, see Colin D. Campbell and Rosemary G. Campbell, "Conflicting Views on the Effect of Old-Age and Survivors Insurance on Retirement," *Economic Inquiry*, 14, No. 9 (September 1976): 369–388.
10. Feldstein, "Social Security, Induced Retirement," p. 924.

11. Campbell and Campbell, "Conflicting Views," p. 385.
12. In 1946 Lord Keynes argued that Americans need not fear stagnation because Social Security would reduce saving. See Alicia H. Munnell, "The Impact of Social Security on Personal Savings," *National Tax Journal*, 27, No. 4 (December 1974): 554.
13. Milton Friedman, *A Theory of the Consumption Function* (Princeton, N.J.: Princeton University Press, 1957), p. 123.
14. Cited in Joseph A. Pechman, Henry J. Aaron, and Michael K. Taussig, *Social Security: Perspectives for Reform* (Washington: Brookings Institution, 1968), p. 295.
15. Philip Cagan, *The Effect of Pension Plans on Aggregate Saving: Evidence from a Sample Survey*, NBER Occasional Paper No. 95 (New York: Columbia University Press, 1965).
16. George Katona, *The Mass Consumption Society* (New York: McGraw-Hill, 1969), Chap. 19.
17. See Pechman et al., *Social Security*. The two studies are cited on pp. 30, 63 and 186.
18. Feldstein, "Social Security, Induced Retirement," pp. 905–926.
19. Alicia H. Munnell, *The Effect of Social Security on Personal Savings* (Cambridge, Mass.: Ballinger, 1974) and Munnell, "Impact of Social Security on Personal Savings," cited above. A comparison of her findings with Feldstein's is found in Alicia H. Munnell, *The Future of Social Security* (Washington: Brookings Institution, 1977) pp. 116–121.
20. Feldstein apparently includes not only Social Security taxes (OASDHI) but other payroll taxes and contributions, including the federal portions of unemployment insurance, railroad retirement, federal civil service retirement, veterans' life insurance, and miscellaneous similar resources. OASDHI receipts for that year were about $42.5 billion. It is apparently assumed that employers shift all of their share of payroll taxes.
21. Using a marginal propensity to consume of .65.
22. Feldstein estimated the marginal propensity to consume SSWG at .021.
23. Personal saving in the 1960s constituted 60 percent of total private saving. Thus, a 50 percent cut in personal saving produces a 38 percent cut in total saving. Feldstein assumes that all savings, at least in the long run, are invested.
24. Assuming a Cobb–Douglas technology and a capital coefficient of 0.3.
25. Assuming a 60 percent decrease in capital stock, and using a Cobb–Douglas technology with a capital eleasticity of 0.3, with fixed labor supply, the wage rate is proportional to $k^{0.3}$ and the rate of interest is proportional to $k^{-0.7}$. Since the Cobb–Douglas technology implies no change in factor shares, this implies a substantial redistribution of capital income to those who now save little because of Social Security. Feldstein does not indicate whether this aspect of the redistribution offsets the maldistribution between wages and capital income.

26. The description of Munnell's analysis is taken from "Impact of Social Security on Personal Savings" and from *Future of Social Security*, pp. 113–133.
27. The series is based on aggregate savings data by components, published by Raymond Goldsmith in 1956 for the years 1900–1948, and by the Securities and Exchange Commission (1970) for 1948–1970. See Munnel, "Impact of Social Security on Personal Savings," pp. 556–557. The purpose is to separate retirement saving from saving for other purposes, and thus to isolate the impact of Social Security.
28. The redistribution of income would reduce saving if workers had a significantly lower propensity to consume than beneficiaries. Munnell argues that both groups have high propensities to consume and that the income transfer has a negligible effect on saving behavior. See Munnell *Future of Social Security*, p. 120.
29. Martin Feldstein, "Social Security and Private Savings: International Evidence in an Extended Life Cycle Model," Discussion Paper No. 361, Harvard University, Institute of Economic Research, 1974; processed.
30. A fourth and more technical reason adduced by Munnell is Feldstein's claim that his evidence is consistent with the Keynesian view that rising income increases the aggregate saving rate unless offset by government policies. A secular increase, however, is difficult to explain within the context of a life cycle model.
31. Robert J. Barro, "Are Government Bonds Net Worth?" *Journal of Political Economy*, 82, No. 6 (November–December 1974): 1095–1117.
32. Martin Feldstein, "Social Security and Savings: The Extended Life Cycle Theory," *American Economic Review*, 66, No. 2 (May 1976): 77–86.
33. Robert J. Barro, "Social Security and Private Saving: Evidence from the U.S. Time Series," University of Rochester, April 1977, processed.
34. Including a modified unemployment variable.
35. Michael R. Darby, "The Effects of Social Security on Income and the Capital Stock," University of California, Los Angeles, Working Paper No. 95, July 1977.
36. That is, the rational individual plans his consumption and saving, subject to the constraint of his income, so as to exhaust his savings upon his demise.
37. Darby experimented with several variations on this, but none altered his conclusions.
38. Darby's careful analysis distinguishes between closed and open economies. By treating the United States as a large and partly open economy, he is able to distinguish between impacts on U.S.-owned capital and all capital used in the United States.
39. It is impossible to do full justice to Darby's careful and lengthy analysis in a few paragraphs, and I have focused on the gist of the matter.

40. For other studies of savings behavior, see Paul A. David and John L. Scadding, "Private Savings: Ultrarationality, Aggregation and 'Dimson's Law,'" *Journal of Political Economy*, 82, No. 2 (March–April 1974): 225–249, and Feldstein's critique of this in "Social Security and Saving," p. 80. After my manuscript was completed, I came across Louis Esposito's analysis of the Feldstein–Munnell–Barro–Darby controversy. Esposito does not believe that further analysis of the data used by these authors will yield different results, and suggests that either (1) time series data cannot isolate the private savings effects of Social Security, or (2) the program does not significantly affect private saving. See Louis Esposito, "Effect of Social Security on Saving: Review of Studies Using U.S. Time-Series Data, *Social Security Bulletin*, 41, No. 5 (May 1978): 17.

**CHAPTER 6: FINANCING SOCIAL SECURITY (pp. 171–216).**

1. In some states, carriers who want to sell autombile insurance must accept all applicants by participating in an assigned-risk pool. However, the premiums are presumably high enough to cover the bad risks.
2. The increase in the rate for self-employed persons is sharper, rising from 8.1 percent in 1978 to 10.75 percent in 1990. This is to restore the original ratio between the tax on employed and self-employed persons.
3. "AFL-CIO Recommendations on Major Provisions of House and Senate Social Security Bills," processed, n.d. (January 1978), p. 1
4. Assuming, of course, no change in the distribution of earnings.
5. Computed from Social Security Administration, *Legislative Report*, No. 17, December 16, 1977, Table 2.
6. U.S. Congress, House of Representatives, Committee on Ways and Means, *Summary of the Conference Agreement on H.R. 9346, the Social Security Amendments of 1977*, WMCP: 95-61 (Washington, U.S. Government Printing Office, 1977), p. 3. The same figure appears in Social Security Administration, *Legislative Report*, Table 2.
7. Congressional Budget Office, "Update on Social Security Legislation," processed, n.d. (January, 1978).
8. Social Security Administration, "Projected Workers with Taxable Earnings," processed, 1978. The estimates in this table are based on assumptions underlying the President's 1979 Budget. Letter from Social Security Administration, February 10, 1978.
9. Proposals for full funding are analyzed in another section of this chapter.
10. Congressional Budget Office, *Five-Year Projections: Fiscal Years 1979–1983 (Technical Background)* (Washington: U.S. Government Printing Office, 1978), p. 124.
11. In theoretical terms, this constitutes a welfare burden on the economy.

For an empirical investigation of the differential tax burden of Social Security on employers by sector, see G. N. Carlson, G. C. Hufbauer and M. B. Krauss, "Destination Principle Border Tax Adjustments for the Corporate Income and Social Security Taxes: An Analysis of Sectoral Effects," National Tax Association, *Proceedings of the Sixty-ninth Annual Conference, November 14–16, 1976*, pp. 104–106.

12. That is, the ratio of the relative change in sales to the relative change in the price.
13. Corporate income tax increases can have a similar effect.
14. For a discussion of pricing policies and inflation, see Nicholas Kaldor, "Inflation and Recession in the World Economy," *Economic Journal*, December 1976, pp. 703–714, esp. p. 706.
15. *New York Times*, October 5, 1977.
16. The Mikva-Nelson bill, introduced in Congress in early 1978, proposed to finance Medicare and Disability Insurance from general revenues. See *New York Times*, February 7, 1978.
17. The dollar "break points" in this formula are indexed to changes in average annual earnings.
18. Alicia H. Munnell, *The Future of Social Security* (Washington: Brookings Institution, 1977), pp. 39–40.
19. *Reports of the Quadrennial Advisory Council on Social Security*, p. xvii.
20. Munnell, *Future of Social Security*, pp. 92–93. Munnell argues for a strictly wage-related benefit structure, with relief for low wage earners by an expansion of the income tax's earned income credit to relieve the burden of the Social Security tax on low wage earners. In addition, she wants expansion of Supplemental Security Income (public assistance) to care for those of the aged who remain needy after Social Security benefits. The effect of this proposal is, again, to shift accounts between the system and general revenues.
21. Social Security Administration, *Legislative Report*, No. 17, (note 5 supra), Table 4.
22. 1977 *Annual Report of the Trustees of the Federal Old-Age and Survivors Insurance and Disability Insurance Trust Fund*, House Document 95–150 (Washington: U.S. Government Printing Office, 1977), p. 37, Table 22.
23. Projection made by the Social Security Administration, using the intermediate assumptions of the trustees. See Social Security Administration, *Legislative Report*, No. 17, Table 4.
24. 1977 *Annual Report of the Trustees*, p. 37, Table 32.
25. For a different view, see George E. Rejda, *Social Insurance and Economic Security* (Englewood Cliffs, N.J.: Prentice-Hall, 1976), p. 147. Rejda emphatically rejects the notion that the fund is a fictitious entity. He is correct, of course, in the sense that a fund exists and holds federal obligations that would otherwise be held by others.

26. The data below are drawn from the 1977 *Annual Report of the Trustees.*
27. Assets are carried on its books at par value or book value (par value plus unamortized premium, less discount outstanding). The market value of some of its public debt holdings, such as 3½s of 1998, is substantially below par values as of 1978.
28. Replacement rates for disabled workers and survivors will also decline until they fall into line with the replacement rates for older workers with similar earnings histories.
29. The "intermediate assumptions" are that the percentage change in the Consumer Price Index will level off at 4 percent in 1982, that the percent change in wages will level off at 5.75 percent in 1983 (yielding a somewhat discouraging annual rise of 1.75 percent in real wages), that the unemployment rate will reach 5 percent in 1981 and remain at that level thereafter, and that the fertility rate will gradually return to 2.1 by the year 2000. "Table 1, Values of Selected Economic and Geographic Factors (Alternative II)" (Baltimore: Social Security Administration, processed, 1978).
30. A. Haeworth Robertson, "The Financial Status of Social Security After the Social Security Amendments of 1977 (Baltimore: Social Security Administration, processed, January 1978) p. 20.
31. Socialists would, of course, quarrel with this notion, However, the problems described below are applicable to a socialist economy where all nonwage claims are redistributive.
32. The analysis is drawn from Donald O. Parsons and Douglas R. Munro, "Intergenerational Transfers in Social Security," in Michael J. Boskin, ed., *The Crisis in Social Security* (San Francisco: Institute for Contemporary Studies, 1977), pp. 65–86.
33. The number of workers needed to support one retired person is simply the reciprocal of the aged dependency ratio, i.e., the ratio of the number of people aged sixty-five and over to the population aged twenty to sixty-four. The series used above is the one used by the Actuary in the 1977 Trustees' Report. It is not comparable to the series of projections issued by the Census Bureau (*Current Population Survey Series* P-25, No. 704). Although the latter has the advantage of more detailed age breakouts, it is based on a narrower sample than the former. Long-range projections are, in any event, not intended to be precise.
34. For a discussion of this and related issues, see Harold L. Sheppard and Sara E. Rix, *The Graying of Working America: The Coming Crisis of Retirement-Age Policy* (New York: Free Press, 1977), esp. Chaps. 2 and 3.
35. This corresponds roughly to the assumptions made in the 1977 *Annual Report of the Trustees*, p. 64. For comparison see Howard N. Fullerton, Jr., and Paul O. Flaim, "New Labor Force Projections to 1990," Bureau of Labor Statistics, Special Labor Force Report 197.

36. 1977 *Annual Report of the Trustees*, p. 63. The reader is reminded that this is not quite comparable to the more detailed projections made by the Census Bureau. The use of age twenty to represent entry into the labor force is arbitrary but does not change the essence of the analysis.
37. See Bernard Okun, "Comment on Gary S. Becker's 'An Economic Analysis of Fertility,'" in National Bureau of Economic Research, *Demographic and Economic Changes in Developed Countries* (Princeton, N.J.: Princeton University Press, 1960), pp. 235–240. Becker's analysis differs in that he expects both the number of children and expenditures on child equality (education, etc.) to increase with income. See his paper cited above, pp. 209–231.
38. Marxists make labor the crucial variable. However, since they treat capital as congealed labor, the tenor of the analysis is not changed by the use of the Marxist rather than conventional economic analysis.
39. George von Furstenberg and Burton G. Malkiel, "The Government and Capital Formation: A Survey of Recent Issues," *The Journal of Economic Literature*, 15, No. 3 (September 1977): 860, 867.
40. The description of Feldstein's full funding proposal is drawn primarily from his "The Optimal Financing of Social Security," Discussion Paper No. 388 (Harvard University, Institute of Economic Research, 1974, processed), and secondarily from his "Toward a Reform of Social Security," *Public Interest*, 40 (Summer 1975): 75–95. Feldstein believes that his proposal is "optimal" only if the current growth of benefits cannot be altered. His preference is for a slower growth of future benefits (letter to the author, August 24, 1978).
41. The 1977 amendments are intended to permit benefits to grow with changes in average earnings but to stabilize the average replacement rate.
42. Feldstein also points out that an alternative, but less efficient, approach would be to tie the tax increase to the worker's current age. Presumably, this would overcome objections of intergenerational inequity, but Feldstein does not explore the extent to which the gain in welfare would be reduced.
43. More precisely, the difference between the social rate of return and the rate at which persons discount future consumption. I am assuming, for purposes of simplicity, that this is the relevant rate faced by workers.
44. This requires the assumption that the incidence of the employer's share rests on workers. I have earlier noted that this is not always a sound assumption.
45. Munnell, *Future of Social Security* (note 18 supra), pp. 127–128. See also pp. 128–133 for an excellent critique of Feldstein's proposal to move to full funding.
46. As shown in an earlier chapter, this was not exactly the case, since actuarial projections made at the time predicted exhaustion of the fund by the 1960s. Presumably, this could have been dealt with by raising

the Social Security tax rate more rapidly than envisioned in the 1935 act.

47. There is a small irony here. Feldstein's proposal requires a *compulsory* bequest from mature workers to their children. The econometric model that he uses to estimate savings behavior excludes *voluntary* bequests from consideration.
48. Munnell, *Future of Social Security*, p. 130.
49. For example, see the latest available projections by the Social Security Administration. The intermediate assumption is that unemployment rates will decline from 7.1 percent in 1977 to 5% in 1981, and remain stable thereafter. The pessimistic set of assumptions include unemployment leveling off to 5.5% in 1984. Only the optimistic assumptions show unemployment at 4.5% after 1980. Even the last is more optimistic than the projections in the 1979 Budget of the President. The data are from "Values of Selected Economic and Demographic Factors Included in Alternatives I, II and III, by Calendar Year."
50. Munnell, *Future of Social Security*, pp. 130–131.
51. The interest elasticity of personal savings.
52. But, according to another writer, not enough to offset the overall rise in national savings. See Benjamin M. Friedman, "Public Pension Funding and U.S. Capital Formation: A Medium-Run View," in *Funding Pensions: Issues and Implications For Capital Markets* (Boston: Federal Reserve Bank of Boston, 1976), p. 173.
53. von Furstenberg and Malkiel, "Government and Capital Formation" (note 39 supra), pp. 847–848. The international effects are also analyzed in Michael R. Darby, "The Effects of Social Security on Income and the Capital Stock," Working Paper No. 95, University of California, Los Angeles, July 1977.
54. Darby, "Effects of Social Security," Chap. 6, p. 3.
55. Martin Feldstein, "The Social Security Fund and National Capital Accumulation," in *Funding Pensions*, pp. 32–63.
56. Martin Feldstein, "Response to Pechman," in *Funding Pensions*, p. 71.
57. Joseph A. Pechman, "Discussion," in *Funding Pensions*, p. 66.
58. Ibid., p. 67.
59. James Tobin, "Discussion," in *Funding Pensions*, p. 211. Tobin says Feldstein overestimates the extent to which national savings are reduced by Social Security and is critical of other aspects of the proposals. See pp. 210–212.

## CHAPTER 7: ANALYSIS: THE NEEDS FOR CHANGE (pp. 217–252).

1. Except to the extent, if any, that employers cannot shift the burden of their contributions.
2. Old Age Assistance until 1973 and Supplemental Security Assistance thereafter.

3. See Martin Neil Bailey, "Stabilization Policy and Private Economic Behavior," *Brookings Papers on Economic Activity*, 1 (1978): 11–50, esp. p. 14.
4. Intergenerational redistribution was not an issue, because the original law provided for full funding of benefits.
5. The reader is reminded that means-tested programs are demeaning to recipients.
6. The original actuaries, however, knew that the scheduled taxes would not suffice for full funding as the system matured. However, the day of reckoning was estimated at thirty years away.
7. Among them are France, Belgium, Sweden, and Germany (Federal Republic). See Organisation for Economic Co-Operation and Development, *Socioeconomic Policies for the Elderly*, Annex 1, Par 1, MAS(77) 18 (Paris: OECD, December 29, 1977, processed), paragraphs 80–88, 108–110.
8. James H. Schultz, "Public Policy and the Future Roles of Public and Private Pensions," G. S. Tolley and Richard V. Burkhauser, eds., *Income Support Policies for the Aged* (Cambridge, Mass.: Ballinger, 1977), pp. 17–18.
9. Ibid., p. 18
10. For analyses of this factor, see Donald J. Cymrot, "The Effect of Tax Incentives on the Rate of Return for Private Pensions," unpublished paper, January 1978, and "The Effect of Private Pensions on Labor Contracts," unpublished paper, April, 1978.
11. U.S. Senate, Committee on the Budget, *Tax Expenditures: Compendium of Background Material on Individual Provisions* (Washington: U.S. Government Printing Office, 1976), p. 115.
12. See *Report of the HEW Task Force on the Treatment of Women under Social Security*, esp. pp. 75–76.
13. Nancy M. Gordon has independently arrived at the same conclusion. See her *Treatment of Women in the Public Pension Systems of Five Countries*, working paper 5069-01 (Washington: Urban Institute, March 1978), pp. 56–66.
14. As reported in Bureau of National Affairs, *Daily Labor Report*, pp. E-1–E-3.
15. Tenured college professors will achieve this protection in 1982. Federal civil servants now have no mandatory retirement age at all.
16. The suggestion comes from Marilyn Moon and Eugene Smolensky, *Income Support Policies for the Aged* (Cambridge, Mass.: Ballinger, 1977), p. 51.
17. Lowering the age of the retirement test from seventy-two to seventy will induce some workers to remain in the labor market past age seventy, in order to keep benefits *and* earnings, and would induce others to retire earlier. Historically, the effect of early availability of benefits has

been to increase retirement, on net balance. The total number of workers involved, however, is likely to be small.

18. For additional support of this point of view, see Joseph J. Spengler, "Population Aging and the Security of the Aged," *Atlantic Economic Journal*, 6, No. 1, (March 1978): 1–7.
19. For a similar view, see James H. Schultz, *The Economics of Aging* (Belmont, Calif.: Wadsworth, 1976), pp. 150–151.
20. Robert M. Ball, *Social Security: Today and Tomorrow* (New York: Columbia University Press, 1978), pp. 478–480. Commissioner Ball wants to tax half the benefit and to dispense with the double exemption and other special tax provisions for the aged.
21. Ibid., p. 56. The proportion paid by employees is slightly lower than that of employers, because they receive refunds for overpayment in the event that combined wages from more than one job in any one year exceed the wage base. Employers do not receive refunds in such cases.
22. However, the proposal would have led to a lower rate of increase in the payroll tax rate, thus reducing the overall distortionary effects of the payroll tax. Whether this advantage would outweigh the disadvantage noted above is a difficult empirical question that cannot be answered here.
23. For a summary of the arguments, see Schultz, *Economics of Aging*, pp. 149–150.
24. A bill to finance Medicare and Disability Insurance was introduced in 1978. I am opposed to treating disability cash benefits differently from cash benefits to the aged, because *differential* treatment of the two groups might lead to invidious distinctions. However, the sharply rising cost of Disability Insurance may make this approach popular.
25. This idea was first advanced by Professors James Buchanan and Colin Campbell. Buchanan later incorporated it into a more complex proposal to replace Social Security with compulsory purchases of public or private bonds. See Schultz, *Economics of Aging*, pp. 146–149.

# Bibliography

"AFL-CIO Recommendations on Major Provisions of House and Senate Social Security Bills." Processed, n.d. (January 1978).

Allen, Everett T., Jr., Joseph J. Melone, and Jerry S. Rosenbloom. *Pension Planning: Pensions, Profit Sharing and Other Deferred Compensation Plans*. 3rd ed. Homewood, Ill.: Richard D. Irwin, 1976.

Altmeyer, Arthur J. *The Formative Years of Social Security*. Madison: University of Wisconsin Press, 1966

*Annual Report of the Board of Trustees of the Federal Old Age and Survivors Insurance and Disability Insurance Trust Funds*, 1974. Washington: U.S. Government Printing Office, 1974.

*Annual Report of the Board of Trustees of the Federal Old Age and Survivors Insurance and Disability Insurance Trust Fund*, 1977. House Document 95-150. Washington: U.S. Government Printing Office, 1977.

*Annual Report of the Board of Trustees of the Federal Hospital Insurance Trust Fund*, 1977. Washington, mimeo, May 9, 1977.

*Annual Report of Financial and Statistical Data for Fiscal Year Ended June 30, 1975.* Washington: U.S. Civil Service Commission, 1975.

Ashley, Sir W. J. *An Introduction to English Economic History and Theory*. New York: Sentry Press, 1966.

Baily, Martin N. "Stabilization Policy and Private Economic Behavior." *Brookings Papers on Economic Activity*, Vol. I, 1978, pp. 11–50.

Ball, Robert M. *Social Security: Today and Tomorrow*. New York: Columbia University Press, 1978.

Barro, Robert J. "Are Government Bonds Net Worth?" *Journal of Political Economy*, 82, No. 6 (November–December 1974): 1095–1117.

Barro, Robert J. "Social Security and Private Saving: Evidence from the U.S. Time Series." University of Rochester, April 1977, processed.

Binkin, Martin. *The Military Pay Muddle*. Washington: Brookings Institution, 1975.

Blaug, Mark, "The Myth of the Old Poor Law and the Making of the New." *Journal of Economic History*, 23, No. 2 (June 1963): 151–184.

Bleakney, Thomas P. *Retirement Systems for Public Employees.* Homewood, Ill.: Richard D. Irwin, 1972.

Board of Actuaries of the Civil Service Retirement System. *Fifty-second Annual Report,* House Document 94-203. Washington: U.S. Government Printing Office, 1975.

Board of Actuaries of the Civil Service Retirement System. *Fifty-fifth Annual Report.* Washington, processed, November 4, 1977.

Bond, Kathleen. "Retirement History Study's First Four Years: Work, Health, and Living Arrangements." *Social Security Bulletin,* 39, No. 12 (December 1976): 3-40.

Boskin, Michael J. "Social Security and Retirement Decisions." *Economic Inquiry,* 15, No. 1 (January 1977): 1-25.

Break, George F. "Social Security as a Tax." In Michael J. Boskin, ed., *The Crisis of Social Security.* San Francisco: Institute for Contemporary Studies, 1977, pp. 107-123.

Brittain, John A. "The Incidence of Social Security Payroll Taxes." *American Economic Review,* 61, No. 1 (March 1971): 110-125.

Brittain, John A. "The Incidence of Social Security Payroll Taxes: Reply." *American Economic Review,* 62, No. 4 (September 1972): 739-742.

Brown, J. Douglas. *An American Philosophy of Social Security, Evolution and Issues.* Princeton, N.J.: Princeton University Press, 1972.

Brown, J. Douglas. *Essays on Social Security.* Princeton, N.J.: Industrial Relations Section, Princeton University, 1972.

Browning, Edgar K. "Labor Supply Distortions of Social Security." *Southern Economic Journal,* 42, No. 2 (October 1975): 243-252.

*Budget of the United States Government, Fiscal Year 1979.* Washington: U.S. Government Printing Office, 1978.

Burns, Eveline M. *Social Security and Public Policy.* New York: McGraw-Hill, 1956.

Burns, Eveline M. *Toward Social Security: An Explanation of the Larger Issues.* New York: McGraw-Hill, 1936.

Cagan, Philip. *The Effect of Pension Plans on Aggregate Saving: Evidence from a Sample Survey,* NBER Occasional Paper No. 95. New York: Columbia University Press, 1965.

Campbell, Colin D., and Rosemary G. Campbell. "Conflicting Views of the Effect of Old Age and Survivors Insurance on Retirement." *Economic Inquiry,* 14, No. 9 (September 1976): 369-388.

Campbell, Rita R. "The Problems of Fairness." In Michael J. Boskin, ed., *The Crisis in Social Security.* San Francisco: Institute for Contemporary Studies, 1977, pp. 125-145.

Carlson, G. N., G. C. Hufbauer, and M. B. Krauss. "Destination Principle Border Tax Adjustments for the Corporate Income and Social Security Taxes: An Analysis of Sectoral Effects. "In National Tax Association, *Proceedings* of the Sixty-Ninth Annual Conference, November 14-16, 1976, pp. 97-107.

Chen, Yung-ping, and Kwang-wen Chu, "Total Dependency Burden and Social Security. "In Industrial Relations Research Association, *Proceedings of the 29th Annual Meetings, 1976.* Madison, Wisc.: Industrial Relations Research Association, 1977, pp. 43–51.

Chiswick, Barry R., and June O'Neill. *Human Resources and Income Distribution*. New York: Norton, 1977.

*City of Los Angeles* v. *Manhart*. Reported in Bureau of National Affairs, *Daily Labor Report*, April 25, 1978.

Cohen, Wilbur J. *Retirement Policies Under Social Security*. Berkeley and Los Angeles: University of California Press, 1957.

Congressional Budget Office. *Five Year Budget Projections: Fiscal Year 1979–1983, Technical Background.* Washington: U.S. Government Printing Office, 1978.

Congressional Budget Office. *Poverty Status of Families Under Alternative Definitions of Income.* Washington: U.S. Government Printing Office, June 1977.

Congressional Budget Office, "Update on Social Security Legislation." Processed, n.d. (January, 1978).

Cymrot, Donald J. "The Effect of Private Pensions on Labor Contracts." Unpublished paper, April 1978.

Cymrot, Donald J. "The Effect of Tax Incentives on the Rate of Return for Private Pensions." Unpublished paper, January 1978.

Darby, Michael R. "The Effects of Social Security on Income and the Capital Stock. Working Paper No. 95. University of California, Los Angeles, July 1977.

David, Paul A., and John L. Scadding. "Private Savings: Ultra-rationality, Aggregation and 'Dimson's Law,'" *Journal of Political Economy*, 82, No. 2 (March–April 1974): 225–149.

Dawson, William H. *Social Insurance in Germany 1883–1911: Its History, Operation, Results and a Comparison with the National Insurance Act, 1911.* London: T. Fisher Unwin, 1912.

Drucker, Peter F. *The Unseen Revolution: How Pension Fund Socialism Came to America.* New York: Harper & Row, 1976.

Dyer, John K., Jr. "Coordination of Private and Public Pension Plans." In Dan M. McGill, ed., *Social Security and Private Pension Plans: Competitive or Complementary*. Homewood, Ill.: Richard D. Irwin, 1977, pp. 29–40.

*Economic Report of the President, 1976*. Washington: U.S. Government Printing Office, 1976.

*Economic Report of the President, 1977*. Washington: U.S. Government Printing Office, 1977.

Ehrbar, A.F. "Those Pension Plans Are Even Weaker than You Think." *Fortune*, November 1977, pp. 104–114.

*Employee Benefits, 1975*. Washington: Chamber of Commerce of the United States, 1976.

*Employment and Training Report of the President, 1978.* Washington: U.S. Government Printing Office, 1978.

Esposito, Louis. "Effect of Social Security on Saving: Review of Studies Using U.S. Time-Series Data." *Social Security Bulletin*, 41, No. 5 (May 1978): 9–17.

"Estimated Trust Fund Ratios for the OASDI System under the Social Security Act as Amended Through Public Law 95-216, Calendar Years 1977–2035." Office of the Actuary, Social Security Administration, February 2, 1978.

Feldstein, Martin S. "The Incidence of Social Security Payroll Taxes: Comment." *American Economic Review*, 62, No. 4 (September 1972): 735–738.

Feldstein, Martin S. "The Optimal Financing of Social Security." Discussion Paper No. 388. Harvard University, Institute of Economic Research, 1974, processed.

Feldstein, Martin S. "Response to Pechman." In *Funding Pensions: Issues and Implications for Financial Markets.* Boston: Federal Reserve Bank of Boston, 1976.

Feldstein, Martin S. "Social Security." In Michael J. Boskin, ed., *The Crisis in Social Security.* San Francisco: Institute for Contemporary Studies, 1977, pp. 17–30.

Feldstein, Martin S. "Social Security and Private Saving: International Evidence in an Extended Life Cycle Model." Discussion Paper No. 361. Harvard University, Institute of Economic Research, 1974, processed.

Feldstein, Martin S. "Social Security and Saving: The Extended Life Cycle Theory." *American Economic Review*, 66, No. 2 (May 1976): 77–86.

Feldstein, Martin S. "Social Security, Induced Retirement and Aggregate Capital Accumulation." *Journal of Political Economy*, 82, No. 5 (September-October 1974): 905–925.

Feldstein, Martin S. "The Social Security Fund and National Capital Accumulation." In *Funding Pensions: Issues and Implications for Capital Markets.* Boston: Federal Reserve Bank of Boston, 1976, pp. 32–64.

Feldstein, Martin S. "Toward a Reform of Social Security." *The Public Interest*, No. 40 (Summer 1975), pp. 75–95.

Fleming, J. S. "Optimal Payroll Taxes and Social Security Funding." *Journal of Public Economics*, 7, No. 3 (June 1977): 329–349.

Friedman, Benjamin M. "Public Pension Funding and U.S. Capital Formation: A Medium-Run View." *Funding Pensions: Issues and Implications for Capital Markets.* Boston: Federal Reserve Bank of Boston, 1976, pp. 156–201.

Friedman, Milton. *Capitalism and Freedom.* Chicago: University of Chicago Press, 1962.

Friedman, Milton. "Payroll Taxes, No: General Revenues, Yes." In Michael J. Boskin, ed., *The Crisis in Social Security.* San Francisco: Institute for Contemporary Studies, 1977, pp. 25–30.

Friedman, Milton. *A Theory of the Consumption Function.* Princeton, N.J.: Princeton University Press, 1975.

Fullerton, Howard N., Jr., and Paul O. Flaim. "New Labor Force Projections to 1990." Bureau of Labor Statistics, Special Labor Force Report 197.

Glick, Paul C., and Arthur J. Norton. "Frequency, Duration and Probability of Marriage and Divorce." *Journal of Marriage and the Family*, 33, No. 2 (May 1971): 307–317.

Gordon, Nancy M. *The Treatment of Women in the Public Pension Systems of Five Countries.* Working Paper No. 5069-01. Washington: Urban Institute, March 1978.

Greenough, William C., and Francis P. King. *Pension Plans and Public Policy.* New York: Columbia University Press, 1976.

Halperin, Daniel. "Sex Discrimination and Pensions: Are We Moving Toward Unisex Tables?" In Richard Adelman, ed., *Proceedings of the 30th New York University Conference on Labor.* New York: Matthew Bender, 1977, pp. 235–256.

*Handbook on Pension Reform Law.* Englewood Cliffs, N.J.: Prentice-Hall, 1974.

Henle, Peter. "Recent Trends in Retirement Benefits Related to Earnings." Reprint 24. Washington: Brookings Institution, 1972.

Hsiao Report. See U.S. Congress, Report of the Consultant Panel.

Johnson and Higgins, *Benefit Bulletin*, March 17, 1978.

Jump, Bernard, Jr. *State and Local Employee Pension Plans: Watching for Problems.* Columbus, Ohio: Academy for Contemporary Problems, October 1976.

Kaim-Candle, P. R. *Comparative Social Policy and Social Security: A Ten-Country Study.* New York: Dunellen, 1973.

Kaldor, Nicholas. "Inflation and Recession in the World Economy." *Economic Journal* (December 1976), pp. 703–714.

Kaplan, Robert S. *Indexing Social Security: An Analysis of the Issues.* Washington: American Enterprise Institute, 1977.

Katona, George. *The Mass Consumption Society.* New York: McGraw-Hill, 1964.

Keene, Kenneth K., and Sandra M. Kazenetz. "Comparing Unfunded Liabilities: Net Worth Provides Good News." Published by Johnson and Higgins, 1978.

Kolodrubetz, Walter W., and Alfred M. Skolnik. *Pension Benefit Levels: A Methodological Analysis.* Social Security Administration Publication No. 72-11851. Washington: U.S. Government Printing Office, 1972.

Lampman, Robert J. "The Future of Social Security." In Industrial Relations Research Association, *Proceedings of the 29th Annual Meetings, 1976,* Madison, Wisc.: Industrial Relations Research Association, 1977, pp. 35–42.

Latimer, Murray Webb. *Industrial Pension Systems in the United States and Canada.* Vol. 1. New York: Industrial Relations Counselors, 1933.

Levitan, Sar A. *Programs in Aid of the Poor.* 3d ed. Baltimore: Johns Hopkins Press, 1976.

McKay, Stephen F. "Computing a Social Security Benefit Under PL 95-216." Baltimore: Social Security Administration, January 23–24, 1978, processed.

Mackin, John P. *Protecting Purchasing Power in Retirement.* New York: Fleet Academic Editions, 1971.

Mantoux, Paul. *The Industrial Revolution in the Eighteenth Century.* New York: Harper & Row, 1962.

Marcus, Bruce W. "Will Public Plans Sink the Cities?" *Pension World,* 13, No. 4 (April 1977): 11–14.

Maxwell, James A. "Characteristics of State and Local Trust Funds." In David J. Ott et al., *State-Local Finances in the Last Half of the 1970s.* Washington, D.C.: American Enterprise Institute, 1975, pp. 35–61.

Mendelson, Mary A. *Tender Loving Greed.* New York: Vintage Books, 1975.

Moon, Marilyn. *The Measurement of Economic Welfare: Its Application to the Aged Poor.* New York: Academic Press, 1977.

Moon, Marilyn, and Eugene Smolensky. *Income Support Policies for the Aged.* Cambridge, Mass.: Ballinger, 1977.

Morgan, James N., Katherine Dickinson, Jacob Benus, and Greg Duncan. *Five Thousand Americans: Patterns of Economic Progress.* Vol. 1. Ann Arbor: Institute for Social Research, University of Michigan, 1974.

Munnell, Alicia H. *The Effect of Social Security on Personal Savings.* Cambridge, Mass. Ballinger, 1974.

Munnell, Alicia H. *The Future of Social Security.* Washington: Brookings Institution, 1977.

Munnell, Alicia H. "The Impact of Social Security on Personal Savings." *National Tax Journal,* 27, No. 4 (December 1974): 553–567.

Munnell, Alicia H. "The Interaction of Social Security and Private Pensions." Unpublished paper, processed, 1977.

Munnell, Alicia H. "Private Pensions and Saving: New Evidence." *Journal of Political Economy,* 84, No. 5 (October 1976): 1013–1032.

Munnell, Alicia H. "Social Security." In Joseph Pechman, ed., *The 1978 Budget: Setting National Priorities.* Washington: Brookings Institution, 1977, pp. 207–247.

Munnell, Alicia, and Ann M. Connolly. "Funding Government Pensions: State-Local, Civil Service and Military." In *Funding Pensions: Issues and Implications for Financial Markets,* Boston: Federal Reserve Bank of Boston, n.d. (1976), pp. 72–133.

Murray, Samuel H. *Analysis of the Pension Reform Act of 1974.* New York: Matthew Bender, 1974.

Musgrave, Richard A. *The Theory of Public Finance.* New York: McGraw-Hill, 1959.

Musgrave, Richard A., and Peggy B. Musgrave. *Public Finance in Theory and Practice.* New York: McGraw-Hill, 1973.

Myers, Robert J. "The Future of Social Security: Is It in Conflict with Private Pension Plans?" *Pension and Welfare News* (January 1970), pp. 38–48.

National Bureau of Economic Research, *Demographic and Economic Changes in Developed Countries.* Princeton, N.J.: Princeton University Press, 1960.

*New York Times*, May 6, 1975.

*New York Times*, July 10, 1977.

*New York Times*, October 5, 1977.

*New York Times*, February 7, 1978.

*1975 Study of Corporate Pension Plans.* New York: Bankers Trust Company, 1975.

Organisation for Economic Co-operation and Development. *Socio-economic Policies for the Elderly*. Annex 1, Part 1, MAS (77) 18. Paris: OECD, December 29, 1977, processed.

Palay, Earl. "Arbitration and Pension Benefits." In Richard Adelman, ed., *Proceedings of the 30th New York University Conference on Labor.* New York: Matthew Bender, 1977, pp. 223–233.

Parsons, Donald O., and Douglas R. Munro. "Intergenerational Transfers in Social Security." In Michael J. Boskin, ed., *The Crisis in Social Security.* San Francisco: Institute for Contemporary Studies, 1977, pp. 65–86.

Paul, Robert D. "Statement Before the Subcommittee on Retirement Income and Employment." Martin E. Segal Company, April 6, 1978, processed.

Pechman, Joseph A. "Discussion." In *Funding Pensions: Issues and Implications for Financial Markets.* Boston: Federal Reserve Bank of Boston, 1976, pp. 65–68.

Pechman, Joseph A. "The Social Security System: An Overview." In Michael J. Boskin, ed., *The Crisis in Social Security.* San Francisco: Institute for Contemporary Studies, 1977, pp. 25–40.

Pechman, Joseph A., Henry J. Aaron, and Michael K. Taussig. *Social Security: Perspectives for Reform*. Washington: Brookings Institution, 1968.

*Pensions and Investments*, July 18, 1977.

*Pension Facts 1976*. New York: American Council of Life Insurance, 1976.

*Pensions: Britain's Great Step Forward.* London: HMSO, n.d. (1977).

Perkins, Frances. *The Roosevelt I Knew*. New York: Viking Press, 1946.

Phelps, E. S. *Golden Rules of Economic Growth.* New York: Norton, 1966.

Pinkus, Norbert. "Workmen's Insurance in Germany: III." *Yale Review*, November 1904, pp. 296–323.

Poston, M. M., E. E. Rich, and Edward Miller, eds. *The Cambridge Economic History of Europe, Vol. III: Economic Organization and Policies in the Middle Ages.* Cambridge, England: Cambridge University Press, 1965.

"Projected Workers with Taxable Earnings, 1973–83." Social Security Administration, processed, 1978.

Quinn, Joseph F. "Microeconomic Determinants of Retirement: A Cross-Sectional View of White Married Men." *Journal of Human Resources*, 12, No. 3 (Summer 1977): 329–346.

Rejda, George E. *Social Insurance and Economic Security*. Englewood Cliffs, N.J.: Prentice-Hall, 1976.

*Report of the HEW Task Force on the Treatment of Women Under Social Security*. February 1978, processed.

*Reports of the Quadrennial Advisory Council on Social Security*. House Document No. 94-75. Washington: U.S. Government Printing Office, 1977.

Robertson, A. Haeworth. "The Financial Status of Social Security After the Social Security Amendments of 1977." Baltimore: Social Security Administration, January 1978, processed.

Rosen, Harvey S. "An Approach to the Study of Income, Utility and Horizontal Equity." Research Memorandum No. 212, Princeton University, Econometric Research Program, February 1977.

Rosow, Jerome M. "Public Sector Pay and Benefits." *Public Administration Review*, 36, No. 5 (September–October 1976): 538–543.

Sacher, Steven. "ERISA Legislation." In Richard Adelman, ed., *Proceedings of the 30th New York University Conference on Labor*. New York: Matthew Bender, 1977, pp. 257–273.

Schulz, James H. *The Economics of Aging*. Belmont, Calif.: Wadsworth, 1976.

Schulz, James H. "Public Policy and the Future Roles of Public and Private Pensions." In G. S. Tolley and Richard V. Burkhauser, eds., *Income Support Policies for the Aged*. Cambridge, Mass.: Ballinger Publishing Co., 1977, pp. 11–36.

Schulz, James H., and Guy Carrin. "The Role of Savings and Pension Systems in Maintaining Living Standards in Retirement." *The Journal of Human Resources*, 7, No. 3 (Summer 1972): 343–365.

Schulz, James H., et al. *Providing Adequate Retirement Income: Pension Reform in the United States*. Hanover, N.H.: University Press of New England, 1974.

Sheppard, Harold L., and Sara E. Rix. *The Graying of Working America: The Coming Crisis of Retirement-Age Policy*. New York: Free Press, 1977.

Simon, William E. "How to Rescue Social Security." *Wall Street Journal*, November 3, 1976, p. 20.

Skolnik, Alfred M. "Private Pension Plans, 1950–1974." *Social Security Bulletin*, 39, No. 6 (June 1976): 3–17.

Sleeman, J. F. *The Welfare State: Its Aims, Benefits and Costs*. London: George Allen & Unwin, 1973.

Smith, Adam. *The Wealth of Nations*. London: Oxford University Press, 1904.

Social Security Administration. *Legislative Report*, No. 17, December 16, 1977.

*Social Security Bulletin* Vol. 38, No. 12 (December 1975).

Spengler, Joseph J. "Population Aging and the Security of the Aged." *Atlantic Economic Journal*, 6, No. 1 (March 1978): 1–7.

Stein, Bruno. *On Relief: The Economics of Poverty and Public Welfare.* New York: Basic Books, 1971.

Stoeber, Edward A. *Pension Reform Act Explained.* Cincinnati: National Underwriters, 1974.

Sulzbach, Walter. *German Experience with Social Insurance.* Studies in Individual and Collective Security, No. 2. New York: National Industrial Conference Board, 1947.

Taueber, Karl E. "Demographic Trends Affecting the Future Labor Force." University of Wisconsin, Institute for Research on Poverty, Special Report Series, SR14, 1977.

Tawney, R. H. *Religion and the Rise of Capitalism.* London: Hazell, Watson & Viney, 1926.

Thompson, Lawrence H., and Paul N. van de Water. "The Short Run Behavior of the Social Security Trust Funds." Technical Analysis Paper No. 8, Department of Health, Education and Welfare, Office of the Assistant Secretary for Planning and Evaluation, July 1976.

Tilove, Robert. "Comment on Schulz." In G. S. Tolley and Richard V. Burkhauser, eds., *Income Support Policies for the Aged.* Cambridge, Mass.: Ballinger, 1977, pp. 37–44.

Tilove, Robert. "ERISA—Its Effect on Collective Bargaining." In Richard Adelman, ed., *Proceedings of the New York University 29th Annual Conference on Labor.* New York: Matthew Bender, 1976, pp. 187–198.

Tilove, Robert. *Public Employee Pension Funds.* New York: Columbia University Press, 1976.

Tobin, James. "Discussion." In *Funding Pensions: Issues and Implications for Financial Markets.* Boston: Federal Reserve Bank of Boston, 1976, pp. 206–212.

Turnbull, John G., C. Arthur Williams, Jr., and Earl F. Cheit. *Economic and Social Security.* 4th ed. New York: Ronald Press, 1973.

U.S. Committee on Economic Security. *Social Security in America.* Washington: U.S. Government Printing Office, 1937. Also cited as U.S. Social Security Board, Publication No. 20.

U.S. Comptroller General. *Effect of the Employee Retirement Income Security Act on the Termination of Single Employer Defined Benefit Pension Plans.* Washington: U.S. General Accounting Office, April 27, 1978.

U.S. Congress, House Committee on Education and Labor. *Interim Report of Activities of the Pension Task Force of the Subcommittee on Labor Standards.* Washington: U.S. Government Printing Office, 1976.

U.S. Congress, House of Representatives, Committee on Ways and Means. *Summary of the Conference Agreement on H.R. 9346, The Social Security Amendments of 1977*, WMCP: 95-61. Washington: U.S. Government Printing Office, 1977.

U.S. Congress, House Ways and Means Committee. *Hearings on H.R. 4120, Economic Security Act.* Washington: Senate Library, Vol. 699, 1935.

U.S. Congress, House Ways and Means Committee, Subcommittee on Social Security. *Decoupling the Social Security Benefit Structure.* Hearings on H.R. 14430, June 18, July 23 and July 26, 1976. Washington: U.S. Government Printing Office, 1976.

U.S. Congress, Joint Economic Committee. Studies in Public Welfare, No. 17: *National Survey of Food Stamp and Food Distribution Recipients.* Washington: U.S. Government Printing Office, 1974.

U.S. Congress, Joint Economic Committee. Studies in Public Welfare, No. 20: *Handbook of Public Income Transfer Programs: 1975.* Washington: U.S. Government Printing Office, 1974.

U.S. Congress. *Report of the Consultant Panel on Social Security to the Congressional Research Service.* August 1976, 94th Cong. 2d sess. Washington, D.C.: U.S. Government Printing Office, 1976.

U.S. Department of Commerce, Bureau of the Census. *Current Population Reports*, Series P-60, No. 104 (March 1977).

U.S. Department of Commerce, Bureau of the Census. *Current Population Reports*, Series P-60, No. 105, "Money Income in 1975 of Families and Persons in the United States." Washington: U.S. Government Printing Office, 1977.

U.S. Department of Commerce, Bureau of the Census., *Current Population Reports*, Series P-60, No. 109 (January 1978).

U.S. Department of Commerce, Bureau of the Census. *Finances of Employee-Retirement Systems of State and Local Governments, 1975–1976*, GF 76, No. 2, 1978.

U.S. Department of Commerce, Bureau of the Census. "Historical Statistics of the United States." Washington: U.S. Government Printing Office, 1960.

U.S. Department of Commerce, Bureau of the Census. "Historical Statistics of the United States, Colonial Times to 1970, Bicentennial Edition, Part 2." Washington: U.S. Government Printing Office, 1975.

U.S. Department of Commerce. "The National Income and Product Accounts of the United States, 1929–1974, Statistical Tables." Washington: U.S. Government Printing Office, 1975.

U.S. Department of Health, Education, and Welfare. *Coverage and Vesting of Full Time Employees Under Private Retirement Plans: Findings from the April 1972 Survey.* DHEW Publication No. (SSA)74-11908, BLS Report No. 423. Washington, 1974, processed.

U.S. Department of Health, Education, and Welfare. *Report of the HEW Task Force on the Treatment of Women Under Social Security*. Washington, February 1978, processed.

U.S. Department of Health, Education, and Welfare, Social Security Administration. DHEW Publication No. (SSA) 73-11915: *Social Security Programs in the United States*. Washington: U.S. Government Printing Office, 1973.

U.S. Department of Health, Education, and Welfare. *Monthly Vital Statistics Report, Final Divorce Statistics, 1975*. Health Resources Administration, Vol. 26, No. 2, Supplement 2, May 19, 1977.

U.S. Department of Health, Education, and Welfare, Social Security Administration. *Benefits and Beneficiaries Under Public Employee Retirement Systems, Calendar Year 1976.* Research and Statistics Note No. 8, July 11, 1978.

U.S. Department of Health, Education, and Welfare, Social Security Administration. *Preliminary Findings from the Survey of New Beneficiaries.* Washington: U.S. Department of Health, Education, and Welfare, June 1973.

U.S. Department of Health, Education, and Welfare, Social Security Administration. *Problems in Financing Social Security.* Research and Statistics Note No. 14, August 3, 1977.

U.S. Department of Health, Education, and Welfare, Social Security Administration. *State and Local Government Employees Covered Under Social Security, 1972–1973.* Research and Statistics Note No. 18, September 30, 1976.

U.S. Department of Health, Education, and Welfare, Social Secuirty Administration, Office of Research and Statistics. *Reaching Retirement Age: Findings from a Survey of Newly Entitled Workers 1968–1970.* Research Report No. 147. Washington: U.S. Government Printing Office, 1976.

U.S. Department of Health, Education, and Welfare, Social Security Ad ministration, Office of Research and Statistics. *Social Security Programs Throughout the World.* HEW Pub. No. (SSA) 76-11805. Washington: U.S. Government Printing Office, 1976.

U.S. Department of Labor, Bureau of Labor Statistics. *Administration of Negotiated Pension, Health and Insurance Plans.* Bulletin 1425-12. Washington: U.S. Government Printing Office, May 1970.

U.S. Department of Labor. *Digest of Selected Pension Plans.* 1973 Edition, Supplements II and III, October 1974 and August 1975.

U.S. Department of Labor. *Handbook of Labor Statistics, 1976.* Washington: U.S. Government Printing Office, 1976.

U.S. Department of Labor. *Three Budgets for a Retired Couple.* Washington: Bureau of Labor Statistics, August 4, 1977, USDL 77-690, and August 19, 1976, USDL 76-1133.

U.S. President. *Eighth Annual Report on the National Housing Goal.* Washington: U.S. Government Printing Office, 1976.

U.S. Senate, Committee on the Budget. *Tax Expenditures: Compendium of Background Material on Individual Provisions.* Washington: U.S. Government Printing Office, 1976.

"Values of Selected Economic and Demographic Factors Included in Alternatives I, II and III by Calendar Year," Office of the Actuary, Social Security Administration. Baltimore: processed, n.d. (February 2, 1978).

Vogel, Walter. *Bismarcks Arbeiterversicherung: Ihre Enstehung im Kraftespiel der Zeit.* Braunschweig: Georg Westermann Verlag, 1951.

von Furstenberg, George, and Burton G. Malkiel. "The Government and Capital Formation: A Survey of Recent Issues." *The Journal of Economic Literature*, 15, No. 3 (September 1977): 835–878.

Walker, J. *British Economic and Social History 1700–1967.* London: MacDonald & Evans, 1968.

Webb, Sidney, and Beatrice Webb, *English Local Government: English Poor Law History, Part 1: The Old Poor Law,* Hamden, Conn.: Archon Books, 1927.

Watts, Harold, and Felicity Skidmore. "An Update of the Poverty Picture Plus a New Look at Relative Tax Burdens," *Focus*, 2, No. 1 (Fall 1977).

Wildavsky, Aaron. "Doing Better and Feeling Worse: The Political Pathology of Health Policy." In John H. Knowles, ed., *Doing Better and Feeling Worse.* New York: W. W. Norton, 1977, pp. 105–123.

Witte, Edwin E. *The Development of the Social Security Act.* Madison: University of Wisconsin Press, 1962.

Yohalem, Martha Remy. "Employee-Benefit Plans, 1975." *Social Security Bulletin*, 40, No. 11 (November 1977): 19–28.

# Index

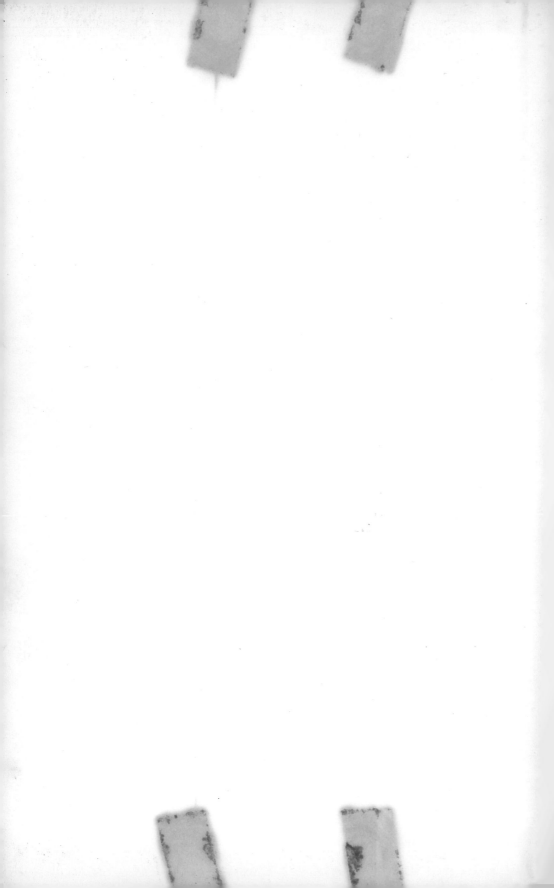